a drink with shane macgowan

a DRINK WITH SHane macgowan

SHANE MacGOWAN &
VICTORIA MARY CLARKE

GROVE PRESS
New York

First published in 2001 by Sidgwick & Jackson, an imprint of Macmillan Publishers Ltd., London, England

Published simultaneously in Canada
Printed in the United States of America

FIRST AMERICAN EDITION

Library of Congress Cataloging-in-Publication Data

MacGowan, Shane 1957–
    A drink with Shane MacGowan / Shane MacGowan and Victoria Mary Clarke.
        p. cm.
    ISBN 0-8021-3790-3
    1. MacGowan, Shane, 1957—Interviews. 2. Rock musicians—Ireland—Interviews. I. Clarke, Victoria Mary. II. Title.

ML420.M1375 A3 2001
782.42166'092—dc21
[B]   00-069465

Grove Press
841 Broadway
New York, NY 10003

01 02 03 04   10 9 8 7 6 5 4 3 2 1

CONTENTS

Acknowledgements

Thank yous to Gordon Wise, Holly Rose, our families, Andrew Catlin, my many agents and millions of friends and admirers everywhere.

VMC

Foreword

by Shane MacGowan

IN MY EARLY HELLBORN NIGHT-
MARES IN LONDON I DREAMED
I WAS CHOPPING UP YOUNG FULL-
BREASTED GIRLS IN A BUTCHERSHOP
THEY GIGGLED AND TALKED GIRL
TALK AS I HACKED OFF THEIR
ARMS AND LEGS AND SOLD
THEM AS MEAT TO PUNTERS —
THEN, SLEEPWALKING OR AWAKE
I WANDERED OUT THE BACK

YARD I MET TWO MALE LIONS-
THEN VERY TALL EBONY
GHOULS IN WHITE MONKS
ROBES IN COWLS - THEY TALKED
IN A TELEPATHIC LANGUAGE

FOREWORD

by Victoria Mary Clarke

Shane MacGowan was calling himself Shane O'Hooligan when I first spotted him in a music magazine, I can't remember which one. I was eleven at the time and I'd heard the Sex Pistols on Dave Fanning's radio show and I was desperate to be a punk. I lived in West Cork, which wasn't a very progressive place, so I had to settle for a black binliner and a pair of fishnets and whatever I could find on the radio, which wasn't much. But looking longingly at Shane, I satisfied myself with the knowledge that one day I too would go to London, which was where it was at, obviously, and be a proper punk.

When I was sixteen, I did move to London, to live with my friend Jo in Golders Green, and in my local pub I met a man called Spider Stacey, who played tin whistle with a new band called Poguemahone. I was distinctly unimpressed because I was a New Romantic by then and I had no time for Irish music, having been dragged up in an Irish speaking hellhole where that was all you ever heard. One night I went to my local, as usual, for a port and grapefruit or two, as was my custom, and I bumped into Spider and on this occasion he had Shane with him. I didn't recognize Shane as being the same man I'd envied a few years earlier and I was put off taking any further interest in him by his aggressive tone and arrogant air. He ordered me to buy Spider another drink, for his birthday, which I would have done, had he not told me to. I told him to fuck off and sat down with my drink. For the rest of the evening I couldn't stop myself staring at him, even though I was annoyed with myself for being compelled to.

I did warm to Shane slightly as the years passed and we encountered each other at Pogues gigs and in pubs. He was

TO ME THAT HIT MY SUBCON-
CIOUS BACK OF THE HEAD, MY
HEART, MY SOUL, BUT BYPASSED
MY FRONT MIND — MY PLEASANT
DREAMS WERE IN COLOUR — A
BLACK-HAIRED SCHOOLGIRL
IN A BLUE GANSEY WALKING
DOWN A WINDING PATH IN
WEST CORK BETWEEN ~~WEST~~
COOLAY AND BALLYVOURNEY —
YEARS LATER I MET HER
IN THE ROYAL OAK IN FINGAL
~~ROAD~~ — SHE WAS SIXTEEN NOW AND
HER HAIR HAD GROWN LONG
I WAS CELEBRATING SPUDS
BIRTHDAY ~~WITH~~ WITH HIM AND

HAD EMPTIED MY POCKETS AS HE
WOULD FOR ME — SHE WAS STARING
AT ME — I WAS GOBSMACKED —
SHE WAS THE MOST BEAUTIFUL
THING I HAD EVER SEEN AND
OBVIOUSLY UNATTAINABLE — SO

sympathetic when I went to a very early Pogues gig as Spider's date and Spider drank all my money and fell asleep. I didn't fall in love with Shane, though, until I was twenty, and two things happened.

The first thing was that somebody told Shane to kiss me, because of it being my birthday, and he did. The second thing was that Shane and I had an argument in the back of a taxi about whether he knew what 'Sean Nos' singing was. I believed that I knew more than he did, having grown up in a Gaeltacht and he said I was full of shit and afterwards I kissed him goodnight and fell in love. The next day I woke up thinking about him and every day after that. I was living with somebody else by then and Shane didn't want to upset the guy, but I had no such scruples. So after a gig in the Mean Fiddler, in Harlesden, I shamelessly threw myself at Shane and we collapsed on the floor together in the dressing room and rolled around, amorously, until the club was deserted.

After that, we had our first date, at the 100 Club in Oxford Street, although we weren't allowed into the club, because of a disagreement with the bouncer, and I spent the evening watching Shane try to persuade the bouncer to fight him. When he finally gave up, we went back to Shane's flat in King's Cross, where we drank retsina and discussed the Irish poets of the seventeenth century in great depth.

Shane's flat was disgusting, one room, red walls, black carpet, a mattress on the floor with nylon sheets, covered in dirty washing and Wendy wrappers, the floor littered with overflowing ashtrays and empty wine bottles, albums hanging out of their sleeves, tapes, musical instruments and bits of paper. He had five tellys, none of which worked properly, and a crappy record player, and he played *Astral Weeks* and *African Brass* all night. I've never been so mesmerized in all my life. When I woke up, the following afternoon, I didn't want to leave, but I had to go home to my boyfriend. When I got there, somebody had already tipped him off and that was the end of him, but I didn't care, I was in love and I was happy. I went out with Shane again that night and the night after that and eventually we moved in together and that was that.

I EVENTUALLY SAID — "BUY SPIDER
A DRINK FOR HIS BIRTHDAY AND
ME ONE AS WELL, WILL YOU?!"
"GO AND FUCK YOURSELF." WAS
HER WITTY RETORT IN THE

SWINEYARD TONGUE — NOT THE
SWEET WORDS OF ELSE I WAS
EXPECTING FROM MY WEST
CORK COLLEEN. — WE BOTH
LAUGHED THEN CARRIED ON
STARING AT EACH OTHER FOR
3 YEARS OR SO, HAVING THE
ODD POLITE CONVERSATION, AS I REALISED
I DID NOT DISLIKE HER AT ALL
BUT WAS COMPLETELY AND UTTERLY
IN LOVE WITH HER. IN THE MEAN-
TIME FAME AND FORTUNE

ARRIVED, MORE OF IT THAN I'D
EVER DREAMED OF. FOR THE
FIRST TIME IN MY LIFE I WAS ALMOST
AS HAPPY AS MY EARLY CHILDHOOD,
WHICH I HAD STUPIDLY DISMISSED
AS SOME KIND OF ROSE-TINTED

It's difficult to say exactly what attracted me to Shane because to me, everything about him was attractive, even the Wendy wrappers. I still come over all romantic when I see cigarette butts and Retsina bottles. But I've noticed that the things that attracted me are also the things I try to change, the things that drive me crazy, like the wild partying and total lack of interest in things like vitamins and yoga and cleaning and tidying and washing up and cooking and exercise and polite dinner parties. It's very annoying, for me, because even though I half despise myself for being interested in having a more 'normal' life, I've spent years trying to make Shane into a more 'normal' person, to no avail whatsoever. And I'm not attracted to 'normal' people, when I do meet them, so obviously I'm a totally dysfunctional type, myself.

Even the things about Shane that I truly admire, such as his total artistic integrity, his courage, total lack of pretension, refusal to conform to anyone else's idea of how he should be; his ability to remain entirely unimpressed by rock stars, supermodels, movie stars, posh people, rich people, etc.; his extreme generosity and compassion for those less well off than himself, without being patronizing or smug or self-aggrandizing about it; his idealism, his sense of purpose, his romanticism, his fearlessness in the face of injury, illness and even death, his sense of the ridiculous and ability to laugh at himself, even these things, I try to change, at times. I have *tried* to make Shane more like other rock stars, more presentable, more domesticated, more respectable, more businesslike, more health conscious, more materialistic, more careerist, more pretentious, more socially acceptable, so we can be in *Hello* and party with Elton and Sting and Bono and live in mansions and stuff. I've tried to get him to be *nice* to celebrities, so they'll invite us to hang out with them, but he won't and they don't! It's not going to work, obviously, Shane is Shane and he's unique and magnificent and besides being a genius, he's the most intelligent man I know and the most interesting and I am proud and honoured to have spent so much time with him and to have been able to write this book.

DREAM - I WAS GRADUALLY DROPPING
MY BAGGAGE - CYNICISM, BITTER-
NESS, SELF-HATRED, RACISM, BIG-
OTRY, CATHOLIC GUILT, SELF-PITY
- AND RECOVERING FAITH, GOD, SELF-
RESPECT, HUMOUR AND HONESTY.

AND I'M STILL ON ON THE SAME
PATH GOD-WILLING - HOW DO YOU
KNOW E.T.'S A PROTESTANT - 'CAUSE
HE LOOKS LIKE ONE - SEE WHAT I
MEAN? - I HAD ALSO GOT INTO
TAOISM, BUDDHISM, ZEN ETC. -
WHICH I PUT BESIDE FREE-THINK-
ING CATHOLICISM, LOVE OF IRE-
LAND, HATRED OF FASCISM, RACISM,
BIGOTRY, BULLIES (ESPECIALLY IM-
PERIALISM), INTOLERANCE, ATHEISM
LOGIC AND STUPIDITY, AND AFTER

A FEW GREAT CONVERSATIONS
WITH VICKY. IN THE DEVONSHIRE
ARMS IN CAMDEN WHERE I WAS
BUMPING INTO HER EVERY NIGHT
AND TALKING TO HER WHILE
HER BOYFRIEND, A FRIEND WHO

Originally this was written as a straightforward autobiography, which means that I interviewed Shane and then edited his answers so it looked like one stream of consciousness, uninterrupted by questions or comments or arguments. It seemed to be working like that, but something about it worried me, and I couldn't figure out what. Then Holly, who was transcribing the tapes, made me read a whole chunk with my questions left in and I realized that what was worrying me was that what I was doing was contrived and Shane has never been contrived, as a songwriter or as a person. So I rewrote the book, with my questions and comments left in and added some more interviews where I got to talk too and that was much more interesting and funny and essentially more revealing of the real Shane. It was more embarrassing for me, because some of my questions don't make me look clever, and because we argue in places and it's more revealing of our relationship and of me, but for the sake of authenticity, I'm willing to make that sacrifice. Maybe I'll start a trend. I apologize to Flann O'Brien for any offence caused and I hope the book entertains you and makes you laugh and does whatever else you want it to do.

I WAS ~~was~~ RAPIDLY LOSING ~~RESPECT~~
FOR, ~~HER~~, ACTED LIKE A COMPLETE
SHITHEAD AND CHATTING UP OTHER
WOMEN IN FRONT OF HER, A
MUTUAL FRIEND, ~~PAUL RONAN~~ ONE OF
THE MOST GAS MEN I'VE ~~EVER~~ MET
~~C??????????????~~
~~FAMILY~~

~~P???????~~ ONE OF THE SANEST, WHO
CAME ORIGINALLY FROM THE SAME
PART OF THE WORLD AS VIC (AND
QUITE A FEW OTHER ~~PEOPLE~~ INCLUDING
SEÁN Ó RIADA) DECIDED TO PLAY
MATCH-MAKER AND GOT ME TO
KISS ~~HER~~ HER ON HER 19TH BIRTH-
DAY – AND THAT WAS THAT, IT
STARTED WITH A KISS, THE THUNDER-
BOLT AS THE SICILIANS CALL IT –
I DROPPED MY GUARD AND ABOUT
7 WOMEN I WAS JUGGLING LIKE
A WANKER, SHE DROPPED HER BOY-
FRIEND AND WE HAD A MAD PASS–

IONATE ROMANCE. 16 OR SO
YEARS LATER I LOVE HER MORE
THAN EVER AND OF ALL MY FAMILY
AND FRIENDS ~~A???? FROM MY PARENTS~~
~~AND A FEW OTHER FARTS ? OLD~~

~~FRIENDS~~ - ALIVE, DEAD OR IN AMERIKAY - I OWE HER MY HEALTH, SANITY AND HAPPINESS - MY BLOOD STILL BOILS WHEN I EVEN THINK ABOUT HER, WHICH IS MOST OF ~~THE~~ THE TIME - I HATE TO SEE HER SAD, I LOVE TO SEE HER HAPPY - DRINKING, EATING, LAUGHING →

AND TALKING - AND SHE'S HEAVEN TO DANCE WITH, TALK WITH, AND SLEEP WITH. GOD BLESS THE DAY I FOUND HER, AND I FEEL LIKE THE LUCKIEST FUCKER ALIVE.

TIPPERARY 1966

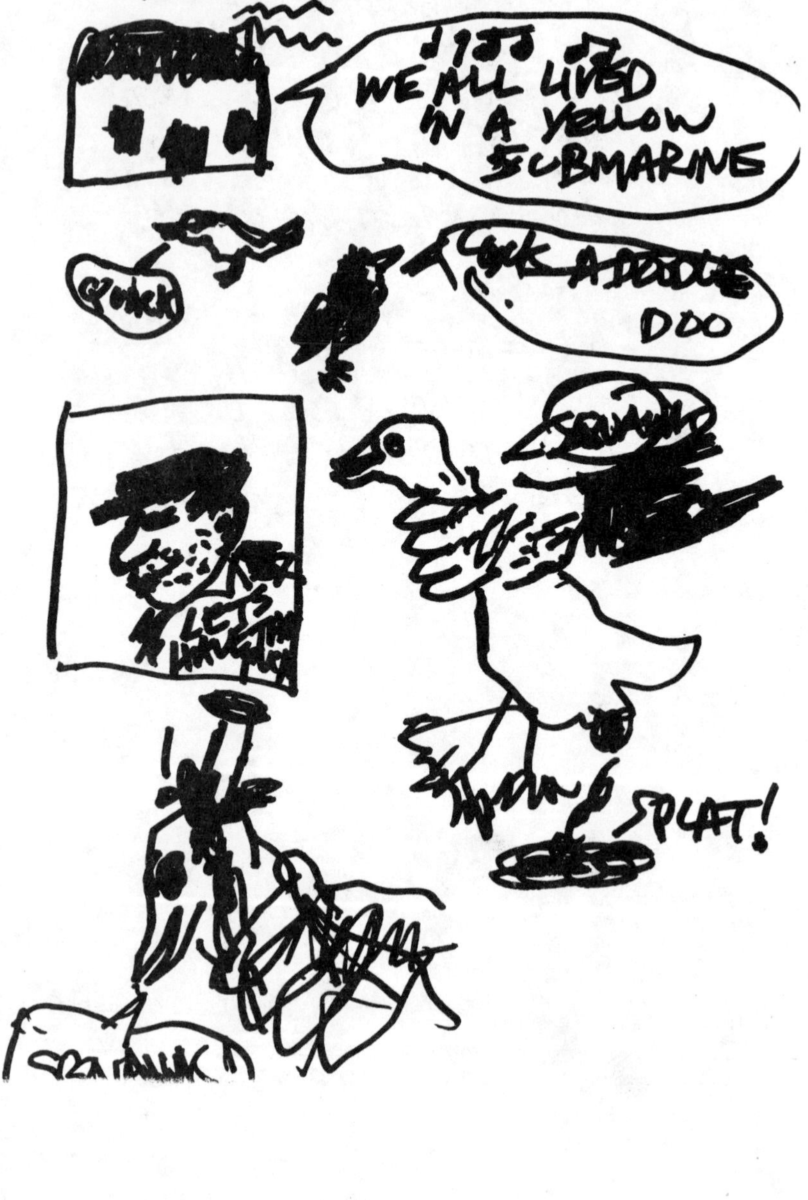

ACT ONE

A rugged Irish cottage, night. A fierce and loquacious wind tears, mercilessly, mirthlessly, at the simple thatched roof. An immodest fire illuminates the shadows, boldly. Out of the ashes, a luminous face looms, magnificently. A trembling hand taps a cigarette, certainly, on a filthy trouser leg. Another, equally pale and blackened, grasps a bottle of gin, half full or half empty, depending on which way you look at it. Shane MacGowan, leaning back against the whitewashed wall, contemplates the portrait of Pope John, contemplatively, spits into the flames, contentedly, clears his throat, aridly, and addresses his companion.

—My Uncle John never said much. He'd sit here, belting his cap off his knee, tapping out his pipe. And cursing under his breath.

His companion, Victoria, a fragile, ethereal beauty, the likes of which will never be seen again, nods anxiously and swallows delicately. Shane eyes her, insistently, and continues.

—My Uncle Jim used to get pissed off about how overcrowded it was, because there were fourteen people living in this house and it's a small house, AS YOU CAN SEE.

Victoria glances around the cottage, obediently, and nods her agreement, assiduously.

—So he used to have to sleep in haystacks in the rain, y'know? You'd be playing in the haystacks and suddenly you'd realize Uncle Jim was lying there, underneath the hay, in the tarpaulin. It was either the haystack or sleep in the same bed as Uncle John and Uncle John used to fight in his sleep. 'Fock yez, I'll fockin kill yez, fock yez, yeh conts.'

He used to knock Uncle Jim out of the bed every time he tried to sleep in it. They were both big men, but Uncle John could easily have

Uncle Jim. So Uncle Jim got so sick of it he would sleep in the haystack and in the end he never slept in a bed at all.

Shane coughs, mightily, and partakes of the gin, healthily. Victoria sips a glass of Chablis, daintily.

—Tell me your earliest memory, Sweet Pea.

—My earliest memory is of the whole family building a bed and not being able to get it through the front door. Couldn't get it through the fucking door. So we had to take it apart outside and put it together inside the house.

Shane leans forward, suddenly, clasps his nose, tentatively, and blows an enormous bogey on to the stone floor.

—There was a shortage of beds, so we shared beds. Every so often, a committee meeting would be held in this kitchen, which was the main room of the house. The men would hold their fingers around their noses and blow the snot on the floor and then spit on it. Which is where I picked up the habit.

Victoria pales, considerably.

—At the meetings, all the men and women of the house shouted at each other and afterwards, everyone's sleeping arrangements got switched around. The main bone of contention was the dying room, over there, which is where people who were dying were moved into. Unless there was a dying person in there, it was supposed to be occupied by my Uncle John and my Uncle Jim, sleeping head to toe in a single bed. With a picture of the baby Jesus looking down at them. These were the people that brought me up for the first six years of my life, my mother's family in Tipperary.

A gust of wind accompanies the lull in conversation, appropriately, blowing open the door of the dying room, where a single bed sits, unoccupied, temporarily. Shane lights a fag and smiles, agreeably.

—Did I tell you about Tom Cahalan? Tom Cahalan was one of three brothers who owned a bigger farm, down the road from us a bit, and Tom used to get dressed up every Sunday night and come round and give me chocolate. And he gave me money and cigarettes. Every Sunday night, a fire would be lit in the parlour, and Tom would arrive on a bicycle and he'd go into the parlour with my Auntie

Monica and they'd have a lamp lighting and they'd sit on the old
settee in front of the fire and talk. I'd go in and interrupt them,
deliberately, and they'd pay me to go away. I caught them kissing a
few times. I suppose they were in their late thirties then and they were
in their forties when they eventually got married, and she moved out.
—Why did Tom and Monica wait so long to get married?
—Jesus Christ, I'm not a bloody sociologist. You know what
happens in Ireland. It was perfectly normal, in those days, for people
to court for twenty years. She was stricken, absolutely stricken. She
never even looked at another man. He was a fucking goodlooking
guy, great sense of humour, strong, but not domineering.
—So you were fond of him?
—Yes. Very fond of him. He was a great Irishman. There were an
awful lot of incredible men in this house. Not to mention incredible
women. It's not for nothing I hold the English in such contempt.
They just don't measure up to those people.
—Not any English people?
—Yeah, some, but they're exceptional. Actually, I wouldn't say I
knew any English people who measured up to any of my uncles.
Shane snorts, acrimoniously, and takes a swig, acerbically.
—My main hero, when I was small, was my Uncle John, who was the
actual owner of the house and the farm. It was up to him to decide
who got the farm and the house when he'd gone and he ended up
being the last one to go. He was a Zen master in the art of cursing
and making short, obvious, but meaningful statements. And gross
dirty jokes. The rest of the time he remained completely and
absolutely silent. He grunted, rather than saying yes or no and he
was an expert in swatting flies with his cap.

I used to go out and help him on the farm, ploughing or making
hay and I used to help him kill the chickens and turkeys and geese.
—Yeah?
—Yeah. I found it fascinating because they knew they were going to
die, before we started running after them and it took two of us to
catch them. Then we'd drag them along and I'd hold them, while he
shoved the knife in. He'd have to bend their necks and cut them and

then they'd bleed to death which took about twenty minutes. As they were dying they started looking really stoned like junkies look. And the other thing that really fascinated me about the hens was when we killed them, we'd find eggs just floating around inside them, without any shells. I found that really disgusting. When my mother was pregnant with me, she was having a boiled egg for breakfast one morning and she opened it up and inside it was a baby chick. She passed out and nearly had a miscarriage. Another time she was at a football match with my dad and the football hit her right where my head was. And when I was four, I had measles which didn't come out, yeah? The spots never came out, they went to my head and I went completely mad for a month. They say I never really came back. In fact, that's when I started making up stories and poems and songs and tunes. That's when I blossomed. Of course, my mum says I was always brilliant.

Victoria nods, knowingly.

—Being small at the time, the farm seemed very big to me, it seemed like a jungle, because everything was overgrown. So, apart from hurling, we used to play war games, we used to play Vietnam war – because the war was going on at the time – and we used to play Black and Tans. Vietnam war was the Vietcong versus the Yanks and Black and Tans was the Irish versus the Black and Tans. I knew a lot about the Black and Tan war because I was always being told stories about it by people who'd lived through it. Our house was a safehouse for the IRA during the Black and Tan war. So we could act out real stories in exact detail, my Uncle Mick having been the local commandant of the IRA. I was on the goodies' side in both wars, obviously. I was the IRA in the Tan war and I was the Vietcong in the Vietnam war. So I got to win all the time. Which is always the way I've liked it, I like to win.

—Yes, dear.

—What now just looks like overgrown fields and little tracks, to me, as a kid looked like the jungle, in the case of the Vietnam war, and in the case of the Tan war it looked like a vast expanse of countryside. So it was a wonderful childhood. It was very primitive.

—Is that why you don't do normal things, like have a bath?

—Maybe. My Uncle Mick Guilfoyle never took a bath from the day he was born. Or at least from the day his mother died, because he didn't see any reason to. He had a big black horse and we used to meet him at the water pump with his big black horse and his oil barrels. We'd have our oil barrels, on the back of our cart, and we'd fill them up from the pump with a bucket, that was how we got our water, in those days.

Mick Guilfoyle looked like a coal miner, he was completely black from head to toe, with a black suit and a black cap and a black horse. Mind you, everybody was black around there, but he was really black. Really, really black. And his horse was huge. He lived until he was eighty-seven, never taking a bath, never washing anything, not even the horse. Then, when he was eighty-seven, he got taken into hospital for a minor ailment and they gave him a bath. And he wasn't immune to the air because he was completely covered in black dirt, so he got sick immediately and he died of exposure to fresh air. That may have something to do with my aversion to taking a bath now.

Then there was Paddy McGrath, who wouldn't make his bike go up hills. He used to say to it, 'I wouldn't make you go up that big hill. I'll walk you up it.' And he'd walk the bike up to the top of the hill then get back on it and say, 'Isn't that better?' Then he'd ride down the other side of the hill. And then there'd be another hill so the whole thing would happen again.

And there was Napoleon O'Guanasa, who survived for forty years, walking home from the pub every night pissed, in the middle of the road. Napoleon was mad and he used to bother everybody in the town for drinks and he burned down the Protestant church several times. And he used to walk home in the middle of the road with cars coming around blind bends at ninety miles an hour and he'd just stand there leering at them. He got away with it for forty years until he met one driver who was drunker than him and the driver hit him and he was splattered all over the road.

The ferocious wind rattles the front door of the remote cottage, ambulatorily. Shane glances at the door, occasionally.

—When I was a kid there weren't many cars, so cars were something you'd run out to look at. The nearest place to buy anything was the post office, a half a mile up the road, and I used to get sent to the post office to buy flour for making bread and I used to get tipped with a bar of chocolate and cigarettes.

All the men used to go into town on the horse and cart, or on their bicycles, and when he was younger, my Uncle Willie got shot at by the Tans for driving too fast with his horse and cart, but he was lucky, they missed him. The Tans used to line up the men as they came into town, on the way into Borrisokane, and play Russian roulette with them. Line them up, facing a wall and go, 'Eeny-meeny, miney-mo. Bang!' They got great fun out of that. So after a bit of that, a whole division of them got taken out in a little town near our house. There's a load of Tans buried down there.

Outside, the wind falls silent, eerily. Shane spits into the flames, noisily.
—In Mayo they didn't have any room to bury the dead from the famine, so they buried them in sand dunes on the beaches. Me and a bunch of mates went down there one time, led by a guy who came from Mayo, and he took us down and showed us the dunes. There was an atmosphere of intense panic and dread and we were trying to be big boys, so we went up and started kicking the sand dunes and all these human bones started coming out. Which is what my song 'The Dunes' is about.

The couple contemplate this information, silently.
—**Why were you brought up on the farm, instead of with your parents?**
—I was a kid at the time, so I don't know, but working it out, it would seem that my parents left me here to be brought up by my mother's family while they got on with their work, because they both had jobs in England. They were very unhappy in England and they wanted me to have as much happiness as possible, before they had to send me to school. And they couldn't send me to school in Ireland, or so they thought, because they didn't want me to be subjected to the Christian Brothers or the Jesuits. They visited me and I visited them, but basically they thought it would be much

IT'S TRUE I WAS A DOCTOR'S SON
AND YET I GAZED IN WONDER
AS WE PERISHED FROM THE RAGING PLAGUE
THAT CAME WITH THE GREAT HUNGER
THAT CAME WITH THE GREAT HUNGER

I TRAVELLED TO THE WESTERN SHORE
SAW HUGE MOUNDS BUILT OF SAND THERE
FULL OF ROTTING BODIES OF SOULS
THAT DIED FROM THE GREAT HUNGER
THAT DIED FROM THE GREAT HUNGER

I SAW DEAD WOMEN IN THE DITCHES
WITH BABIES ONE OR YOUNGER
POISON BERRIES IN THEIR MOUTHS
TO TRY TO ESCAPE THE HUNGER
TO TRY TO ESCAPE THE HUNGER

BRITANNIA'S WHORES TOOK ALL OUR GRAIN
TO PUT BREAD ON THEIR TABLES
WHILE WALKING SKELETONS CRAWLED TO THE
                                    BOATS
TO ESCAPE IF THEY WERE ABLE
TO ESCAPE IF THEY WERE ABLE

I SAW THEM SCURRYING ON THE BOATS
PANICING AND FRANTIC
YET MOST OF THEM THEY PERISHED STILL
TRYING TO CROSS THE BROAD ATLANTIC
TRYING TO CROSS THE BROAD ATLANTIC

better for me to be brought up in the nice healthy countryside. It was an obvious place for a kid to spend his childhood.

—So you didn't miss them?

—Not really, no. Being a kid, you don't miss people when they're not there. Of course, when they came over and went away again, I'd cry for a couple of days, but I was having the life of Reilly. I had a great time here and I think they should have left me here longer. My mother feels guilty about it, but everything turned out for the best. I'm sure if I'd had a normal childhood I wouldn't have turned out the way I am.

Victoria smiles, faithfully.

—That would have been a tragedy.

Shane agrees, instinctively.

—Yeah. I'd be a different person. Maybe I'd be more famous and more successful. I could be a multibillionaire. Maybe I'd have gone through school and college and university and become some sort of genius, academically. It's very unlikely though. I don't have any talent, apart from musically.

—Yes you do. You once cooked me stir-fried lasagne.

—Yeah. That's true. Okay, I do have other talents.

Shane stubs out a fag, lights another fag and eyes a picture of JFK, respectfully.

—I want to talk about my Uncle Sean. My mother only had one brother and that was my Uncle Sean who was a great singer and a really flash dresser. He was a rocker, he wore wrap-around shades and a flash black suit and winklepickers. He went over to England and worked on a site and he spent all his money on clothes and taking women out. He was a brilliant dancer and he could do any kind of dance. He could sing Irish ballads, country ballads, Elvis Presley. And he had a really cool delivery. He could have been on the stage, just like my mother, they should have been a double act. He was a loveable rogue and women found him irresistible. He taught me about women and how to charm them.

Shane leers, intriguingly.

—Oh yeah? How do you do it?

—His method was just to go up to them and ask them if they wanted to dance and then to dance with them, until they were breathless and they had to sit down. Then he'd sit down with them and put an arm around them and start talking to them about themselves. He said always talk about them.

—**You don't do that. You don't talk about me.**

—I suppose I was so successful with women that I didn't bother with chat-up lines and anybody that I had to bother chatting up, I couldn't be bothered with. But women always like talking about themselves. This was his trick. He was a real piss-taker. He put on a front of being a very cool, sarcastic man, but in fact he was a very warm, loving individual, easily hurt.

—**Just like you.**

—He influenced me a lot. And his singing inspired me a lot. He had the same figure as me and he had blue eyes like me. And he used to really take the piss out of me if I took a girlfriend home. He'd always get her to milk a cow and then we'd stand and watch and comment on her wrist action. Anybody who took themselves seriously, he'd rip them apart. And he could also handle himself in a fight, but he wasn't into starting fights. He got me out of a couple of situations that I got myself into. In the area he was generally known as a man that you didn't fuck with.

I've always been surrounded by older men and women that I looked up to. I have a lot of respect for older people, even people slightly older than me. Because I was the oldest in the family, I suppose I wanted a big brother or a big sister. But I did have hundreds of uncles and aunts and loads of older friends that have taught me about life, what to expect. Who have prepared me for things.

—**Like who?**

—Like my friend Joanne, who told me about my Saturn return, before it happened to me, so that when it did happen, I knew what it was. And my friend Jock Scot, who's been there for twenty years, always giving me fresh hope and optimism. And my Uncle John, who to me was what a man ought to be. And my father and mother.

I'm not saying that their example is necessarily what every man should be, because it's up to you what you want to be. A man should be what he wants to be, that's the important thing to remember. A man should shape his own future and make his own present. Deal with his own past. Charlie Maclennan was a great man also, I'll talk about him later, a man who taught me very deep things about loyalty and trust and paranoia and machismo and how to conduct yourself. *Shane pauses, reflectively. The wind rattles the door, affectionately.*
—My Auntie Ellen was a brilliant concertina player. She could show Terry Woods a thing or two. She used to hide the IRA under her bed behind the pisspots, behind the full, ranking, stinking pisspots. And the Tommys used to come in and they were such wimps that they couldn't go any further once they saw the pisspots. So the IRA guys were safe. It wasn't very pleasant for them, mind you, but better than getting a bullet in the head.

They were all safehouses, all our family houses. My Grand-uncle Mikey, who was the postmaster in Cloughjordan, was the local commandant of the IRA. Which is a handy guy to have being the commandant of the IRA. Tipperary was a *gaeltacht* in 1900, and my great-grandad, John Lynch – whose picture is in the parlour – spoke fluent Irish, and so did my great-grandmother. And so did all the people, in their day. Because they had been alive in the time of the famine. My great-grandad was in the Land League, with Michael Davitt. He was a co-founder of Shannon Rovers. And my uncles and aunties, that brought me up, taught me all my history, the real stories about what happened to them in the Black and Tan war, and the civil war.

But there was only one full-time farmer, and that was my Uncle John, the oldest brother, who actually looked after the farm. My Uncle John, and all that lot, they were real Irish layabouts. I mean, if it came to hiding people on the run and all the rest of it, then they'd move at lightning speed. But what they liked doing was sitting around talking rubbish. But it wasn't all rubbish, of course. I learned a lot from listening to them. And I would be allowed to pipe in. One of the main arguments was, had de Valera had Michael Collins shot or not? And my Uncle John used to say, 'Fuck off . . . don't be so stupid.' Cause he was a really clever man, and he could read your mind. Anyway, when the rest of the men would be squabbling about Dev, the women would be joining in, but they'd be told to shut up, because what did they know about it, sort of thing. And some of them would be piping up for Dev, saying, 'He gave us electricity. Imagine if we were still using the old gas lamps. And because of electricity, we have the radio, and we can know what's going on outside.'

—**But radios don't need electricity.**

—It wasn't a transistor!!! It was a fucking 1930s fucking radio!!! Anyway, my great-grandad, Big John, inherited this kitchen from his father. His younger brother was Tom Lynch. Who ran two pubs into the ground. He was a screaming alkie. But eventually he was cured, while praying to Our Lady. And then he started a third pub which he built into a thriving business. A gold mine. And when all that was done, at the age of about sixty, he gave a lot of money to Big John Lynch, cause he was the one who had fucking fourteen children and was trying to build an extension, to give him bedrooms. Which were all going to be slept in four or five to a bed. And he had to build an upstairs because there were so many of them.

He was thinking modern. He built the parlour as a way of getting people out of the kitchen, and making it a two-room house. You know, a very modern idea in 1901. But the parlour only ever got used to house religious statues. And a grand piano, which they bought at a big house auction for fuck all, because it didn't work. But it looks great! Have you seen it?

—**The piano? Yeah. It's out of tune, though, you're right.**

—Yeah and it's covered in religious statues. There's a harmonium in there as well, which has been kicked to shit by somebody who got frustrated by the fact that they couldn't work out how to play it. Probably my Uncle Mikey, who thought, like, he'd have a go on it. Cause he'd gone as far as he could on the accordion. You know, he lived till ninety-nine.

Hubert, my Uncle Mick's son, Hubert, married Nancy, who was

11

beautiful, and they were both fond of a drink, Hubert and Nancy. Her daughters are all very beautiful, too. Blonde, beautiful with blue eyes.

—I met one of them.

—Yeah, you met Carmel. Did I tell you about Frank and Tony Gleason? Frank and Tony were in a band with my cousin Gerry Lynch. A Dubliners type band. And when I was a kid, Tony Gleason used to bounce me on his knee. He was a fresh-faced youth then. And they all grew beards and everybody was going, 'This is shocking. Isn't this shocking! They've all grown beards!'

Shane laughs, indulgently.

—They were the wild men of the neighbourhood because they'd grown beards. They were like hippies, before hippies arrived. And they'd all grown beards to be like the Dubliners. They had a ballad group, Frank and Tony Gleason, and my cousin Gerry Lynch. My cousin Gerry Lynch originally started off wearing Arran sweaters, and being clean shaven. Looking like one of the Clancy brothers, yeah? Then he stopped wearing Arran sweaters, and grew a beard, and started wearing an old suit. And everybody said how shocking it was that they had beards. They were the first bearded ballad group in Tipperary. I'm just outlining my musical heritage a bit, for you here.

Victoria glides to the dresser and makes two cups of tea, efficiently.

—Who was the milkman? You said something about a milkman?

—Tommy Keane, the milkman. He was another guy who used to bounce me on his knee.

—You got bounced a lot?

—I got bounced a lot, yeah. Bounced on people's knees a lot. And he was always pissed out of his head, right. He used to come round, collecting the milk, y'know.

—Delivering it.

—No, collecting it. The extra milk that you had from the cows, you'd give it to him, and he'd put it in big churns, and he'd take it off and sell it for you in town. But then he'd come around, about three or four every morning, just as we were dousing the fire, and everybody was getting ready to go to bed. Or, people who didn't go to bed weren't getting ready to go to bed, cause a lot of people didn't go to bed. I didn't go to bed much. And Tommy used to turn up pissed out of his head at three or four o'clock in the morning. And in came Tommy, and he'd say, 'Sorry to wake you. Sorry to get you up. Sorry to keep you from your bed.'

—**But he wasn't really sorry, was he?**

—He was sorry, but he needed company. Cause he'd run out of . . . all his pals were comatose, know what I mean. He was one of these men who could drink all night. So he'd sit around the kitchen for the next couple of hours and I'd give him another bottle of stout, and that meant I could get another bottle of stout, too.

—**How old were you?**

—When Tommy used to come around at three or four in the morning?

—**Yeah.**

—I suppose I was about five.

—**Five?! And you'd get another bottle of stout?!**

—Yeah.

—**And how many bottles had you already had?**

—Two.

—**Two!?!?**

—Yeah.

Shane grins, hideously. Victoria nibbles a digestive, attractively.

—**Gosh. That's a lot for a kid.**

—I used to get two a night.

—**Two a night?**

—Yeah.

—**And who gave you that?**

—My Uncle John. He used to bring it in from the boozer . . . when he got back from the boozer.

—**So that'd be quite late.**

—Yeah. He'd get in from the boozer about one o'clock in the morning.

—**And you'd still be up.**

13

—Yeah, I'd still be up.

—**Did nobody try to make you go to bed?**

—No.

—**Why not?**

—I forgot to mention my Auntie Monica.

—**She tried to put you in the bathtub.**

—She did put me in the bathtub, yeah. She used to try and make me go to bed, too, but . . .

—**But what? So why didn't you?**

—I was a disobedient child, y'know.

—**I thought you were a good child.**

—I was a good child, apart from with my Auntie Monica, because she asked me to go to bed, and have a bath, and things. And I didn't want to. So I didn't. And they'd all say, 'Leave the child alone. Leave the child alone.'

—**Did they?**

—Yeah. She used to get so frustrated.

—**I bet.**

—And my granny used to have a go as well, being my granny. But they used to say, 'Leave the child alone. Leave the child alone.' To her, as well.

—**So the men ruled the roost.**

—No, the men and the women used to say, 'Leave the child alone.' There was my granny, right, and she had fucking three sisters, and four brothers. And there was my Auntie Monica, who was my cousin . . . well, my auntie, you know. My cousin really, but I called her my auntie, cause she was like forty. I was six. And even when I used to go back, afterwards, it was the same scene, you know. She didn't leave the house until she married Tom. I told you about her courting Tom in the parlour, and all of it. Basically, they got married, and she left the house, and I never had to have a bath again.

—**So, your granny didn't make that much of an effort, obviously?**

—She made a small effort.

—**But not enough of an effort to make any difference, really.**

—No, not really, no.

—Did they not think that, like, it might be bad for you?

—What?

—Sitting up all night drinking at the age of five?

—They believed in letting the child do what it wanted, as long as it went to Mass.

—And did that include . . . ?

—I mean, not sex, you know. But the child was too young to have sex. I was allowed to smoke, drink and bet, as a child, all of which are regarded by puritans as bad habits, because I came from a very anti-puritan background. Sex was the one thing that was a no-no, sex and blasphemy. You were allowed to say fuck as much as you wanted to, but that isn't blasphemy, that isn't saying anything against Jesus or His Holy Mother. Fuck, itself, is the most popular word in the Irish vocabulary. And I was brought up to say it from a very early age. And I was smoking and drinking and gambling before I could hardly talk.

The first horse I ever bet on was called Maxwell House and he came in at 10–1. I was five years old. So I was a regular gambler after that. And the way my Auntie Nora taught me the gospel was we used to do the Irish Sweepstake together and she used to buy me packets of cigarettes. She was a heavy smoker, she didn't drink but she allowed the men to buy me drink, she told me there was no crime in having a drink, she told me the crime was in worshipping the devil. So with one hand she was dishing out cigarettes and the Irish Sweepstake, which we used to do religiously every week, the two of us and we used to win again and again because it involves a certain amount of intelligence, the Irish Sweepstake, because it involves a crossword puzzle, and then when she had me pissed and smoking like a chimney, she'd start teaching me the gospels. Hideously devious. Jesuits couldn't touch it. So I became a religious maniac at the same time as becoming a total hedonist. And it worked because I'm still a religious maniac and a total hedonist.

It nearly tore me apart, when she died. She died a reasonably dignified death, but unfortunately she was getting out of bed and she was in the process of putting her knickers on when she had a heart attack which killed her immediately. They found her lying on her bed with her knickers around her knees. When I heard, I cried for a week. Just like Hendrix all over again. I'm a very emotional person, however cold I appear on the exterior. A lot of people think I appear cold, but why shouldn't I be, with strangers? I don't know them, they don't mean anything to me. I'm always warm with people I know, if I like them. I'm not a hypocrite.

—**What about stealing and killing? Were they allowed?**

—Stealing and killing were all right.

Victoria scrutinizes her companion, outragedly.

—**No! You didn't try that, did you?**

—I didn't have to steal. I mean, what do you steal for when you're a kid? You steal to get cigarettes, you steal to get booze, you steal to get sweets. I was given all the sweets and cigarettes and booze that I could fucking handle.

—**Did you get drunk?**

—Well, I suppose originally, I got drunk. But you soon get used to two bottles of Guinness a night.

—**Do you remember getting drunk?**

—No. Yeah, I did used to get drunk a bit, yeah.

—**Do you remember the first time you got drunk?**

—I remember the first time I got drunk on whiskey, but I think I've said that.

—**Have you?**

—Well, I'll tell you again, in case I haven't. I used to spy on Tom and Monica, right? In the parlour. So Tom bought me a bottle of whiskey, a baby Powers, one day, in Hannigans, in Kilbarron, the town my mum and dad were married in. And, he said, 'Don't tell anybody I gave that to you!' A baby Powers, right, and I was about eight, I think, when that happened. I wasn't still living here, I was on my school holidays. But I suppose as far as I was concerned I was still living here. School was just an interruption, know what I mean?

—**Yeah.**

—A baby Powers. You know how big that is? It's two doubles, yeah. Two Irish doubles. 'Don't tell anyone I gave you that'! I don't know why he did it. I asked him, that's why. And he worshipped the ground I walked on.

—Why?

—He was just really fond of me, know what I mean. And I used to say to him, 'Tom, don't marry Monica. For God's sake!'

—Why did you say that?

—Cause she'll make you have a bath! Know what I mean. And she'll fucking try to make you go to bed early, and stuff like that.

Victoria chokes on her biscuit, audibly.

—Shane, that's ridiculous. Think about it. I often try to make you have a bath and go to bed early too.

—Yeah! But you're not like Monica. You're more submissive than Monica. She used to get really tough, you know.

—Maybe I should have gotten tougher.

—No, no! See, I will have a bath.

—Yeah . . .

—You'll see.

—Perhaps next year.

—Before that.

—Okay, so he gave you a bottle of Powers whiskey, what then?

—A baby Powers he gave me, yeah. So, I kept it for a while, thinking about drinking it. I was keeping it for a special occasion, know what I mean? Cause I had this whiskey in my pocket, and I was just a kid. And I thought I'd never have another bottle of whiskey in my pocket. But that's the way you think when you're a kid. A bit like an animal.

—Yeah. Hoarding.

—Yeah. I hoarded it, but then one day I said, 'What the fuck!' I drank it in the middle of the day, and I went out in the farmyard, and the geese started talking to me.

—What did they say?

—They were just talking gobbledegook, but I was thinking gobbledegook, know what I mean?! I was out of my fucking brains. I had one belt and I went, 'God Almighty!!!' . . . I got a fantastic rush! And then I went, 'Fucking Hell!' and had the rest of it. And got another fantastic rush! I think they all thought I'd gone a bit loopy, cause however drunk I was, I couldn't say that I'd just had some whiskey, and that I'd got it off Tom. I wasn't that sort of kid.

—No.

—That's why he bought it for me, he wouldn't have bought it if he thought I'd split on him. But the farmyard animals were talking to me, and I was talking back to them. And my Uncle John actually showed some interest in something, for once. He was carting a bucket across the yard, and he sort of looked at me, and he said, 'What the fuck!?!?' I think he sussed it out actually, you know. Well, I was laughing my head off for hours. I remember that really vividly, the first time I got drunk on whiskey.

—**That's a lovely story, Sweet Pea, and I'm sure that's an inspiration to a lot of other people as well.**

—How come?

—**I'm sure millions of people will be following that example, won't they?**

—Yeah, well, this is a book of don'ts!

—**But you're still here.**

—I'm still here, yeah. A few bottles of whiskey later.

—**Yeah. So, you didn't have ill effects?**

—No, I didn't puke. I didn't have a hangover.

—**Weird, huh?**

—Then you couldn't keep me off the stuff.

—**So, their philosophy didn't work, did it?**

—I don't think they thought it really would, y'know.

—**Didn't they?**

—They just couldn't deny me anything. Old people get really mischievous around young people. But it was the old folks who bought me the Guinness and gave me the fags, and started me gambling, and all the rest of it.

—**They were just playing with you, weren't they?**

—It was just like having a little man around the place. They used to call me 'little man'.

—**Did they?**

—Yeah. 'Where are you off to, little man?'

—So they were just wicked.

—Yeah, they were wicked fuckers, yeah.

—It sounds like a fairy story, doesn't it? It sounds like Snow White or something. It would make a brilliant movie for kids.

—But if anybody ever questioned them about it, they would say, 'Well, you know, if you give them enough when they're young, they won't over burden it later on.'

—Well, obviously they were right!

—Well, I can handle my drink, you know.

—You don't beat anybody up.

—No.

—So, I suppose in one way, it did work.

—Yeah. It taught me to respect the stuff, know what I mean.

—But don't you think it's given alcohol a sort of mythical quality in your imagination?

—But there's nothing mythical about it. It already happened, yeah.

—Also, you've never actually experienced life at all without it, have you? You've never experienced life without alcohol.

—Not really, no.

—Cause you've had it since you were a small child. So you don't have memories of not drinking.

—No.

—Like, most people have got a fair stretch where they didn't drink at all, which they can remember, they can remember being happy without even having ever tasted the stuff.

—I was happy without it.

—Were you?

—I wasn't hooked on it . . . at that stage.

—But you had two every day, so you maybe wouldn't know. Were there any days when you didn't have it?

—Well, some nights I didn't get any booze at all, you know. I didn't miss it if I didn't have it.

—Didn't you?

—Well, it was a nice enough place anyway. I know you don't think much of it.

—But when you're a child it's different. Places are different.

—It was a wonderful life anyway. I used to enjoy walking, and running, and . . . all the things that I can't do any more, y'know.

—You can still walk.

—No, I mean going for long walks.

—You could still do that if you wanted to.

—No, I'm not saying I can't do that any more, it's that I don't do that any more. That's what I'm saying.

—Yeah. So, you were a normal-ish child apart from . . .

—I was normal except I had the biggest playground in the world! I had a whole farm. It wasn't a big farm, but I wasn't a big boy. It was like being in a Western.

—Yeah?

—Yeah. I mean, we kids used to fight a family who lived opposite and they used to fight us. Bloody IRA games and Vietnam games were just training for fighting . . . for real, you know. It was just instinctive, like crack dealers and coppers, you know what I mean.

—Did you fight the Protestants? When I was a kid, I went to a Protestant school for a while and the Catholics used to get their heads kicked in every day, in the playground.

—No, but when I would go back to Ireland, after I had moved to England, I'd say to them 'What's the matter with Protestants?' Because now I was mixing with loads of Protestants. So I'd say, 'What's the matter with Protestants?' and they'd say, 'They're going to hell.' Well, they didn't say they'd go to hell, they'd say, 'They're wrong, they've got it wrong.' And like . . .

—But weren't Protestants supposed to go to hell?

—No, no, they spent time in purgatory. And our next-door neighbour, Jim Ralph, was a Protestant, and had his meals with us, you know, because his parents were dead, and he didn't have any brothers and sisters – and he was a very cool guy, you know, a very funny guy. Anyway he was instrumental in a trick I had for avoiding saying the rosary. Everything in my life was a paradox, so even when I was a religious maniac, the rosary used to kill me. And it killed . . .

—Everybody!

—Yeah, everybody, you know what I mean. Except the religious maniac who led the rosary. And everybody was dying for it to finish, and everybody was trying to find an excuse to get out of kneeling down. We used to kneel on chairs, around the kitchen table. Wouldn't be very comfortable, you know. And my Auntie Nora, who led the rosary, even I could see that she was a bit over the top, because she had special novenas for everything, so instead of it being over in forty minutes, it would be an hour and a half.

—**Did you pray on your own?**

—Yeah, I prayed on my own, yeah.

—**What did you pray for?**

—I prayed for all my relatives, and things. And I prayed that I wouldn't die in my sleep.

—**You prayed that?**

—Yeah, and I prayed that I wouldn't wake up in a coffin.

—**Were you afraid that you would wake up in a coffin?**

—Yeah, that was a big fear of mine.

—**And why was that?**

—Dunno. Premature burial thing. One of the big stories that they used to tell me before I went to bed at night, to give me a really good night's sleep, was about the young woman who died, and she wasn't really dead, she was catatonic and was put in a coffin, right, and in the middle of the night, the priest heard banging in the church, but by the time he got there she really was dead.

—**Is that a true story?**

—That has happened, yeah, lots of times. It does happen.

—**Why did they tell you that story before you went to bed?**

—I don't know why they did it. But the only theory that makes sense is that they were preparing you for a heavy, hard life. A life where you were going to have to suffer a lot, and be afraid a lot, and be facing up to fear, right. So, they'd tell you ghost stories . . . horrific stories, before you went to bed. With the result that I didn't like to go to bed.

—**I know, and you still don't.**

—And I still don't.

—**And you're very imaginative.**

—Yeah, but catalepsy does happen, you know what I mean, and ghosts do exist. If I did go to bed, it was always three in a bed, with a couple of girls . . .

Victoria frowns, jealously.

—**With a couple of girls?**

—I found out that girls are much more easily frightened. And all I'd have to say was, there's a fox outside, you know what I mean, and they started shrieking, and had to be calmed down. So, I got my revenge. But I was always obsessed by the macabre. I don't know why. I don't know if they made me obsessed by the macabre, or whether I was naturally macabre. But I mean, some of the stories I was told . . . ! Like, the one about the non-believer who got his girlfriend to nick the host from the church. And then he said, 'This is what we think of the body of Christ', and he cut it in half, right, and blood spurted out all over the place, and all the walls started crumbling, and they all had to run out of the place. And I believed that completely.

—**Did you?**

—Yeah. As a small child, yeah.

—**Well, kids do believe the things they're told, especially by the grown-ups.**

—Yeah, and I believed that Protestants were yellow. My Dublin gran told me that. So, anyway, the best trick for avoiding the rosary was to be out in the fields where Jim Ralph was, cause they were too polite to . . .

—**That was the neighbour, the Protestant?**

—Yeah, he's a Protestant, and they were too polite to shout loud enough for Jim to hear the shout, 'The rosary, the rosary. Time for the rosary!' And of course I felt quite guilty about it, but I also felt like I got away with it, know what I mean.

So it was a very pleasant way of living. I used to go and get lost in the field, and have my own world. And that's when I thought of making up music. I would start making up tunes.

—**In the field?**

—Yeah.

—**How old were you then?**

—Five or six. And then when I'd come back on my school holidays, I'd go back to my field . . . I had a little spot which was my spot, you know what I mean. I can't really explain how exciting it all was, and how much fun it all was. Like, I didn't have to go to bed. And I was allowed to drink. Me and my Auntie Nora, who was a compulsive gambler, would gamble with me. And like, at the same time, would drum into me about catechism, so I imagined hell exactly as it is in the book, with writhing bodies, and flames.

—**Tell me about your dreams.**

—When I was about three or four, I dreamt of naked ladies in a butcher shop. I was working in a butcher shop, and I used to cut off their legs, while they were still alive, and wrap them up, and sell it to customers. And they'd just sit there, while I did it. And uh . . . that was the dream.

—**Was it a sex thing do you think?**

—I dunno . . . I think it was, yeah, I think it was a sex thing,
Shane laughs, beatifically.

—. . . Well, I was dreaming about naked women. I started having erections when I was about five. But I had these dreams before I had erections.

—**Do you have any idea at all where these dreams came from?**

—I was just a kid having dreams . . . I didn't question them.

—**Do you question them now?**

—Well, they seem a bit strange all right, but . . .

—**Do you have any idea where they came from?**

—No, not any more than the lions in the backyard. There were lions in the backyard. And there were tall, statuesque, jet-black people, in white cowls.

—**Yeah?!?**

—Yeah.

—**And what did they do?**

—Nothing much. They were there, you know . . . they were just there. They didn't talk to me. They were quiet.

—Did anyone else see them?

—Nah.

—Did you ever tell anyone about your dreams?

—No. But my dreams used to begin like the beginning of a movie, with a cavalry charge. Yeah, a cavalry charge. The cavalry used to come charging out. Medieval cavalry. In black and white. And then it used to go into colour.

—Did it?

—Yeah.

—And had you seen colour telly? . . . They didn't have colour telly, did they?

—No. I hadn't seen colour telly, no. I hadn't seen any kind of telly.

—Had you seen movies?

—No.

—You'd never seen movies?

—No.

—So you'd have never seen medieval stuff, horses . . .

—Nah . . . I must've seen telly. I must've seen it, somewhere.

—Maybe you were Cecil B. de Mille in a previous life.

—Maybe I was Cesar Romero. No, no . . . George A. Romero. *The Zombie.*

—Did he die? He died in the seventies, didn't he?

—No, he didn't die. He isn't dead.

—Couldn't have been him then. No, you must've been Cecil B. de Mille, he's the one who made all those big epics.

—Yeah.

—You don't know when he died?

—Nah.

—So did you not have any happy dreams?

—They were happy dreams.

—They were happy dreams?

—Well, they weren't unhappy, y'know. But my life was a happy dream when I was a little boy.

—That doesn't sound very happy to me . . . chopping up people, and selling it.

—That's when I was asleep! I've always hated going to bed, going to sleep.

—**Is that because you always had bad dreams, all your life?**

—I've always had mad dreams, yeah.

—**What other kind of nasty dreams have you had?**

—Through the years I've had all sorts of nasty dreams. I've had a recurring dream that I murdered someone and stuffed them in the cupboard in my flat in Cromer Street.

—**But I had that dream!**

—Did you have that dream as well?

—**Yeah.**

—Well, I had the same dream.

—**It must be true! You must've done it!**

The fierce and loquacious wind whistles horrifically in the chimney and a pitter-patter of tiny rodent feet is heard in the rafters. Victoria shudders, appropriately.

—I didn't do it!

—**How do you know?**

—How do I know?!? Cause I know I didn't do it!

—**But how do you know?**

—Because I'd remember if I'd done it.

—**Would you?**

—Yeah.

—**Do you remember everything you've ever done in your whole life?**

—Of course not! But I didn't ever murder anybody and stuff them in the cupboard in Cromer Street.

—**Sure?**

—Yeah.

—**So why did I dream that too then?**

—I dunno.

—**Maybe I'm just psychic.**

Shane grins, reassuringly.

—. . . Now I have recurring dreams about the shop.

—**What shop?**

25

—The record shop.

—The one where you used to work?

—Yeah.

—What happens in them?

—I'm meant to be at work, but I'm late, and I'm trying to get there.

—So what does that mean, dreaming about trying to get to work? That might mean something.

—I dunno.

—Oh . . . Have you seen *The Butcher Boy*?

—Nah.

—That's about a child who works in a butcher shop and chops up a lady.

—Yeah, I know what it's about. I tried reading it.

—Weren't you mildly interested in the fact that you've had similar dreams?

—It never really occured to me.

—Didn't it?

—Nah.

—There's a picture of you as a child, trying to saw the legs off some woman. Tell me about that. That might be a clue.

—That's Mrs Lamb. She was someone we lived with, in England. I thought about sawing her legs off.

Shane chuckles, jovially.

—And that's why there's a picture of me about to saw her legs off.

Shane continues to chuckle.

—And what happened? After the picture was taken, what happened?

—I can't remember.

—Did she think you were cute?

—Yeah. She had endless patience. She had endless patience with me.

—Didn't you do something to her goldfish?

—I fed her goldfish to the cat.

—That's really nasty, isn't it!?

Shane nods, sniggering, quietly.

—Isn't it, Shane?

Victoria leans forward, accusingly.

—Isn't that nasty?!

—Yes, it's nasty. It's nasty.

—Do you regret it now?

—Of course I regret it!

—What did she do then, when you did that?

Shane howls, helplessly.

—She just cried and cried.

—Awwwww. How old was she?

—I dunno . . . well, I was about fourteen.

—That's too old to be feeding somebody's goldfish to a cat, Shane.

No response is noted, apart from muffled laughter.

—Isn't it?

Still, no response is apparent.

—You like children, don't you?

Victoria pleads, ineffectually.

—You do.

—No I don't.

—Why not? Why don't you like children?

—I didn't like being one. I didn't like the ones I met when I was one, know what I mean? And I still don't like them. They give me the creeps.

—Why? Why do they give you the creeps?

—Because they're such cruel, fucking horrible little bastards, know what I mean?

—Yeah?

—Yeah. They've got no fucking shame, y'know.

—No shame?

—No shame, no.

—Would you like to have children?

—Not particularly.

—No?

—Not particularly, no.

—So if we had children, what would happen?

27

—You could look after them.

—Ahh-haa . . . That doesn't seem very nice, does it?

—I'd teach them how to smoke crack.

—Don't you have any nice feelings about children at all?

—Yeah, I quite like children when they get to a certain age.

—What age?

—Eight, nine, ten, or eleven.

—Why?

—Well, cause then they get perky, and you can have a conversation with them, y'know.

—Yeah. They can be very astute, can't they?

—Yeah, yeah. They see things that we don't see.

—Yeah.

—I was a child myself once. I have to remember that, y'know.

—We don't really believe that, do we?

—And I saw things that other people didn't see. But I was lucky, cause I was brought up in a family who did see the things that I saw.

—Yeah?

—Yeah.

—What did they see that you saw?

—The ghosts, and the banshee [*bean sídhe*].

—And did you really see them?

—Yeah.

—What did you see? Tell me.

—I saw ebony people in white cowls.

—Yeah?

—Yeah. And I saw lions in the back yard. But they would say, 'That's all right, I saw them myself!'

—And do you think they did see them?

—I don't know. I don't know whether they were . . . what's the word . . . indulging me, or whether they saw them, y'know. I think they saw them.

—Did you think they were really there, these ebony people?

—Yes. I know they were there.

—How do you know they were there?

—Because I saw them.

—Oh, right, of course. And what did they do?

—They just pointed.

—That's all?

—Yeah.

—They pointed at you?

—They just pointed in some weird direction, know what I mean? No particular direction, y'know. As if there was something more for me to see. But I never saw what it was they were pointing at.

—Maybe they were showing you enlightenment.

—Maybe they were. I get a strong feeling they were. But I couldn't see it. Not when I was a kid.

—Can you see it now?

—I can see it now.

—And what is it?

—It's a huge beautiful light that comes all around you.

—Yeah?

—And like, you see everything it's made out of. Everything is made with squidgy plastic dough.

—Yeah?

—It's all around you all the time, y'know. I'm touching it as I move my hands right now.

—Yeah?

—But there are colours you can hear, and colours . . .

—You can hear the colours?

—You can hear the colours. You can see the sounds.

—You can see the sounds?

—Yeah. And there's all squidgy plastic dough all around you, and you can float on the ceiling, on a magic carpet.

—You know, I'm reading a book about that. It's called *The Nature of Personal Reality*. A channelled book.

—Yeah?

—Describing what reality is made of, yeah. And how we don't normally see all that stuff.

—It's true. Well, I've seen it, and I know it's there.

—**And about how our bodies are actually creating music, you know, with musical vibrations and sounds. And they're eternal.**

—Yeah, over time. Eternally.

—**And if we hear a piece of music that we like, there's actually a physiological change. It changes our physiology.**

—Yeah. Gives you a rush.

—**And it can actually bring you into a state of health, listening to music that you really enjoy.**

—Yeah, I can believe that, yeah.

—**Your cells enjoy music. It makes them happy.**

—Happy cells.

—**Yeah. You know that your cells have feelings and thoughts?**

—Is this going in the book?

—**I don't know. All right, anyway . . . you carry on.**

—I've said all I have to say.

—**Okay then. So, you had a family that understood?**

—Yeah, about things not seen normally.

—**Are there any psychics in your family?**

—They were all psychic. They were all psychic in my family.

—**Did they tell people's futures?**

—Yeah. Well, my great-granny had a dream the night before my Uncle Tommy fell into the threshing machine and got shredded. A threshing machine is what they used before they had combine harvesters. You have a fanbelt with a traction engine and the fanbelt rolls through the motor on the threshing machine, which is a box on wheels that you can pull around on the back of the tractor. People stand on the top, raking in the raw barley, or wheat or oats, and it comes out at the bottom, one end wheat or barley, or oats, and the other end chaff. So there's all this stuff going on inside.

My Uncle Tommy was sixteen years old. He tripped and went into the hole and through the whole machine and came out the wheat end. At least he didn't come out both ends. He lived for two days. How the hell he managed that, I don't know. I would have thought he would have been shredded into little bits and come out both ends. But he didn't, he went through the whole machine and came out with a recognizable human body, still alive, but with absolutely no chance of living and he was nursed for two days and then he died.

Like I said, my great granny's dream told her that Tommy shouldn't go to the fields that day. And she told him, she warned him and she poured God knows how much holy water over him and she begged him not to go, but he went, he was the youngest and he wanted to be one of the lads. Sure enough, when she saw them carrying him back, she knew what had happened.

—This was your great granny on your mother's side?

—Yeah.

—Did you inherit it from her?

—Yeah. I talk to dead people all the time.

—Do you talk to Tommy?

—Yeah, I talk to him a lot.

—What does he say?

—He's sort of cheerful, y'know? He's looking after me. He's looking over my right shoulder.

—Wow! How do you know?

—Cos I can feel him and see him.

—You can see him?

—Yeah. Unless it's me, unless I'm a reincarnation of him. And it could be my imagination, but I've had the description of his death from him, the exact details, minute by minute, of the threshing accident and the four days he took to die. Him out of it all the time on morphine and poitin. He saw heaven, days before he died, and he was telling his mother he could see it.

—So have you asked him why he's hanging around?

—Yeah. Cause we're mates.

—But you never met him. He died before you were born.

—We would have been mates, if we'd lived at the same time.

—But why is he hanging around NOW? Why doesn't he go off to his next life, or whatever people do? Why is he staying with you?

—He's happy with me. He's got a job.

31

—What's his job?

—He's a guardian angel.

—**What does he do, as a guardian angel? Does he guide you?**

—He's never guided me, he's just brought me comfort.

—**He doesn't? Do you have other ones that guide you, other dead relatives?**

—No, they don't have to guide me. They all reckon I'm doing all right.

—**Uh-huh. What about your father? What were his family like?**

—My father's family were MacGowans and the MacGowans were from the North. My great-great-grandfather moved down from the North and made a load of money building. My great-grandad inherited a bit of money and blew it all on whiskey and women and gambling and left my grandad to fend for himself. So my grandad became a civil servant. He also became a barrister and was a gas character.

My father was born in Rathmines, they moved around a lot. They were middle class without much money.

My dad had one brother and two sisters, but one of them died of tuberculosis, when she was about twenty-one. The other sister married a guy who was half French and half English from Belfast. Who was christened Rene, but of course nobody called him Rene, they called him Rennie because he was from Belfast. Rene's so close to Rennie that it didn't really matter. And he had quite an exciting career in the British army during the war because he joined up when he saw a German plane fly over Belfast, and he decided the Germans were the enemy. Before that he wasn't sure whether to join up or not. And he got a great job, he worked as a liaison officer with the Italian resistance. So he spent most of the war drinking wine and shooting Germans. And Italian blackshirts. So he spent his time in classic Hemingway style. And that's my dad's family background. His dad was called Maurice like him. And his mother was called Eileen. She went to Mass every day of her life. She was the one who told me Protestants were yellow.

My dad's family were a bit urban for me. I got on better with my

Auntie Sheila, who was my grandad's brother's wife. My grandad's brother Noel died tragically of cancer just after he retired from the ESB and they had about twelve children. She eventually died a few years ago. She had twenty-three grandchildren.

My father was interested in literature and wrote a bit. His brother became a doctor. And my old man got a job in C&A in the Dublin office. There were only two people in the Dublin office. I don't know what they did there. Then he got posted to England to a job in charge of a department at London head office.

—**How did your parents get together?**

—My parents met each other in a pub in Dublin. Courted for about seven years. My birthdate was perilously close to their marriage, in 1957. Their honeymoon was two weeks driving around Ireland, in a Ford which they'd borrowed, a pretty crappy car. We didn't have a car until I was seven, and that was a secondhand 1956 Hillman. A really horrible car. That was the family car for many years until we moved on to a Mini.

My mum's father died of alcoholic poisoning when she was three and they went back to live on the farm in Tipperary, her and my Uncle Sean and their mother. She and my uncle were a year apart, but they had the same birthday. Quite a strange family really. She went to National School and she was so good at Irish that she won a scholarship to an Irish-speaking school in Carraigaholt. She hated it because they'd go into the town to practise speaking Irish and the minute the locals heard them speaking Irish, they'd start speaking English. And they'd say to the kids, 'Get out of here with your book Irish', they weren't given much of a welcome, which is probably why she hated it. Carraigaholt is a very barren region, on the edge of the Burren, in Clare. Very mean people.

But my mother should have been a Marine. She overcame, adapted, whatever a Marine is supposed to do she did. Improvised. In the end she ran away and went back to the farm and went to the local school. Then she decided she wanted to be a model, so she left the farm and went up to Dublin. She moved to Limerick, first, the big city, then she went to Dublin, the really big city and she lived there in horrible little digs with just room for her and her flatmate and the stove which kept them warm. And then she met my old man in a pub and he used to come round and bring them cakes his mother would bake. I've never thought of asking him how he chatted her up, but knowing my old man he would have said something pretty rude. Something about her being a culchie, probably.

Apparently my old man was a hundred times worse than I've ever been. A real bastard. And she was attracted to him. Women seem to have a thing about bastards. Being a nice guy never seems to get you anywhere. I suppose it works for Tom Hanks. I wouldn't be surprised if he turned out to be a bastard too.

I know that at first she detested my old man, though, and it was his mate she was interested in, this guy called Tony Portley. He wasn't portly though, he was thin and he was from Limerick, so they hit it off, both being from the country. And my old man used to get pissed and obnoxious and Tony Portley would be all charming. But it didn't get him anywhere because she was actually into my old man, I don't know why. She doesn't know. She can't understand it herself, why she was attracted to him, but she says there was a little-boyish charm about him, about this obnoxious turd. She found him boyishly charming. He still lived at home, he didn't move out of home until after they got married.

So in the meantime she became a successful model and she was Colleen of the Year in 1954 and she was photographed with three Irish wolfhounds on the front of the *Independent*. She's looking really nice in a white knitted jumper. The female wolfhound is nearest to the camera and she's looking straight ahead, disinterested. My mother is in between the two of them. The male one is obviously trying to fuck my mother from behind, you can see he's got his paw around her neck. She said it was a very uncomfortable photo shoot. So she became a successful model for a few years. Then she was hoping to get into being an actress and singer. I forgot to mention that she is a brilliant singer. She's won loads of cups for her traditional Irish singing. And dancing. And she's also good at Broadway ballads and jazz ballads. So she was hoping to become an actress. It could easily have happened. And then she goes and marries my old man and that's the end of that. She said she thought he'd grow up and become a responsible husband when they got married and had a kid, but on the contrary he started drinking more than ever and gambling more and whenever he was looking after me I spent my time sitting outside the bookies or in the pub. I was a happy child.

My mum met Patrick Kavanagh when she lived in Dublin. Patrick Kavanagh used to pick up young girls from the country, but he couldn't pick her up. He used to lie in wait for them under a certain bridge in a dodgy part of Dublin, where it wouldn't be safe for a girl to walk on her own and he'd offer to escort them to their doorsteps. And he used to read them poetry and eat raw onions to keep his health up, being an alcoholic. And she was the sort of girl that he was on about in the poem 'Raglan Road'. And my Auntie Catherine used to work at the reception desk at the *Irish Times* and Brendan Behan used to come in to collect his money, in cash. He always wanted it in cash so he could go out and blow it at the boozer. *A stray mouse ambles across the stone floor, casually. The fragrant fumes from the still immodest fire tickle the nostrils of our hero and his heroine, fondly. Outside, in the sleepy dawn sky, a light rain descends, soporifically, as Victoria drifts into a slumber, snoring elegantly. Shane continues to contemplate, contemplatively, whilst puffing cigarettes, industriously, and composing great masterpieces, effortlessly.*

DRUNKEN MIX

ACT TWO

Filthy MacNasty's Whisky Café, London, night. A fierce and loquacious barman mops the gleaming mahogany bar with an immaculate dishrag, determinedly. A pristine pint of Guinness awaits a valued customer, proudly. Shane MacGowan takes a cigarette from a packet of Carrolls and a light appears, as if from nowhere. A large martini sits on the bar in front of him. His companion, Victoria, radiant as ever, in pale green silk – which becomes her – consumes a plate of chips, hungrily. A tape-recorder is activated, eventually. Victoria addresses her beloved, respectfully.

—So, when did you move to England?

—When I was six, nearly seven, I started going to school in England. My mum came to the farm and collected me. I ran away and hid, but they found me and I cried and they cried and we all cried and off I went to England, to live with them in Brighton.

—Why Brighton?

—I don't fucking know why they chose Brighton. Do you think parents are going to tell a six-year-old kid why they're moving to Brighton? I didn't ask. Anyway, Brighton was boring, after Ireland.

—Wasn't it full of mods and rockers chasing each other?

—There was mods and rockers, yeah, but that was the only thing it had going for it, in the early sixties. And I was too young to take advantage of stuff like that.

—So what did you do? Did you go to school?

—I went to a convent school, yeah, where my mum was a typist. And when it was half-term, I went to Uncle Frank's and when it was the holidays, I went back to Ireland.

—Why did you always go to someone else's house, when you weren't at school?

—I think for some reason my parents didn't particularly want me around. I must have been a pain in the arse.

—**Probably. I mean, you still are difficult to live with.**

—Although there might have been other reasons. They were both busy working, y'know, and they were depressed about being in England and they didn't want to dump it on me, unless it was absolutely necessary, but seeing as they knew they were going to be in England a long time, they decided I'd better go to school in England, so when it was time for me to go to school, they fucking had to cart me over to England, I think that's the reason they did it.

—**Did you miss Ireland?**

—Of course. My Uncle Frank was the only link to Ireland that I had, when we moved to England. At half-term, I used to always go and stay with him. Frank gave me James Bond books, which my parents would never have done, they thought James Bond books were trash. But they turned me on to sexuality and to being cool and dressing well. After reading James Bond books, I wanted to wear mohair suits and I wanted to wear Fred Perrys, stuff that I never thought of, down on the farm.

My Aunty Catherine was into Joyce, Behan, Russian stuff. My dad, and or me, permanently 'borrowed' *Ulysses* and *War and Peace* off her. Also, she turned me on to Mikhail Sholokov – *Quiet Flows the Don*.

So when my mother made her effort at educating me, by giving me Edna O'Brien's *Girl with Green Eyes* to read, I just thought it was a beautiful novel and I admired the writing – although it's not one of her best books, my mum had all her books – that was the cleanest one, which is why my mum gave me that one. The one sex scene in *Girl with Green Eyes* is pathetic, it doesn't explain anything to an enquiring mind. All my dad did was to say to me, 'You know where you came from? You came out of my dick.' And left it to me to imagine the rest.

Uncle Frank was a great historian. Being from Mallow, he had an expansive brain.

—**Being from Mallow?**

—I mean *considering* he was from Mallow. I don't mean that being from Mallow you would have an expansive brain, that's not the truth at all, of course it isn't, anybody who's been to Mallow knows that, Frank and Catherine (only joking!). Both knew a lot about Irish history, which my parents were good on and which I had been taught by the old folks on the farm. So he was a link with Ireland for me, he ran a great pub in Dagenham for the Irish Ford workers, which is what Sally MacLennane is based on. My dad helped out there sometimes.

[sings]

Well Jimmy played harmonica in the pub where I was born
He played it from the night time to the peaceful early morn
He soothed the souls of psychos and the men who had the horn
And they all looked very happy in the morning.

Now Jimmy didn't like his place in this world of ours
Where the elephant man broke strong men's necks
When he'd had too many Powers,
So sad to see the grieving of the people that he's leaving
And he took the road for God knows in the morning.

We walked him to the station in the rain
We kissed him as we put him on the train
And we sang him a song of times long gone
Though we knew that we'd be seeing him again
(Far away) sad to say I must be on my way
So buy me beer and whiskey cos I'm going far away (far away)
I'd like to think of me returning when I can
To the greatest little boozer and to Sally MacLennane.

The years passed by the times had changed I grew to be a man
I learned to love the virtues of sweet Sally MacLennane
I took the jeers and drank the beers and I crawled back home at
   dawn
And ended up a barman in the morning.

I played the pump and took the hump and watered whiskey down
I talked of whores and horses to the men who drank the brown
I heard them say that Jimmy's making money far away
Some people left for heaven without warning.

We walked him to the station in the rain
We kissed him as we put him on the train
And we sang him a song of times long gone
Though we knew that we'd be seeing him again
(Far away) sad to say I must be on my way
So buy me beer and whiskey cos I'm going far away (far away)
I'd like to think of me returning when I can
To the greatest little boozer and to Sally MacLennane.

—Speaking of Sally MacLennane, the elephant man in that song was
a real bloke, who used to come in the pub in Dagenham and he was
a huge bloke and he used to get into terrible fights and he'd crunch
people and one night he got in a fight with another huge bastard and
he won the fight, but he got a broken neck in the process. And he
went around with a cast around his neck for the next six months,
which is why they called him the elephant man. The elephant man
broke strong men's necks when he'd had too many Powers. Powers
whiskey, obviously.
—So, did you like school?
—The convent school was great, it was all Irish nuns and Irish kids.
They were Franciscans, the followers of Saint Francis, who said
'Brother Sun, Sister Moon'. He talked to the animals and he dressed

in beggar's clothes and the Franciscans are an order that believes in the love of Jesus, not the wrath of God.

I didn't like living in England, though, and all I looked forward to was going home to Ireland, when the school holidays came, which I did, every year of my life. I also loved staying with my Uncle Frank, of course, because he ran boozers and I loved being allowed to stand behind the bar, watching all the fights and the band playing Irish songs, which I knew.

—**How did you feel when your sister was born, were you pleased?**

—Siobhan arrived when I was five and I wasn't particularly pleased, because any attention I did get automatically went to her, so I got jealous as hell, which is a natural thing for kids.

—**Yeah.**

—I called Siobhan 'it' for most of her early childhood. I remember when she started walking, I was the first person to see her walking and I said to my mum, 'Look, it's walking.'

—**Shane! That's horrible.**

—But anybody will tell you I was one of the nicest children you could meet. I said my prayers, I ate my dinner, I only had to be smacked two or three times.

—**What for?**

—That was for sociopathic behaviour. Like locking my sister in a cupboard.

—**Did you deserve it?**

—I didn't feel I deserved it at the time.

Actually, I was quite violent, as a kid. I tended towards violence. But all the other kids did as well. That's what growing up in London is all about. I became violent when other people became violent to me, which was when we moved up to London. We moved around a lot, I went to various different schools, I'm not going to go through all the different places we moved to, but it was about five different places, I suppose. I was eight when we moved up to London.

—**Where did you live?**

—The first place we moved to was Ealing. In the convent, I didn't feel cut off from Ireland so much, because I was surrounded by nuns and other Catholic kids, but I had to leave that school when I was eight, because you had to leave at eight, if you were a boy, because they reckoned you were a danger to the girls, after that.

—Were you a danger to the girls?

—I don't think I would have been a danger to the girls, I wasn't interested in them, sex was something people of your mum and dad's age did.

—Yeah, but you told me you'd read *Venus in Furs* when you were six!!!!

—Yeah, that's right but the people in *Venus in Furs* are not kids, it's just unusual for a kid to read it.

So what's *Venus in Furs* about? I haven't read it.

—*Venus in Furs* is about a dominatrix. For the stupid people, that means a mistress with a whip. She was completely naked, apart from a fur around her neck and it was about her relationship with her sex slave, Severin. Steve Severin of the Banshees named himself after her. It also inspired the Velvet Underground song 'Venus in Furs'. It's about her whipping him and him fucking her and then her whipping him and him fucking her; it's a very erotic book and it gives you an instant stalker, if you're liable to those things, at the age that you're reading it, and I read it when I was about eight.

And it had the illustrations, as well, which made it particularly graphic, so I regularly wanked off over that, dry, without any cum, because I wasn't pubescent yet.

—Did you want her to whip you? Did you fantasize about being whipped?

—I was clever enough to realize that it was the woman that was the important part of the book, unless you were a sado-masochist. The book can be read two ways. If you're a sado-masochist, you get off on the whipping scenes, but if you're straight, like me, you get off on the fucking scenes. The fucking scenes were very lurid and realistic, looking back, so I knew what it was all about, at the age of eight.

I was interested in doing it and I fantasized about doing it, but I fantasized about doing it with grown women, not with little girls that didn't have tits. I was a tit man, from the word go. Probably because in the illustrations in *Venus in Furs*, she's got massive tits. I used to get horny about the Venus de Milo and stuff like that. I've never been into little girls, not even when I was a little boy. I was always into big women. There was a tinker girl I used to play with on the farm, when I used to go in the holidays. I had a sort of weird kind of a sexual relationship with her. We used to sort of cuddle each other and stuff, we were just playmates, really, but she was fourteen and I was eight, so she was always a few years older than me and the youngest woman I fancied was her. But I didn't really think about her, when I got hard-ons, even though she was a lovely looking girl and she had big tits. And it wasn't because she was a tinker girl that I didn't think about her, we weren't prejudiced against tinkers in our family, I just used to think, 'There but for the grace of God go I'. Anyway, later, when I was about eleven or twelve, I started getting interested in a girl called Trudy Brereton, who was a big-breasted beauty with black hair, a bit like you, with more than a passing resemblance to you. She left a torch in my heart.

Anyway, so we moved to London and my parents were very depressed and I was very depressed and Siobhan was very confused, because we were all so depressed. Although Siobhan used to go to Ireland as well, she didn't have quite the same attachment to it that I did. But she formed an attachment to it. Siobhan lives in Ireland now, she felt the urge to move back stronger than I did. I do feel it all the time, but I don't feel like I've made enough money yet. The idea is to come over here and make the money and go back. And in my line of business, you have to come over here.

So my time in England was just boring and depressing, until I became an adolescent, and I couldn't wait to get back to Ireland.

—**Didn't you have any friends?**

—I did make some friends, most of them were Irish Catholics. There was an exception, a real thug who was into reggae, this was when I was about ten or eleven, in London, so it was the late sixties and he was into reggae and I was into reggae and he had a gang and he initiated me into his gang by putting a dustbin over my head and banging on it for half an hour, that was the initiation ceremony and because I didn't scream or anything, he was so impressed by my lack of fear – because I didn't give a shit, they'd already kicked the shit out of me God knows how many times by then, for being a Paddy. He was a half-caste, so it was a half-caste and a Paddy bonding. We both hated the Brits. And we both loved reggae. And what's more, I knew more about reggae than he did, I was cooler on the new releases than he was. I was always into music and I spent my pocket money on singles. So every two weeks, I got a new single. And it was all Motown and stuff. My parents had the Irish stuff and I knew all the Irish stuff off by heart, so I was getting into pop music, by this stage. And reggae and soul were particular favourites of mine and also particular favourites of this guy.

He was definitely a sociopath, as you might imagine, putting a bin over someone's head and banging it for half an hour. So we got to be great friends and I had his protection from then on and he made me his Minister for Torture, so I got to do the stuff with the bin to lots of other people. And I loved it. I was getting back at those Brit bastards who'd beaten me up.

—**Were you beaten up a lot, then?**

—I was beaten up a lot. They used to say, 'Oi, Paddy, sing us an Irish song.' And I used to go, 'Which one?' like a dope, every time. 'That one "Kevin Barry".' And I'd sing 'Kevin Barry'. When it got to the bit where it goes, 'Another murder for the crown', they'd go, 'The crown never murdered anybody, right?' And beat the shit out of me. I fell for that four times, before I clocked on.

—**Is that why you hate English people?**

—I think my hatred for them came from the old folks back at home, originally, but it was re-inforced by the fact that they turned out to be as big a bunch of bastards as I'd been told they were.

—**But Shane, you do have friends who are English.**

—I have made some English friends, I'm not saying there aren't any good English people, just that I didn't have a very good experience with them, growing up. And I didn't like the country.

So, at school, I was Minister of Torture, for a while. I put dustbin lids over kids' heads and banged them for half an hour, I got stinging nettles and rubbed their balls with them, tweaked their nipples and generally abused them. That was before I read the Marquis de Sade. I got into sadism without reading the Marquis de Sade, but sadism is a fairly normal human condition. Particularly for kids, although some people don't grow out of it.

—So, did you grow out of it?

—Yeah, I grew out of it because I got into drink. If I hadn't got into drinking, it's quite possible I might still be into sadism. I enjoyed it, for a while.

—Didn't you feel sorry for the kids you were torturing?

—I didn't feel sorry for the bastards, they'd beaten me up enough times, it was just payback time. That's when I got my payback and then I forgot about it. I didn't feel bitter about being beaten up, after that. I still felt bitter about being in England, though. But as I gradually became an adolescent, it occurred to me that there was a lot more happening in the way of skirt and drink and drugs and parties and discos and gigs and all the rest of it in England than there was in Ireland. So I still went back to Ireland, but I started enjoying myself more in England. I had great fun going to the dances in Ireland, too, of course, but I was a bit of a celebrity by then, because I lived in England and they all thought I was sophisticated, coming from London. I don't think that inferiority thing that Irish people had then exists any more, Ireland's a hip country now.

—Yeah. It's more hip to be Irish than English. So what else happened at school?

—Well, there was also a kid called Jimmy at the convent school and he was definitely a sociopath. He was a hoodlum and a bully and a real fucking tearaway and I instantly befriended him. I've done that all through my life, I've always been attracted to sociopaths. Jimmy and me used to lock each other in the coal bunker at the back of the house, just for the hell of fighting and then we used to beat each other up. We were best friends. That's what we did to each other so you can imagine what we did to the rest of the kids. But the reggae thug was a psychopath, he was the first psychopath that I ever met.

He was a genuine psychopath, with that cold look in his eyes, the twenty-thousand-yard stare, like a Vietnam war veteran. 'Listen to him scream,' he'd say. 'Isn't it funny? Ha ha ha ha. Hahahahahha. Have you heard the new Trojan single by the Heptones?' And then he'd start singing a reggae song, while the guy was screaming in agony. He was like Michael Madsen in *Reservoir Dogs*. He was psycho. He put a chill down my spine. I've always liked living on the edge, not just with drugs and drink and jumping out of cars and stuff, but also with the human beings that I deal with. I've always loved taming psychopaths. I've always been able to do it, that's why I'm still alive.

—Yeah? How do you tame a psychopath?

—You do it by flattering them and finding an interest in common, that takes their mind off violence. Music is a great one for doing it. Or just making them laugh. Making a psychopath laugh is a very difficult thing, but if you can do it, you're away, you're his bosom pal.

—I suppose the Pogues have attracted quite a few psychopaths.

—We get a few psychopaths in our audience, but they're just mainly boozy bozos who like having a good time. I like to think that I can control the psychopaths in the audience, we've never had a serious fight at one of our gigs and we've never had anybody get killed.

So, anyway, on the home front, my mother was even more depressed by now, because she'd been denied the sacraments, for taking the pill. I was a difficult birth, Siobhan was even more difficult and she was told that if she had a third baby, she would die and so would the baby, so she went to the priest. Now this happened in England, this was an English priest, so this is not a horror story about the Catholic Church in Ireland. She went to the priest and she told him, 'I've been told that if I have another baby, I'll die, and the baby will die as well, so I've got to use the pill.' No contraception was allowed, by the Church. The priest said she could come to Mass, but she couldn't go to Communion. That was a massive blow for her and I think it was one of the main factors that contributed to her nervous breakdown, later on, apart from hating this godforsaken country anyway. That was what she got from the English Catholic Church, for needing to take contraception for medical reasons and I've never forgiven them for that. So she was even more depressed than ever by now, but she was holding herself together, she was a strong woman.

I'm not going to try to work out why she had a nervous breakdown, but I can't understand why she didn't have one earlier. I told you my parents were both very unhappy. I was unhappy too, obviously. I couldn't understand why we had made ourselves unhappy by leaving Ireland and coming to live in this shithole. I asked my dad and he said we came here because of work, but he agreed with me that it's a shithole. You've seen the picture of my dad when he was skinny?

—The one on the beach? He's not that skinny.

—Well, he wasn't always that skinny. He was like a young Reggie Kray. He was a goodlooking bloke.

—Reggie Kray's not goodlooking.

—He was when he was younger. My dad was a Reggie type. I don't mean he had people blown away, but he looked good in a suit and my parents looked great when they went out together. I never got over the amount of shoes he had. Most of them were Densons and Eatons. When Dr Feelgood first came on the scene, they were aping the look of the average early sixties men of my father's kind. A young man who was into dancing and drinking. Unfortunately, my father was more into drinking than dancing. And he was a compulsive gambler, but a brilliant one.

—You still haven't said why your mother had a nervous breakdown.

—Yeah, I'm getting to that. Years earlier, my mother had started complaining of fibrositis, which is an old person's disease. She had spent less than twenty years living in that damp old house. She's a very healthy individual and no one in her family had ever complained of even the slightest twinge of fibrositis which is the beginning of arthritis. She didn't get fibrositis from nowhere, BUT she didn't get it in Tipp, where it would have been logical for her to get it, because we'd all run around in the rain and we'd run out to have a shit in the middle of the night, in the pissing rain and it hadn't done any of us any harm. So what I'm suggesting is that she didn't have fibrositis, she had extreme depression, which she was telling herself was fibrositis. So she lay in a room and looked at the ceiling.

—That's what I do, when I'm depressed.

—Well, you're a complete fuck-up. Look, it's not natural for a woman of her age and strength and health to be suffering from what's basically arthritis.

—So why was she depressed?

—She hated it here. And he never came home until three in the morning, arse-holed usually, and possibly with a few friends in tow, so they could carry on the party at home.

—But you did that to me.

—Yes. I'm not denying it. I thought my old man was a great guy, he was a very entertaining guy. But if I was a woman, with a child, living with him it would be a different matter. In those days, if you were married with a kid, you didn't stay out drinking until three in the morning. Well, in Ireland, you did. But the whole point of moving to England was that they were going to have a modern life. So he must have said, of course I won't spend every night on the piss. I'm guessing he said that, but he must have said that. England was supposed to be a great place to be, you could get divorce, abortion, trendy clothes, stuff like that and nobody went to Mass or said the Angelus and you couldn't be excommunicated. The English priests were devout, educated men from rich families. To be an English Catholic you have to have come from one of those Cavalier-type families, you know what I mean. So in England, even Catholicism was supposed to be easygoing and air-conditioned.

—So what was the reality?

—England was full of fucking immigrants fighting each other for low-paid jobs. And there was an epidemic of drugs. The West Indians brought over blues, which are a mixture of amphetamine and pheno-barbitol. That's what the mods lived on. And Irish kids of my age got split down the middle, really heavily. They either decided that they would never be English, however long they spent in England, they would always be Irish, or they became ashamed of their own parents and their own roots and believed the general belief that Paddys were stupid and violent and drunken and that that was all there was to them.

—What's this got to do with your mother having a nervous breakdown?

—Well, I was being confronted by Paddys who didn't want to be Paddys. And I had a strong Irish accent. My mother was really into getting away from the bog and staying away from it forever, so why the fuck she left me there so long is beyond me, but I was fully Irish, by the time I left there, you know what I mean? I spoke with a Tipperary accent and I was fanatical about hurling and the IRA. And I always defended myself, so I got into a lot of fights. You wouldn't catch me running away from a fight, you know what I mean?

And my father was drinking in pubs where nice people didn't drink, because that was where you got the best racing tips and that was what he was into. And I became an adolescent and I started hanging around in cafés, with hippies and greasers and peanuts.

—What's a peanut?

—A peanut is a late mod, a neo-mod. Halfway between a mod and a skinhead. Peanuts were around about '68, '69, '70. They looked more like mods than skinheads, but they were more aggressive looking than mods.

—Were you a peanut?

—No, I was a greaser, I wore my hair long and quiffed up and I wore a black t-shirt, black jeans and winklepickers and a leather jacket, sort of James Dean, Elvis Presley, Cliff Richard kind of look. Like John Lennon used to wear, that's called a greaser. So I used to hang around with other greasers, hippies and peanuts. This was when I was twelve or thirteen. When I was thirteen, I had my first joint, at a festival in Kent.

—Which festival?

—I don't know. A downmarket festival, it wasn't anything to write home about, but I got my first ride on a motorbike and my first go on a joint, from a hippy.

—Did you like it?

—It didn't really do a lot to me, actually. I was drinking beer and that seemed to do a lot more to me. That's quite common with your first joint, it doesn't do anything to you, apparently. After that I used to go to gigs and get given joints regularly and it started having an effect on me. And then I went to Westminster.

—How did you end up going to Westminster?

—My mother was a great believer in education. And I was regarded as a gifted child. I was speaking and taking part in conversations at the age of two.

—Two?

—Yeah. So the priest was saying to the family, 'I think you've got a genius on your hands, he could be a priest, a Jesuit'!!! They looked at my drawings and my stories. When I was three, I was writing IRA stories. I'd had first-hand accounts of Irish twentieth-century history from my relatives. And I was drawing hurling pictures. We used to listen to the hurling on the radio, and I used to draw pictures all the time, during the matches.

So the priest tested me on my religious knowledge, which was phenomenal. I could recite the catechism by heart at three. And he said I should be a priest.

—At three?

—Yeah. I could do it at two. So, no one in my family was very keen on the idea of me becoming a priest, but my mother was excited about me being a genius and she decided that I had to have the best education possible. My dad was pissed off about that I think, because it meant going to a fee-paying convent in England and he wanted the money for drink. But after that it was all scholarship schools. Westminster was regarded as the best school in England, academically, and we could never have afforded the fees, so I got a scholarship.

I was told I was incredibly good at writing, even though I didn't think I was. Every time a teacher looked at a piece of writing I'd done, it would blow their minds. And I was good at history and French and art, as well. I had written an essay about Eliot's Preludes, which got used for teaching the English class I was in, the term before I arrived, so they used to take the piss out of me about it all the time. But I was just doing what I could do naturally, I didn't think anything about it, I did it because I had to do it for school. I didn't want to be good at school, I just wanted to get school over with and get into life. Being good at English literature and the use of the English language, I'd learned from Irish people, ironically enough, who speak the best English in the world. Well, it's a toss-up between the Irish and the Scots. It certainly isn't the English, or the Americans.

When I went to Westminster, we were doing pills and acid and going to the pub and smoking cigarettes, which were all illegal and I got kicked out quite soon.

—**Do you think that contributed to your mother's nervous breakdown?**

—Well, it didn't help.

—**Why did you get kicked out, did they catch you?**

—I got nicked, while I was at Westminster, which is why I got turfed out. Me and a bloke called Charlie had been nicking records down Liverpool Street. We used to do this regularly, we used to go on nicking sprees, like all teenagers do. It was a Sunday, this particular day and we'd had a really good day, so Charlie said, 'Let's be really free and smoke a joint out in the open.' We were standing outside my house at the time. So we had a joint out in the street and some old biddy who was looking out her window called the cops.

The next thing I knew, two dodgy-looking characters in plain clothes came up to us. We'd finished the joint, but they said, 'Let's have a look in your pockets.' And in my pockets, I had the stuff. We both got taken down the nick, but he got sprung, because he didn't have anything on him. And they rang up my parents and my dad had to come down and bail me out. Later on, I got taken down to Tower Hamlets juvenile court and fined five pounds. They had three magistrates at the juvenile court, there was a black guy, a woman and a normal boring old beak. They gave me a five-pound fine and a year's probation, so I was on probation for a year. I used to have to go and see this probation officer, who was a really nice guy, actually, and just tell him I wasn't taking drugs and stuff. He believed me, even though I was stoned out of my head every time I went to see him. I never made any attempt to even pretend I wasn't. But he was a nice guy, I think probation officers generally are nice guys, the ones who really want to help people.

—**What did you do then?**

—I got a job, the minute I was thrown out of Westminster, as a shelf-filler in a supermarket, but it involved unloading lorries as well; it's called a shelf-filler, but you don't just fill shelves, you unload massive loads off lorries, I'm talking about massive loads. I was a strapping lad, I had muscles bulging out of my shirt. If Boyzone had been around at the time, I would have joined. I would have been a bit young, maybe, though, at fourteen.

—**Did you like your job?**

—I enjoyed getting paid, but I didn't enjoy the work. I've never enjoyed work, but it did keep me fit, considering all the stuff I was doing with the money that I made. I saved my money and I went back to Ireland as often as I could. I had a series of jobs. Then I spent a bit of time in limbo, while my mother had a nervous breakdown and my father got really fucked up on the booze and Siobhan got even more confused. My parents didn't have any control over me by then, my mother had had her nervous breakdown and she stayed in bed, pilled out of her head. She looked like she was dying. Acted like she was dying. I thought she was dying. I was quite upset. My old man was pissed all the time and he came in and just shouted at people, at whoever dared show their face and the only people who dared show their faces were me and Siobhan. But I was too big for him to beat me, so it ended up with me attacking him at one point and my mother broke it up. She was

still stronger than either of us, because of her Tipperary breeding. My mother can carry two sacks of potatoes. Up a hill on a wet day. And in 1975 I went on a trip to Tipp, with Peter Gates. De Valera had just died, and was lying in state.

—I remember that. But do you think there might be people who don't know who de Valera was?

—De Valera was the man who they attempted to set up for the murder of Michael Collins, thus destroying the Republican movement altogether.

—I mean they might not know anything about him . . .

—He was a great Irish patriot and he was the father of the modern nation.

—Yeah, but can't you just tell them he was the President?

—All right!!! He was the President SEVERAL TIMES. AND he was the Taoiseach several times and he was the leader of the IRA and he was the founder of the Irish Press . . .

—That's what I meant.

—And we missed the coach, so we got the boat train.

—Just the two of you?

—Yeah. Up to Liverpool. We got pissed on the train. And we had a row straight away. He put on some classical guitar music, and I said, 'What's that fucking crap?!' Y'know. And he was the kind of guy who used to get shirty about things like that, so he said, 'What do you mean, what's that fucking crap? That's fucking Julian Bream,' or whatever. So we were at each other's throats all the time. And it was the usual boat trip. Doors banging, people getting sick, babies screaming, fucking football supporters all over the bloody place.

Anyway, we got to Dublin, and me and Pete were squabbling so much by then that we split up in Dublin. And he went up to O'Donahues, and some idiots down there tried to recruit him into the IRA.

—Yeah?! How come, if he's English?!

—He was second-generation Irish Catholic, and they didn't care anyway, they were only taking the piss. But he took it seriously. And he nearly joined up. Anyway, we'd both brought guitars with us, right, and we went down to Tipp, and we arrived on the farm.

—**Hang on. How did you get back together again if you had split up?**

—Well . . . we met up later on in the evening, y'know, we split up for the day cause we were getting on each other's tits. The point of this is that we got to the farm, right, and my Uncle Sean was shovelling shit in the farmyard, y'know, that's my mother's brother; and they instantly hit it off, because Pete had worked on the sites, and my Uncle Sean worked on the sites for years. Pete worked on the sites for about three days!

Shane chortles, fondly.

—But he was giving it all this, 'Oh, I worked on the sites', you know what I mean . . . 'Can I help you round the farm?' So my Uncle Sean had him milking the cows, mucking out the sheds, fucking doing everything, while I sat there with my feet up, drinking Guinness and whiskey, and talking to my Uncle John.

Every night we used to walk into town, and go to the boozer, with our guitars, and we started a jam session going at the back of Reddan's bar, also known as the Yank's bar. You could fit about three hundred people in there and in the end there was about three hundred people coming every night. And we were playing with this guy Donal Quinn, who was the local guitar genius at the time.

We were mixing it with rock and roll and the Rolling Stones. And we had really massive jam sessions where one minute we'd be playing 'The Rocky Road to Dublin', the next minute we'd be playing a Simon and Garfunkel track.

There was a bunch of us, there was me and Pete and a whistle player who jammed with us. And Donny Quinn.

So that was really the original Pogues. I've never understood why it took me so long to make the connection. It never occurred to me to take it seriously and try and make a career out of it. I had a mental block that said Irish music is one thing and pop music is another. I didn't think about it, but that was just the way it was sectioned off in my brain, because of the different ways I'd got into the two different kinds of music.

The Irish stuff I'd learnt from childhood, totally naturally. The pop stuff I'd learned off the radio later on, although I did start listening to the radio from a very early age too. The Beatles, the Stones, I liked, all good music. My dad had jazz, country and Irish. My mum liked Roy Orbison and Tom Jones, so I grew up liking all types of music. And still it never occurred to me that you could play Irish music to a rock audience.

Even when the Specials went and did it with ska. It was glaring me in the face. The Specials took old ska and made a new kind of beat music out of it. But it was when these people started playing World music, there was a trend for white people playing African Highlife music, and Latin music, there was a lot of that shite, when that happened I thought hang on a minute, we've got our own cultural folk tradition sitting here in the Irish pubs, why isn't there a band doing that? Then it finally clicked. Start a London Irish band playing Irish music with a rock and roll beat. The original idea was just to rock up old ones but then I started writing. So Pete was the first guy that I experimented with, mixing rock and roll and Irish.

—What about the guys you hung out with in London? What were they like? Were you close?

—There was a guy who I'll call John, who was a really nice guy. He was a big guy, he could really do you a lot of damage but he wasn't an aggressive bloke. He looked after me. I used to start arguments, he used to finish them. I was an obnoxious little fuck. It was a kind of game of ours. I'd wind somebody up so much they couldn't handle it any more and then John would kick the shit out of them.

We also did a bit of thieving together. We'd do things like breaking into restaurants, into the kitchens, and getting those big catering size tins of baked beans and peas. A lot of the time the back door was left open, when everything was fairly quiet and they were closing up. And there would be nobody in the kitchen because there would be nobody cooking. But if we did have to break into anywhere, because we did have to break into dive bars of pubs, we'd just smash the glass and open the door from the inside, or if that didn't work just kick it in.

—Kick it in? That must have been hard.

—It's not very difficult, forcing a door.

—Weren't you afraid you might get caught? I would have loved to have done stuff like that, but I was too afraid to.

—We weren't afraid of getting caught because we were just getting kicks. It's like are you afraid of OD-ing when you take smack? Of course you're not, it's part of the kicks; the danger.

—I would be . . .

—And we knew we'd be able to run away.

—Anyway, what posessed you to nick tins of beans?

—We took the tins of beans because we knew we could take them down to Petticoat Lane the next day and flog them for a fiver. Housewives would see these tins and one of these tins would feed their family for a month, for a fiver. We had no problem getting rid of them. Or anything we nicked.

I'm not saying we were the greatest thieves in the world, but we were opportunists. We should have nicked the blenders and knives, I suppose, but it was just so much easier to load up with the peas and beans.

—I think that sounds pretty stupid. You could have loaded up a van with stuff, if you were going to go to the trouble of breaking the door down . . .

—We didn't HAVE a van. We travelled on foot, with the tins of beans and they were big. Four each. We'd run away with them and then we'd come back and get another load. It was late at night, there weren't a lot of people around and who's going to stop a couple of yobs carrying beans and peas? Who's gonna be interested? They're only going to get their head kicked in, aren't they? Would you stop a couple of drunken loonies with a bunch of baked beans?

—Probably not, no.

—The only people who would have stopped us were the coppers and we were lucky with the coppers.

But we weren't lucky with the coppers the time we bricked the front window of Bourne and Hollingsworth. This is the sad part. It was an upper-middle-class, hoighty-toighty store. It was an institution.

—So why did you brick the window?

—We bricked it because they wouldn't give me a job.

—Why wouldn't they?

—Because of my criminal record.

—Why did you want to work there?

—I didn't particularly want to work there, I just wanted to work somewhere. Just a fucking sweeping-up job was all I wanted.

—But you had a job.

—I had jobs on and off all the time. What I was looking for was a full-time job. I was sick of doing all the dogsbody jobs. Shifting heavy loads isn't my scene. It fucking kills you. It keeps you fit though, I must admit. You know you've done a day's work. There's nothing like lifting heavy weights for keeping you fit. I developed biceps that I couldn't get my shirt over.

—Did you?

—Yeah. I was a big lad when I was working. Anyway, don't interrupt. So, we smashed the front window, the display window of Bourne and Hollingsworth with a brick. It's big and it made a big crash, then the fucking alarm went off. But we would have gotten away with it, easy. Except we hadn't noticed there was a car parked across the road. And knowing our luck it was full of plain-clothes pigs, waiting to bust people coming out of this disco up the road.

So we started running and we couldn't understand why there were already coppers on our tail. Thirty seconds after we'd done it. And I was saying, 'What the fuck's going on?' And John was going, 'Run, you cunt!'

It wasn't that far to my place – I was living on the north side of Oxford Street then, in my dad's company flat. There was quite a lot of low-rent accommodation on the north side of Oxford Street in those days.

Well, anyway, we would have made it if these coppers hadn't fucking been there. No problem. What was going to stop us? We were both fit and able to run really fast and we were running really fast. We could have beaten the coppers.

—So what stopped you?

—But for these two fat bouncers who hated us because we were always trying to get in the club drunk, this club that was just up the road, called the Countdown, which was for ultra-smoothies and we weren't ultra-smoothies.

—What were you?

—We were lads. Actually we were soul boys at that time. Well, John was more of a long-haired scruffy git. He just looked like a criminal, John, basically. He had a Dennis Waterman haircut. And I had a classic soul boy outfit. Baggy trousers, wide-collared shirt, wide-lapelled jacket. Casual Italian shoes. And a jacket. If you were dressing up you'd wear a suit and shades of course. Layer-cut hair, like Darryl Hall used to have, when he had short hair. It's layered down all the way and parted in the middle and it's sort of spikey on the top.

Everybody had them in the mid-seventies. Layer cuts were real smoothie soul boy haircuts. Just over the ears, razored. Perfectly shaped. With a bushy bit on the top and a middle parting. People don't really wear them any more. It's a really neat haircut. Quite short, but not short enough to be yobbo.

Anyway, they wanted older office workers at the Countdown. Office shags. They didn't want gangs of guys coming in. One of whom looks like Minder and the other one of whom looks like a proper little nerd in shades and a layer cut who thinks he looks fucking marvellous. I did think I looked fucking marvellous. There's something about a layer cut that makes you feel great. Clint almost has a layer cut in some of the Dirty Harry films.

So, these bouncers were quite happy to step out on to the pavement and block us off for the pigs. I got brought down by a Welsh rugby-playing copper who said, 'Don't move, boyyo, or I'll break your arms, I play rugby every Sunday.' And I was going, 'My fucking shades are broken, you bastard, my shades!' So he thumped me.

Back in the station, fucking John falls asleep. Which is great for him. Leaving me to stay up all night being grilled. So I can't shop him. I'm quite prepared to admit to it myself because I know I'm only going to get fined, but I can't shop him.

—But he threw the brick.

—He actually threw the brick, but I told him to. I picked it up and said, 'Shall we throw this through the window?' And he said, 'Why not?' And I said, 'All right then.' And he said, 'No, let me do it.' And he did it.

So they wore me down and then they scared me. I was saying, 'What brick?' I just kept saying, 'What brick?' I was denying any knowledge of a brick. That's what you do. And asking for a lawyer. Unless they get a confessed statement saying 'I did it' you didn't do it. That's the law. And I knew the law, because I'd had quite a bit of experience with it by then. I was first nicked when I was fourteen, for drugs.

Anyway, after about six hours of me saying 'What brick?' and them getting more and more angry, they didn't even punch me. It's funny, some of them do and some of them don't. I have been punched about badly, other times, but they didn't punch me this time.

But they did do something much worse, something that scared me. They said, 'You know what, Shane? We think you take drugs.' I said, 'No I don't. I don't take drugs. No way, man. No way.'

And they said, 'Well, you know we can go round to your place any time and search it?' And I went, 'Oh yeah?' And I thought, 'Oh shit.' And they said, 'Yeah. How would you like us to do that?' So I gave in and signed the most ridiculous statement saying, '*We* threw the brick through the window.' I thought that because it didn't make any sense, it wouldn't stand up. Because '*We* threw the brick through the window' is an impossibility. It implies that we each took hold of one end of the brick and threw it and it's obvious that that's not what happened so I just said we did it so that later

I could say it was a load of rubbish. *We* couldn't have thrown the brick.

It was a mistake. I should have stuck to 'What brick?' But it meant I could go home and they didn't do me for drugs. I'm not sure if they really could have gone round my place and searched it. But I wasn't going to take the chance. Now John got really annoyed with me for making the statement. But it was all right for him, the cunt, he was fast asleep. And I was up all fucking night with these cunts, just saying 'What brick?' Trying to keep a straight face. I did point out that they didn't have a brick. But being smart didn't get me anywhere.

So John woke up and got in a really bad mood when he found out I'd made a statement and said, 'You stupid bastard, why didn't you just stick to "What brick?" And I said if anybody got done I'd get done because I signed the statement. All he had to say was he didn't throw the brick and he'd be home free. But he thought I was a wimp. He was an unreasonable bastard. He was a bit bossy, John. He was the kind of guy who always thought he could have done it better, but if he'd been in the same position he would have fucked it up a lot worse. He would have gone for one of them, because he had a thing about coppers which got him into trouble later on. If they got him in a temper, he'd hit them. Which isn't a good way to carry on if you want a nice quiet life.

So we went down to the court the next morning, the headmaster of John's old school happened to be the duty sergeant that day and they had a chat about old times. Right bastard he was. It took ages for our case to come up, because it was delayed and there was a pub across the road called the Marlborough, where all the criminals and lawyers drink and we went in and got arseholed. We could hardly stand up when we eventually went into court.

They read out the statement. We were both pleading Not Guilty. The magistrate said, 'I don't understand this statement, "We threw the brick." I think you're trying to waste police time so I'm going to find both of you guilty of throwing the brick. If that's what you say you did, then that's what you did.'

It was meant to be nonsense, of course, but the beak just looked us over and thought, 'These don't look like particularly healthy members of society.' And that was it.

A while after this, John nobbled a copper and went down to DC, detention centre, which is worse than prison. The short sharp shock. It's meant to be a really heavy Borstal-style treatment to stop young offenders from carrying on being offenders. So they make it much worse than prison. They don't stop them killing each other basically. They let them carve each other up and bugger each other. And they're very strict on them, they're always putting them in punishment cells for the slightest reason. Like John said, he used to get up in the morning, when he first got there, and a mirror would come sailing across the bathroom and smash in front of his face. Just because he was there. He was in there with murderers, rapists, fucking armed robbers. It was much worse than prison, though, because they were all much younger, sixteen to eighteen. Because they were younger, they didn't have the sense that older people in prison have, that you've got to do your time and make it easy on yourself and everybody else and keep out of trouble. Instead of that they were all aggressive and feeling quite proud of themselves that they'd finally managed to get put away.

So John had assaulted a copper, which put him quite high on the taking down list. A murderer who wants to make an impression doesn't like that, doesn't like it that there's some guy who's done something classier than him. The classiest thing to do is to take out a copper and that's what John had done. So that meant he was a really hard guy and he had to prove he was hard.

So they never stopped. It was like a John Woo film, he had to beat up about four or five people a day. And he was the least aggressive person you could ever meet, unless he lost his temper. He was into music, he loved rock and roll, drugs, booze and sex and partying, he was an ideal friend. John was into people being nice to each other, respecting each other.

So it really fucked John up, the six months in DC. It didn't break him the first time but he came out and he was shook up. Really shook up. By that time punk was happening and he got into punk. So he had all the pleasure of getting into punk. He'd seen the Pistols with me before he went inside and we both thought they were a really obnoxious, posey, silly band, but that they were good. John pointed out that Rotten had a habit of running his hands through his hair and he said, 'I can see he's just had his hair cut, because that's what I do, when I've just had my hair cut. He's a faggot, he's a ponce.'

John was a bit old-fashioned. He didn't like ponces. I didn't like ponces. But I knew Johnny wasn't really a ponce. John was fooled. John had a different sense of humour to me. I could see the joke and John couldn't. I said, 'But listen, they're playing real rock and roll, that's what we've been waiting to hear.' And he was going, 'Yeah, but they're all fucking Soul Boys.' Because they all had layer cuts. I had a layer cut and I was a soul boy, but John wasn't a soul boy. He didn't particularly approve of me, either. We liked the same kind of music, but he was more traditional. I also liked soul. He liked old soul, but he didn't like modern soul, he didn't like disco, he didn't like rare groove, seventies soul. And I did. John would never have a layer cut. Too poncey. John was a real slob. Real sort of leather jacket and jeans bloke.

—Anyway, so you got caught by the police, and John went down, and then he came out, and then what?

—You could see that it had really shaken him, and that he changed a bit. He was tenser then he used to be, he was more aggressive. He'd lost his inner warmth. You couldn't feel absolutely safe around him any more, as a friend. It was a vibe. The guy was wired. He'd had six months of fucking being attacked on all sides, and having to defend himself. And he had gone back to the jungle, in a way. Because he was a sensitive guy, he cracked . . . a bit. A bit, yeah? If it had stayed like that he would have recovered. Cause when he got into punk, it was loads of fun, and he forgot all about it. And when he saw how good the Sex Pistols really were, he was going, 'Oh yeah, I don't know why I didn't like them that first night we saw them.' I said, 'Well, I didn't like them that much, I just knew they were really good.'

He cut his hair short, he got the right gear and he came along to the gigs with me, to see all the punk bands. And things were fine. He got himself a new guitar, and he was thinking of starting a band, and all that. It was great. And then he did it again.

—**What?**

—He got in a situation with some coppers. They were all winding him up. They were provoking him, and he went for it. He beat the shit out of one of them, and this time it was a second offence. It was an ABH against a police officer – and that's really heavy in the Crown Court. I went to the trial, with his family and his mates and all that, cause I knew them all, y'know, and to comfort his mother and stuff. Everybody knew what was gonna happen. He knew what was gonna happen. He was looking really fucked off. It had become a pathological syndrome in him: Copper = Kill.

—**Why?**

—Why do you think?! He was full of bitterness and hatred about the first time he'd gone down. But he hated coppers anyway, cause one ran over his old lady. Deliberately. Cause this copper had been married to his sister. A copper got married to his sister. And they broke up. The marriage didn't work. And forever after that, the local coppers persecuted the family.

—**How?**

—They ran over his mother.

—**Wow.**

—They arrested his brother . . . for something. And they were always looking out for him. Luckily he had moved up to North London, but one night he went back down to fucking where he was from, and one of these local guys came across him and thought, 'This'll be an easy nick', know what I mean. And he was drunk, so they said, 'We're taking you in for being drunk and disorderly.' And one grabbed him very roughly and he beat the shit of him. And the trouble was he was a strong, big guy, so he did a lot of damage. It wasn't like he just fucking hit them . . . he used to send them halfway to the morgue every time he did it. So, you know, it was heavy, and he went down for six months.

—That's not much.

—I've already told you that the DC fucked him up. And he was still trying to overcome it in a way. This just finished him off. When he came out of prison after six months . . . he was a different person. He was a pyscho. He was violent, paranoid, and . . . I dunno . . . he lost his sense of humour. His sense of humour was so important. A big guy like that has to have a sense of humour or he'd go around beating up everybody, y'know. He changed, and the change was horrible. And we'd been so close, y'know. All the stuff we'd been through together. And we tried to keep it together, know what I mean, but it was like he was always freaking out, and starting fights with me and stuff like that. And I started to get the feeling that he might actually plant one on me, know what I mean? And that was an awful feeling . . . and in the end he did. But that's after the next police story, which comes later. The one I call 'The Chair'.

—So was Westminster the end of your education?

—No, when I was sixteen, I went to Hammersmith College for Further Education, to please my mother, because they'd kicked me out of Westminster before I got a chance to get some O-levels and A-levels. She was being quite sensible. She wanted me to go there because she wanted me to go to university and stuff like that. She thought that with a talent like mine for writing, I should give it a shot, rather than become a bricklayer.

—Did you agree with her?

—I didn't agree with her, no. I was intending to go back to Ireland and become a musician. I went to about two classes before I was kicked out. I used to go there to meet up with Bernie. All the long-haired guys were immediately drawn together. I had long hair, at that time. Me, Moisey Boisey, Bernie, Pete and a few other guys automatically formed a group. Everybody else had layer cuts. That was when I was sixteen. Back then, I was a freak.

—What's a freak?

—A freak was someone who was too young to be a hippy, who didn't believe in Peace and Love or Space Trips or Ley Lines or any of that shit.

—**What did you believe in?**
—We just believed in Hard Drugs, Loud Rock and Roll and Reasonably Long Hair.
—**Long hair? How long?**
—We didn't wear really long hair. More chin length. We despised hippies, who wore afghans. We wore leather jackets and brothel creepers or winklepickers, with jeans or leather pants. We were more rock and roll. Hippies weren't into rock and roll, they were into Pink Floyd, all that shit. We were into the Stooges, the Small Faces, MC5, the Pink Fairies, Humble Pie, Black Sabbath, Led Zeppelin, Roxy Music. We were into Roxy Music, who were a soul boy band. So we were into Roxy and we were into the soul that soul boys were into but we weren't into the soul boy boring straight lifestyle.
—**What was that?**
—Their Cortinas and their girlfriends and football on Saturday and stuff. Getting pissed on two pints of lager and having a fight at the disco wasn't our idea of a good night out. Later it was. Later it was what we used to do. You change rapidly when you're that age.

But the lads used to fuck up the discos. You needed to be speeding to be on top of it. You needed to be cool. Because the lads aren't cool so you've got to make sure that you don't give them an excuse to start a fight with you. Because you're there to dance. Maybe pick up a woman, but that's only secondary. Because we were into music and the whole scene. When you're a teenager, your physical appearance and the music you like are usually reflections of what's going on in your head.

The freaks all got together. You just saw a guy with long hair and went up and talked to him. It was that simple. And the lads talked to each other.
—**What were lads like?**
—Lads were soul boys gone wrong. Football hooligans who were more interested in football than soul. And they were fat and gross. They had layer cuts but they didn't get them cut often enough. They were slobby. And they were into a few pints and a fuck if they could get one, which wasn't often. The soul boys got the fucks because

women want a guy who can dance her into submission, not talk to her about football, and who hasn't got a beer gut. So the soul boys got all the women. The freaks got the freak women, we didn't have any problem getting women because the freak women were all such sluts.

—**Shane!**

—Mattresses. But the state of them was pretty awful. All the track marks and scabs and crabs.

—**What did they wear?**

—They wore sort of printed dresses, they never got the clothes together, at all. Their hair was never clean and they were always spotty. There was the odd really beautiful one. I fell in love with a really beautiful one, but she was too out of it, she'd blown her mind on acid and she wasn't coming back. But anyway, that's how the freaks got women and the lads tried really hard and occasionally managed to get a leg over. The lads had to compensate with fighting, football and drinking. And harassing the freaks and the Asians. They were typical racist, bigoted, drunken, fat stupid English slobs. Although an awful lot of them were London Irish. The cool London Irish guys weren't fat. And they were all heavy Republicans. They used to sing IRA songs at football matches. And they used to take mescalin at football matches. We got on with them, the clued-in London Irish ones, who didn't think they were English. The ones who thought they were English hated us. The ones who regarded themselves as Irish got on with us. Partly because we were nearly all Irish ourselves. Also because anybody intelligent enough to realize that they were Irish rather than English was intelligent enough to realize that the freaks were more interesting people than the bootboys, the lads.

And the lads used to hassle all the women. There were a lot of rich bitches at Hammersmith. Mummy and daddy had insisted that they get their A-levels and they were so thick that they'd been to the best schools but they couldn't get an O-level between them. And everybody was after them, because they were high-class hippies. They weren't real hippies. They dressed in beautiful white fur coats and had beautifully conditioned long gleaming hair, everybody was after them. For some reason there weren't any soul boys at Hammersmith. Actually the reason was that soul boys always went out and got a job, however difficult it was, because they had to run a car, look after a girlfriend, or several girlfriends and go out every night of the week drinking and dancing. And they had to buy new clothes every week and get their hair cut. They were like mods, they had to earn a lot of money. Freaks didn't. Although it helped, but it all went on drugs.

Anyway, everybody was trying to fuck the upper-class bitches. And the freaks were in the lead, obviously . . .

—Why?

—Because we were alternative and wild. And we were a shock to their parents. You know what I mean . . . after Blacks, and Asians, who didn't make any attempt to fuck them, the freaks . . . well, we were definitely on to a good thing there. But the lads got ugly about it. And there was a feud between the freaks and the lads about who was gonna fuck Jennifer, Samantha, Judith . . . and all the rest of them. And they hadn't even said 'yes' yet!

And me and Bernie got jumped outside the toilet, and got threatened by this London-Irish guy, and a few of his mates, going, 'You fucking leave those chicks alone, they're for us, all right!!' I said, 'You're a fucking disgrace to your nation!!' He said, 'My nation is England, mate. Don't give me your IRA bullshit!' I said, 'I'll tell Jimmy you said that.' Jimmy was this total psycho, who later joined the IRA. I met him ten years later and he had a gun on him, and he was in the IRA. But at college, we used to have really long talks, cause he was very clued in on history. He's from a heavy Republican family. It was great, hearing this guy going, 'Well yeah, Collins, and de Valera, man . . . You know, de Valera used Collins, didn't he . . .' You know, this guy looks like he has a mind like a packet of fish and chips, and I'm discussing 1920s politics with him, and stuff like that.

Jimmy always said he was gonna join up. And I said, 'I don't know. I don't know if I've got the guts.' And he said, 'I don't blame you if you don't, mate, but I'm gonna do it. Those bastards have got to be done by somebody.' I said, 'Well, that's true.' I did used to go around with IRA stickers on, and all that. But Jimmy was great, you know. Jimmy would go up to people and go, 'What's all this about you being English!?!?' You know what I mean . . . cause like, this London-Irish guy was twice his size, but Jimmy could beat the shit out of him. Jimmy was the kind of guy the IRA needed, know what I mean! Intelligent, enthusiastic, and psychotic! 'Psycho Killer, qu'est ce que c'est', know what I mean! There would've been nothing left of the London-Irish guy if I had told Jimmy what he said about being English. Cause the only reason Jimmy tolerated the London-Irish guy was cause he was a Paddy, and there was this sense of Paddys stick together, you know.

There was an actual homegrown Paddy there, called Maurice O'Toole who was thirty-five, who was an ex-teacher, who, in an accident, got his hand mangled. He was a little guy, with glasses, you know the type. He wore awful clothes. Maroon v-neck jumpers, sports coat, jeans, flares, you know what I mean. And he used the word 'frigging' more than anyone I've ever met. He used frigging between the friggings.

—How?

—'I'll frigging tell ye what I'm frigging frigging going te frigging tell ye now! I was frigging up there with the frigging frigging children, and I frigging frigging frigging told them that I'm not frigging standing for any more of their frigging rubbish'!! Know what I mean!

—Why did he say frigging?

—Well, you know in Ireland, some people swear a lot . . . everybody swears, but some people swear pathologically, don't they? Like shagging, in Kerry, 'Ah it's shagging, man, like, shagging this, shagging that', you know. But frigging was his own particular one. He never said fuckin', or fecken, or shaggin', or anything . . . it was always friggin' . . . and reams of it, y'know. Like something out of Joyce. And you'd have to pick the friggings out, to make any sense out of the guy. You know, he was talking sense, but there was so much frigging going on, you'd lose track of the plot, know what I mean?

But the thing about him was he had the sympathy factor with the girls. They all fucked him! This thirty-five-year-old fucking oxymoron! I mean, he was an intelligent guy, but he acted like a mongoloid, y'know . . . looked like a mongoloid! Not exactly a dreamboat, and I shouldn't think a great conversationalist with women. But because of his mangled hand, it was always, 'Oh, poor Maurice. Poor poor Maurice', and all the rest of it, and he'd be up on the pull before anyone knew what was happening. He fucked nearly every girl in the fucking college! Could you imagine the pillow talk?!?! 'Oh what a frigging great friggin' shag that was! You frigging friggin' friggin' . . .' I don't think any of them repeated it. But this guy just effortlessly fucked his way around the college. So he was one in our corner, as well. Bernie used to have these hysterical conversations with him, because Bernie knew the subjects to lead him on to, to get him going, like, 'What sort of tricks did you used to use over in Ireland, for picking up the birds, Maurice?' And he'd say, 'Ah it's very frigging simple picking up frigging birds in Ireland . . .' The fact is, he couldn't pick up frigging birds in Ireland!

—Why?

—He'd never been fucked till he came to England!!! Because in Ireland, they don't go for the sympathy fuck.

—Don't they?

—No.

—Why?

—I don't know! But they don't. But English women do. Particularly the upper-class ones. The upper-class ones, he had them first. The ones that everybody wanted to fuck. I got pretty close to fucking one . . . Stephanie, I think her name was. But I never actually got round to it. I kept nodding out at the crucial points.

—Like when?

—Well, you know, when it was the right time to be inserting my tongue into her mouth, I'd sort of slump over on to my knees and dribble for the next five hours. And the next time I saw her, I couldn't say, 'Oh sorry about that, but I've been taking downers', cause she didn't approve of downers.

—**So what did you say?**

—I said I had . . . uh . . . what do you call it?

—**Narcolepsy?**

—Narcolepsy, yeah. None of the freaks, and none of the lads got round to fucking the upper-class girls, in the end. But Maurice O'Toole did. And he was already thirty-five years old!

—**What was he doing there?**

—He was taking some amazing O-levels. He was doing a thesis on fucking *Ulysses*, or something like that.

—**So he was an intellectual, as well.**

—Well yeah. He was a genius, yeah.

—**Well, that's why they fucked him, then.**

—But he didn't talk like a genius!

—**But they must have been aware of what he was studying.**

—Yeah, I suppose so.

—**Well, that would do it.**

—You think that had something to do with it!?

—**Yeah, the combination would do it.**

—Yeah, the combination.

—**It would have to be the combination of the genius, and the sort of disability, or . . . but it's not a disability, it's kind of like a . . .**

—But a sympathy fuck is sympathy.

—**Yeah, but it's not just sympathy, cause the genius comes into it.**

—A GENIUS MAIMED!!! Tragic! A tragic figure!

—**A tragic genius, yeah.**

—Yeah!

—**You haven't got that yet? You haven't understood that yet?**

—No, I just thought it was the sympathy fuck. And with the upper-class girls, being Irish was a big, big draw as well.

—**Being the Irish genius.**

—That would've helped as well. And being thirty-five . . . being older than them.

—Clever, older, Irish . . .

—Disabled . . .

—. . . slightly disabled. Yeah, that would do it.

—And those birds, those upper-class birds, they probably thought all Irish people speak that way.

—**Yes. So, did you pull any birds?**

—Well, Saturday nights at Henneky's, and Sunday nights at the Roundhouse were the places to score drugs. And I used to score at Henneky's off a guy called Zombie, who was an ageing Hell's Angel. He had a record for armed robbery, and for possession of deadly weapons, and stuff like that. And he had his old lady, and his old lady was always made to go and get the drinks, y'know, 'Go and get the drinks!' and all that. And he treated us as . . . like his little clique, know what I mean, that he preached to. He was always trying to get us involved in going on an armed robbery with him. Luckily I didn't do it.

—**Why not?**

—Well, I didn't have the guts.

—**You surprise me!**

—If I HAD had the guts, I probably would have made up my mind to be a career criminal, so it's just as well I didn't. But one night me and that hippy guy were down there – this is how me and him fell out – and he had picked up this girl who we both knew and we scored some very strong acid off Zombie, and we went back to my place, and we started tripping and all that. My mum and dad were in the house, y'know.

—**They were?!**

—Yeah. We were playing records quietly.

—**In your room?**

—Yeah. My room had the advantage of having a lock on it. And my mate freaked the girl out by doing the classic hippy chat-up line, y'know: 'Wow, you're really beautiful, I'd like to fuck you', and all of that crap.

—**Is that a classic hippy chat up line?**

—Yeah. Whereas I was being courteous. So she was going for me and

74

not him. But then she started freaking out, and having a bad trip. And she went running out of the room. She went out on to the balcony, a sixteenth-floor flat, and she was gonna throw herself off. So I gave him a kicking, for fucking . . . putting her on a bad trip, y'know. And I said, 'I never want to have anything to do with you again.'

—Yeah?

—Yeah. You know, he was going like, 'What's the matter, man?' But anyway, I went out there and I started talking her down, y'know.

—Hang on, so she hadn't thrown herself off?

—No. I was talking her down.

—So where was she?

—She was on the balcony, about to throw herself off. And I had to try and talk her out of it. And she was very paranoid, and tripping, but I'd just managed to talk her down she was calm, when my father appeared. He was in a really bad mood, y'know, pissed, just out of bed, and he said, 'What's that slut doing in my flat!?! What's that slut doing in my flat!?!' And he started shouting and I said, 'Listen, Dad, we're both on acid.' And he went, 'Acid!?! What are you doing on acid!?' and all the rest of it. And I had to explain to him that if he didn't stop shouting . . . people's parents don't look very good on acid, know what I mean, particularly if you're having a bad trip.

—Your father came in and said she was a slut?

—Yeah, I had finally managed to talk her into not jumping, and him into calming down, and going back to bed, y'know, which was a gargantuan effort.

—How did you do that?

—I'm just a genius basically. I mean, how would you have done it?

—I don't know.

—Exactly. I used every trick in the book. I think that was the most dangerous situation I've ever been in. Definitely. No situation that's involved danger with me, has ever come close to that. Talking a woman from jumping off a balcony, and at the same time persuading a fifty-year-old drunken Paddy into going back to bed, know what I mean. So I stopped hanging around with the hippy after that.

—Why was it his fault?

—Well, he made her have a bad trip, y'know.

—Did he?

—Yeah. Then I fucked her afterwards. And that was an amazing fuck cause she was going different colours while I was doing it. I woke up the next morning with her in the bed beside me, and my dad trying to kick the door down. And they had to get my mother in on it, know what I mean, they had to get her out of her sickbed to go, 'Open up, sweetie, please! Please open up for Mum.'

—Why?

—So I opened up for her, and I said that I wanted Sarah to live with us.

—You'd only just met!

—Well, we'd met a few times.

—Oh, you had?

—Yeah. And she was my girlfriend for a while. They wouldn't let her . . . it didn't happen – her moving in, obviously. My mother talked us both out of that.

—Why?

—Why?!?!

—Yeah.

—What do you mean, why?!?!

—Why did your mother not want her to move in?

—Because it was a completely mad . . . WHAT DO YOU MEAN?!?! There was . . . she had her own family at home in Croydon!!!

Shanes purples, ominously.

—All right, okay, calm down . . .

—She lived at home herself!!!

—Right. How old was she?

—Fifteen!

—Fifteen?!

—She was only fifteen, and I was seventeen, y'know.

—She was only fifteen?

—And I was seventeen.

—So she was under age!

—Yeah, I suppose so.

—You didn't . . . did you know it was illegal for you to have shagged her at all?!

—. . . Anyway, she had this guru-type Svengali figure hanging around, who was a thirty-five-year-old guy who had read a lot of those books that you read, know what I mean, and he spouted mystical bullshit, as his method of picking up young girls, who he used to influence. And I was constantly fighting with him. I kicked the shit out of him, in the toilet at Henneky's one time. I told him I was taking him in there to give him a hit and I kicked the shit out of him.

—Why were you so annoyed with him?

—Because she was my first serious girlfriend.

—Yeah?

—Yeah.

—Why did you like her?

—She was very beautiful. She had long blonde hair, and she wasn't thin and scraggly, she was well built. And she had a very nice face, and huge blue eyes . . . she was very nice. And she was a very nice person. Unfortunately, this guy had his hooks into her, and uhm . . . I ended up losing out in the end, when I went into the loony bin. Okay. Should we do the loony bin?

—Yeah, go on then, the loony bin. Sounds good.

—Well, I agreed to enter a loony bin because, if I hadn't entered of my own accord, I was going to be sectioned, which meant that I wouldn't know when I could get out. So I agreed to go in there for six months, while they weaned me off the drugs.

—What led up to that?

—Well, I think I had a mental breakdown which is slightly different to a nervous breakdown. I had acute anxiety, depression, hallucinations. Bad. Demonic stuff. I was drinking and taking a lot of pills. Uppers, downers, acid and I was on a script for valium, a hundred milligrammes a day.

—A hundred milligrammes a day? Who gave you that?

—We had a mad GP, he was definitely using some of his own stuff, the guy was hyperactive or on speed or something. He used to say, 'Yes, yes, point of view, point of view' all the time.

He used to tell me that if it was up to him he'd have me out there playing the guitar until my fingers bled. And he used to go on about how I should be in the army. He was completely neurotic. He used to talk to the wrong chair. Not the chair you were sitting in, the chair beside you.

He put me on a prescription for valium because the whole thing was getting to me. I was beginning to show signs of a nervous breakdown. Getting hallucinations. Like acid flashbacks, sort of seeing things going in and out of focus all the time.

I used to see hieroglyphics when I tried to go to bed. They were like Egyptian hieroglyphics on the wall. They seemed to have some meaning to me but I couldn't work out what it was. It freaked me out. It was as if I'd taken acid when I hadn't and that bothered me. I felt anxious all the time. Anxiety about nothing in particular, just anxiety. General sense of menace. Afraid of being alone. So I stopped going to bed altogether. And took valium instead, which got rid of the anxiety.

He had my mother on huge doses of all sorts of things. I used to nick them. Then I needed more of them. So, by the time I went in the bin, I was a multiple drug abuser.

—**And how old were you when you went in the bin?**

—I was seventeen. The night before I went in, I went out drinking with Pete. Remember Pete? We went to the Hope and Anchor, and 'Ace' were playing.

—**Ace?**

—Yeah, you know.

Shane sings, melodiously.

—'How long . . . has this been going on?' That was when it was a hit for the first time. We got really drunk, and the next morning my dad drove me to the bin. And this horrible matron took over. We called her Barrel on Matchsticks, cause she was shaped like a barrel; fat, with spindly little legs. She had glasses and she was very strict. She explained the rules, and all that, and introduced herself to my dad.

—**What were the rules?**

—I was to be given drugs, but to have them gradually lessen the amount. When I arrived, I met Joe, who was in his forties, he'd been an amphetamine addict for twenty years. He was a masseur, and he was in a very bad mood cause he was on a comedown, y'know. Then there was Grāinne, who was an Irish woman. Her husband had beaten her up, and stuff like that. She was an alkie, and also had a barbiturate habit. Heavy barbiturate habit. And Jenny O'Keefe, who was only fifteen, and was a barbiturate addict. And I think that was everyone on the ward at the time . . .

—Mixed ward, huh?

—Yeah, it was a mixed ward. You had two wards, you had the needle ward, and you had the non-needle ward. We were in the non-needle ward. I mean, there were loads of other wards in the hospital, but there were two drug wards, the needle ward and the non-needle ward. We used to have to give a urine specimen every day to make sure that we hadn't taken anything. Apart from that, we spent most of our time sitting around watching telly. And doing group therapy or occupational therapy. Occupational therapy was painting, and things like that, but my paintings were freaking out the other patients so much that I got myself a whole room, and a guitar to play, on the condition that I taught this young schizophrenic girl how to play the guitar. She was a black girl, and she was a naturally good guitarist, so I taught her the guitar, and we got on very well. But she was schizophrenic . . . So anyway, that was easy OT for me, and then . . .

—What was wrong with your paintings?

—Well, they were all sort of, horrific . . . like, demonic paintings, know what I mean? I did it deliberately to upset the other patients. *Shane laughs, nastily.*

—Oh I see.

Victoria responds, disapprovingly.

—Shane . . . why would you want to upset the other patients?

—Cause I was sick of the painting thing, and uh . . . I wanted to play my guitar. So I did. And I gave that girl lessons. We formed a close bond. And I got very friendly with all the other people in the ward.

There was one main building where you went for occupational therapy and cigarettes and chocolates, and things like that. You could have a meal in the canteen, or whatever, if you didn't like the food on the ward. And then there were the grounds, with trees and birds, and stuff like that. All the patients mixed together at occupational therapy in the main building, so we mixed with psychopaths and exhibitionists . . .

—And what do they do?

—Well, take their trousers down in public and things like that, y'know, shit in the street.

—How come you weren't one of them?

—Well, I just wasn't one of them, you know.

—I'm surprised.

—We had interviews with the doctor, individually, and we had group therapy. In group therapy everybody sat around and shouted at each other and I refused to join in, but in the end I got pulled into it, and became one of the most obnoxious members. I was always starting fights between the other patients, know what I mean?

—What was the idea?

—God knows what the idea was. The idea was that talking it over with other patients was supposed to be part of the cure – but all it did was get people wound up. One of the doctors was known as Creeping Jesus because he wore desert boots, so you wouldn't hear him coming. So, you'd be talking about him, and suddenly he'd be behind you. And he talked in a very, very quiet voice. He had slightly receding hair, and glasses. In my private sessions with him, I totally reversed the psychiatrist/patient relationship, and got him telling me all his problems.

—Oh yeah?

—Yeah. Now I don't know whether that was part of his technique, but . . .

—So what kind of problems did he have?

—Well, he seemed to be very, very insecure about his wife and children. I used to grill him about that. He just came across to me as a generally insecure guy. And I reckon I even got him to admit to me that he didn't know what he was doing stuck with psychiatry – that it was one big black hole, that no one could know what was going on at all, really. There were no answers. I got him to admit that to me. So I got out of there pretty quickly, because by then the doctor had become my patient.

—Did you cure the other patients?

Shane ignores the question, nonchalantly, and lights an upside-down cigarette, absent-mindedly.

—After a while, more people came to the ward. Grāinne, the Irish housewife, was a real character, battered by her drunken Paddy old man, know what I mean? And she used to shout and scream and cry, and she had some great stories. Joe had some really funny stories, too, about massaging Sir Michael Redgrave, and people like that, cause he was a masseur in Jermyn Street, in a very flash massage parlour. You used to get Robert Morley coming in, and people like that. Fat old slobs, drunk out of their heads, you know, going in for a massage. And they'd always ask for Joe.

But after a while, some REAL loonies started turning up. All these other people were sane, no doubt about it. I was sane, y'know. I knew I was sane, we all knew we were sane. But then the loonies started arriving. There was this English battered housewife who was really fucked up. Then there was a seven-foot-tall acid casualty, who kept on having attacks where he thought he couldn't breathe. And there was an exhibitionist, he had a drug problem so he was in the drug ward, but he was also an exhibitionist, y'know, so he used to take his bum out in the common room. Nurse McKenna had to be sent for, and she had to say, 'Put your bottom away immediately!' And then if he wouldn't, he used to be restrained by the male nurses.

And there was this guy called Fred, who was a biker from Gypsy Hill. He was another barbiturate addict. Me and him did a breakout one time, and went into the town. We didn't actually have a drink, but we did have some Collis Browne, so we were both in a lot of trouble about that.

When you come straight off barbiturates, unless you're taken off

FIXED UP
SET UP
SMACKED UP
JACKED UP
SCREWED UP
SPEWED UP ~~SET~~
FUCKED UP
LOCKED UP
SITTING THERE
                IN CHOKEY

14 YEARS OLD
NO LOCK ON THE DOOR
BUT NO WAY OUT
~~PINNED DOWN~~
~~PINNED DOWN~~
NO JOKING
NO HOPING
NO NOTHING
PINNED DOWN

①

gradually, you have an epileptic fit – and they allowed him to have an epileptic fit, to teach him a lesson, cause it was his second time in there. Which I thought was a bit odd. I was there when he had it. I was the only person there, and I was scared out of my fucking wits. I called for help, and they came and managed to get him under control and took him away. And the neurotic English housewife fell in love with the seven-foot-tall acid casualty, and they started having an affair, which wasn't allowed. Although it was a mixed ward, you weren't allowed to have affairs or anything like that. I had quite a thing for Jenny O'Keefe, but we couldn't do anything about it.

—Which one was Jenny?

—The one who was fifteen. She'd been on hunger strike for six months when I went in there.

—Gosh, she must have been really thin!

—She was, yeah. They decided they were going to give Jenny an enema, and you could hear her screaming all over the fucking ward. Cause she'd been on a hunger strike for six months, they would force feed her, you know.

—Why would you give someone an enema if they were on a hunger strike?

—I don't know. They force fed her first, and then gave her an enema, presumably to keep her bowels working. It was barbaric.

—Why was she on hunger strike?

—Cause she wanted to get out, but she was sectioned and they wouldn't let her out. And her boyfriend was in the needle ward next door, so she occasionally could catch a glimpse of him. The whole thing is very cruel, very barbaric. The dragon nurse de-loused me, even though I didn't have lice. It was a punitive act for calling her a Barrel on Matchsticks and throwing an ashtray at her. She combed my hair really straight – at the time it was styled like Johnny Thunders, so she totally ruined my hair-do.

—That's barbaric, Sweet Pea.

—Apart from her, all the rest of the nursing staff were nice people. I formed a very deep friendship with a nurse called Maureen from the north of Ireland. She took me to see Man at the Fairfield Hall in Croydon and I had to show remarkable powers of endurance because there was a bar there and I wasn't allowed to drink.

That was the most difficult thing about it. They reckoned that if you started drinking it would become a substitute for the drugs. They were right. But to me, I didn't see what harm a couple of pints would do, she said I couldn't have one because she would get blamed if I did, so I didn't do it.

I also went with Joe and her to see *Jaws*. I was freaked out by the opening scene, it was quite a horrific movie for the time. That made me feel pretty sick. Maureen was holding my hand on one side and Joe's hand on the other. She was scared.

—**How come you were allowed out to a movie at all?**

—We were allowed out with a nurse, because we were drug addicts and we weren't regarded as a danger to other people.

—**Yeah, but you could have run away.**

—We could always have run away, any time we wanted, in which case we would have been caught and sectioned and not allowed out at all. It was allowing you a bit of responsibility, allowing you out with a nurse, and seeing if you could deal with it.

When I left, Maureen ran up to me in tears and gave me a huge open-mouth kiss and threw her arms around me and then ran off crying. She was only nineteen. She was still studying for her SRN. She wasn't allowed to shag me, because of the rules, but we used to talk about it, we'd say if we went in the bushes no one would know. She'd say she was thinking about it and I'd say, 'Think harder about it. I'm going to give you a really good time if you do it.'

She said, 'That's the trouble, I know.' It was against the rules, whatever age I was. Joe was gay, so when she squeezed his hand and screamed, in *Jaws*, it was like squeezing another girl's hand, but when she squeezed my hand it was very much a sexual thing. And we canoodled at the Man gig, we kissed each other and I put my arm around her. I was a big boy for my age. I wasn't any sort of let's-go-fishing type of seventeen year old, I was a street kid. And we could talk openly about adult subjects. I don't just mean sex, I mean politics, philosophy, whatever. So there was no way it was a woman/child relationship. It still haunts me to this day. I was very much in love with her and I think she was very much in love with me. She acted that way, when I left. She was a typically beautiful, slightly plump, freckly curly-haired Irish girl, with knowing eyes. Her eyes knew a lot more than she said.

—**Why do men always go for nurses? I'm surprised at you.**

—I don't know why men find nurses so attractive. But this one was a very special case. We went out on lots of expeditions together. But I was annoyed by not being able to have a drink and I was annoyed by being away from London. I wasn't that far from London, I could have hitched it in an hour, if I'd decided to do a runner, but I decided to do my time and be sensible.

I've always been very sensible in hospitals. When I haven't been sensible, it's been for a reason. To make them hate me so much they want me to leave.

The psychiatrist used to ask me things like how I felt about my mother, how I felt about my father, how I felt about my sister, if I had any girlfriends. I said I loved my mother and I hated my father and I loved my sister and I did have a girlfriend.

He said, 'Why do you think you take drugs?' I said, 'Because I like them.' I'd read a bit of Jung. I was interested in Jung, he was the only one who seemed to make any sense. I didn't believe in all that Freudian shit. And anyway Freud was just a bloody coke freak. And in a lot of his books he said coke was the answer to most mental problems. For the obvious reason that it gives you self-confidence and cheers you up. It's an obvious thing for depression. If you're feeling depressed and you have a line of coke, you feel great. And Freud was heavily into it, he was seriously addicted to it. Which is how psychiatrists' bills got so big.

—**Did you have ECT?**

—No, but they were prepared to use it if someone wasn't controllable by any other method. So, I'll always sign a petition against ECT . . . I think it's disgusting.

—**Did you spend Christmas in there?**

—Yeah, my mum and dad came in. I said, 'Can I have a drink, seeing as it's my birthday?' And they said, 'No!' And they were being even wittier than usual and they had all the patients and the nurses rolling around laughing. And there was an Irish nurse and an Irish patient and they were bonding with them, you know the old Irish bonding trip. We were all being treated like criminals. And not even adult criminals, it was more like a reform school than a prison.

While we're on the subject, I'd like to say that for most of his life, my dad had a savage Dublin wit, comparable to Flann O'Brien's. And his father and my Auntie Sheila both had great senses of humour and were very witty people. So they got on really well with the old people, my mother's family.

—For most of his life? Hasn't he got one now?

—Now he's turned into Mr Collopy, out of *The Hard Life*, by Flann O'Brien. As far as I'm concerned. With everybody else, he's fine, still. As his performance on *The Late Late Show* with Pat Kenny showed. However, bridges are gradually being built and peace will soon be restored, I think. As long as I don't do a Frank McCourt on him. Ha ha ha ha ha.

Anyway, so, I was in a really lousy mood, because I couldn't have a drink and I'd lost my sense of humour, so I was sitting there psychotically staring at everybody laughing and telling me what great people my parents were. 'Well,' I said. 'If they're such great people, why haven't they brought me a drink on my bloody birthday?' It was a horrible day . . . my eighteenth birthday. But at that point, I was completely detoxed and I got out about two months later.

—How d'you get out?

—Well, I was off the drugs, and I just kept hassling them, and hassling them, and hassling them . . . making their lives miserable, know what I mean.

—Mmmmmm.

—What I usually do in hospitals.

—Yeah!

(2)

ANIMALGESIC

I'M AN ANIMAL JESUS
I'M AN ANIMAL JESUS
IT'S AN ANIMALGESIC
TO ME.

I'M A CERTIFIED LUNATIC
DING-DONG DING-DONG DING-DONG
PAVLOV'S BELL, DOWN IN HELL
DOWN AT THE BOTTOM OF
THE DISUSED WELL
DING-DONG
DING-DONG
DING-DONG

DOING!
DOING!

SAID I'M AN ANIMAL
JESUS I'M AN ANIMAL
JESUS IT'S AN
ANIMALGESIC
TO ME

—And eventually they let me out. So out I came.

—**What was it like? Coming out?**

—Very strange . . . very strange. Very strange. They gave me a practice walk to the O.T. section, cause I hadn't been alone since I was in there. I wasn't allowed to go anywhere unless I was accompanied by a nurse. So, I was allowed to walk to the O.T. without anybody with me. And I got about half the way and then I had this massive panic attack, and went running all the way to O.T., sweating like fuck. I tried to get a nurse to come back for me, but they said, 'Try going back on your own.' And I did, and I was all right. So they decided I was ready to go out.

—**How do you feel it affected you?**

—Well, it convinced me that I was sane. It cleaned me up, so that I could fuck myself up again. But it was . . . not an experience I would like to repeat.

—**But you did repeat it, didn't you?**

—Not a whole six months. It taught me how to deal with hospitals really, cause I never spend longer than a couple of weeks in hospital now.

—**Yeah. Did you ever feel like maybe you wouldn't be able to convince them you were sane?**

—I wasn't sure if I was sane or not, until I got out.

—**Yeah?**

—Yeah, I felt a bit unsure, you know.

—**Why?**

—Because I'd been institutionalized. Been heavily institutionalized, inside myself, know what I mean?

—**Not really, cause it's never happened to me. What does it feel like?**

—Well, you're just not used to going anywhere on your own, or without asking someone's permission. I suppose boarding school must do it to you as well, but I'd never been to boarding school.

—**I think being on tour is a bit like that.**

—Being in a band, on tour, institutionalizes you, yeah. Which is why I was always such a heavy customer on tour, I wouldn't take orders, like the rest of them. I refused to be institutionalized again. It's only happened to me once in my life, and it will never happen to me again.

—**Were you angry about it?**

—Yes, incredibly angry, yes. Seething. And then along came an incredibly angry band. It was like fate, that one of the first bands I should see when I came out was a bunch of people who looked like they ought to be in a loony bin.

—**Who's that?**

—The Pistols. So . . . I have found myself in danger of being institutionalized on the road, but I've never allowed it to do it to me. I refuse to be institutionalized, and if you refuse to do it then there's no way they can do it to you.

—**Were you ever scared that . . .**

—They can torture you or something, but there's no way they can do it to you the other way. What?

—**Were you scared that you wouldn't ever get out of that place?**

—No, I always knew I was gonna get out . . .

—**How did you know that?**

—. . . it was just a matter of when.

—**How did you know you could get out?**

—Because I knew that basically, I was sane, and I knew that the doctor knew that. The doctor had told me that I was sane – that there was nothing the matter with me. Except that I had acute anxietal paranoia or something like that, in other words, my home life had done it to me, had fucked me up.

—**You don't think it had anything to do with your basic personality?**

—No, that was the same before. I had the same basic personality before.

—**Before the hospital?**

—Yeah.

—**Okay, is that all you're going to say about loony bins?**

—I might say some more later on.

—**Okay, we'll stop talking about it.**

Victoria orders cheese sandwiches and lashings of ginger beer, copiously. *The couple eat, indelicately.*

INTERVAL. *Reader, feel free at this point to urinate and take refreshments, also.*

ACT THREE

Scene One

Plethora restaurant, Islington, London, early winter evening. Grey, concrete walls and post-post-minimalist, interesting chrome furniture compete for attention with etiolated waiters in purple velvet flares and shiny lurex t-shirts. Shane MacGowan, resplendent in Armani, cradles a dry martini, suavely, and smokes a Marlboro, enigmatically. Victoria, radiant in orange crêpe de Chine and violet lipstick, toys with a beetroot, suggestively.

—Do you like beetroot?

—I've been a lover and a hater of beetroot all my life. The first few years of my life, I hated beetroot. Then I grew to love it.

—How?

—I dunno. You don't like something when you're a kid, and then suddenly you try it cause you're forced to, and you find out that you actually like it.

—Yeah, like spinach.

—Well, I always liked spinach, actually, it was always called 'greens' when I ate it. Greens.

—Eat up your greens.

—Yeah, greens. But I got into beetroot in a big way, then I ate so much of it I got sick of it.

—I've seen you do that with other things.

—Well, yeah, I do it. I've got a terrible habit of doing it with everything.

—Everything?

—Pretty much.

—Which is why I like to get you to a new restaurant occasionally.

—It was nice food.

—Yes, lovely.

—But it's a good thing I wasn't starving, you know, cause there wasn't exactly much on the plate.

Victoria clutches her ample stomach, contentedly.

—I'm stuffed.

Shane reaches out a pale, sensitive hand for Victoria's leftovers.

—Let's try the beetroot again, seeing as I'm still hungry, and I haven't had it in ages.

Shane chews, thoughtfully. Victoria watches, tenderly.

—Funny you know . . .

—I LIKE IT AGAIN!

—. . . when you're eating . . .

—I LIKE IT AGAIN!!

—. . . when you're eating you have these muscles on the side of your face that go in and out.

—I LIKE BEETROOT AGAIN!!! We all have those muscles in our faces.

—Yeah, but they're really prominent on yours. I think it's because of your haircut.

Victoria chortles, affectionately.

—You said I looked like 'rat boy' once. Yeah, that really got to me.

—That got you? I was only joking.

—I thought that was a really cruel thing to do.

—Yeah?

—Although it's true.

—Of course it isn't true.

—It is true!

—It isn't.

—I do look like 'rat boy'!

—You don't. You don't. You're much too beautiful to be . . .

—I wouldn't say I was beautiful.

—Yeah you are. You are beautiful.

—What is it? My eyes?

—Just your whole face – although your eyes are particularly beautiful – but your whole face is beautiful.

—Well, you really are beautiful.

—So are you. You really are too.

—Nah.

—It's the truth.

—No it's crap. Nice bread.

—Yeah, it's lovely bread. It's got rosemary in it.

—What's that you're drinking, decaff?

—Yeah. I do everything now that I didn't used to do.

—What do you mean?

—I have coffee, I have sugar.

—That's not coffee!! It hasn't got any caffeine in it.

—Yesterday I had real coffee.

—Did you?

—Yes. With sugar in it. And I drank wine. And I ate a pizza.

—So you eat all that now?

—Yeah, it's great. I'm really starting to appreciate the basic pleasures. You know, coffee, wine, sugar . . . What did you eat, in Tipperary? Bacon and cabbage?

—We used to have bacon and cabbage and potatoes, most days, except for on one day of the week we'd have Colcannon, which is made with scallions, milk, mashed potatoes and a knob of butter, which you put on the top after it's all mashed, and you let the butter dribble all over it and then you scoop up the butter with the potato. It's a really beautiful dish.

—Did you have that on Fridays?

—No. On Fridays, we had fish, fresh from the river.

—What kind of fish?

—Salmon, trout and eel.

—What was your favourite?

—My favourites were trout and eel. The eels were great, the way they were cooked. You'd heat a knob of butter on a pan and then cut up the eels while they were still alive and fry them to death, in the pan. And then once they were dead, you'd serve them up, with a bit of butter.

—Alive? They cooked them alive? What would happen if one of them was still alive, on the plate?

—They always made sure to cook them well and you'd know if one was still alive because it would still be wriggling. There was no way you'd serve them up still alive, that's how you knew when they were done, because they'd stop wriggling.

—**Right.**

—Some days we'd have turkey or chicken and very occasionally we'd have goose. That's when we weren't having bacon. We'd kill the geese ourselves.

—**You're a vegetarian.**

—I wasn't a vegetarian in those days, I was a sadist. A very extreme sadist. I was a monster. After we'd killed them we'd hang them up. Sometimes we'd shoot rabbits and I'd watch the skinning and everything. A goose is the hardest thing to catch. And a turkey could easily kill a small child.

—**Didn't you feel sorry for them?**

—I didn't feel sorry for them at the time, but later on I became a vegetarian.

—**Why?**

—Because animals suffer and I don't believe in humans suffering and I don't believe in animals suffering.

—**You eat fish.**

—Fish, the Indians call the 'fruit of the sea'. And all Eastern philosophy regards fish as not being proper animals. You can eat fish and still be regarded as a vegetarian, according to Eastern philosophy. My own personal philosophy is that I need the protein, so I eat them.

—**If you did eat meat, what would you eat?**

—I love steak and rashers and boiled bacon with cabbage and potatoes. I love all the stuff I don't eat. It's a matter of self-control. I occasionally give way and have a steak. If I do give way to eating meat, it will be red-blooded meat. Bloody red meat. And it will be steak. Not a hamburger or a fry-up, a good steak. I occasionally have one of those, but I find it hard to digest. I do get a tremendous feeling of satisfaction and a massive adrenalin rush from steak. I could go out there on the street and take on any man after a steak.

When I need a shot of adrenalin is when I'm likely to have a steak. I notice the adrenalin in meat because I eat it so rarely.

I eat for pleasure as well as for sustenance. Eating just for the sake of eating makes me feel ill, y'know? I have to enjoy my food. I get hooked on certain foods and eat them every day for a while and then I eventually go off them.

—**Like caviar and Marmite sandwiches.**

—And smoked salmon and cream cheese bagels.

—**And fettucine with smoked salmon and cream sauce.**

—And Greek food, for a while, taramasalata and hummus and fetta cheese.

—**And snails in garlic butter.**

—And mashed potatoes.

A tray of glasses is heard, suddenly, crashing on to the austere concrete floor. Much disquiet is overheard as the sodden diners comment. An argument ensues, immediately, at the next table. A waiflike waiter in brown Gucci is seen to slap a smart older woman in gold Versace. The waiter retires to the kitchen, defiantly.

—What's happening? Who do you think they are?

—**I don't know.**

—What are they trying to do?

—**I don't know. Get their money back? Get their dry-cleaning bills paid? Who do they think they are!?!**

—Yeah!

—**Well, they're rich people, aren't they?**

—Lawyers . . . or film critics.

—**No.**

—Or what? Businessmen?

—**Yeah.**

—What do you mean? You mean like the stock market?

—**You know, people with shops. People with bars, clubs . . .**

—Oh . . . I thought you meant crooks for a minute. They're not crooks. They hate crooks.

—**They hate crooks? Yeah, maybe.**

—You mean they're small small-business people.

—Well, business people with money.

—No, but I mean small-business people . . . like they work for big companies.

—No, they own their own.

—Yeah . . . their own small businesses.

—Maybe they have a chain of restaurants. Maybe they've got a string of properties. Or whatever. They're ostentatious. Not the men, the girls, I'm talking about the girls.

—Who's talking about them?! I'm talking about the men at *that* table.

—Oh, I thought you were talking about the other table. I'm talking about the girls.

—This lot over here?

—Yeah. Big gold jewellery, foreign . . . well, not English.

—What about them over there? The chattering lot?

—They're just girls whose parents have a lot of money, I think. Yeah, their parents have all the money.

—That's not hip anyway.

—Of course it's hip, to show off your money.

—Don't talk to me like I'm an idiot!!!! I mean, when I said it's not hip, I meant it's not meant to be hip! You know.

—Okay. Maybe it isn't meant to be hip, I don't know.

—No, it's not meant to be hip.

—It is for rich people. People who want to spend money, and talk about spending money. But not for people who come from the aristocracy, because they don't like to look like they're spending money. They don't like to spend it, not their own anyway.

—You're not gonna get an aristocrat spending twenty-four quid on a bottle of wine.

—Not unless they wanted to impress someone. Maybe they would if they went somewhere really expensive, and that was one of the cheaper bottles.

—What's polenta?

—Polenta is like a corn bread. It's sort of tasteless. The chocolate cake is nice.

—You wouldn't get Harry Palmer eating in here.

—No? Well, maybe not. Yeah, but that was in the sixties. When he wrote that book, posh people ate in trattorias, and ate tagliatelle and stuff, didn't they? If they were writing that book now, they would have him eating somewhere like this, probably.

—No I think he'd go to Belgo.

—Would he? No he wouldn't.

—Huh?

—I don't think he'd go to Belgo. I think he'd go to the Ivy. Isn't that George Michael?

—Where?

—Over there, just going in the men's loo?

—Yeah, it is. I think I'll follow him.

Shane saunters across the restaurant, cheekily. Victoria waits, eagerly. Shane reappears, eventually.

—Well? What did he say?

Shane smirks, serendipitously.

—He said he was just thinking about me.

—I'm sure. Do you want to go now?

—Why? Do they want the table back?

—Yeah.

Shane frowns, markedly.

—Just let me finish my martini.

—I think that's Gwyneth Paltrow just coming in.

—Who's Gwyneth Paltrow?

—She's a film star. Don't you know who she is?

—No.

Victoria orders another decaff and toys with it, irritably. Shane dozes, amiably.

—Uh . . . Shane . . . do you still want to do this book?

—Yeah.

—Okay, cause the tape is running.

—What should we talk about?

—Let's talk about you.

—But I'm a mixture of loads of people, you know.

—Are you?

—All right, we'll talk about me. We have been talking about me.

—Yeah. You like . . . uhh . . . rested . . . for a moment there.

—You know what I think? I think about film as being like a great painting.

—You do?

—It is, you know.

—Did you make that up, Shane?

—Yeah. People waste films a lot.

—They waste them?

—Yeah. Film, to me, is an art form. It's like bringing a painting to life. All the greatest paintings have an incident happening in them, or if they don't have an incident happening in them, they're a study, an intricate study. Like all art forms, you don't see a painting or a film until you've really looked at it and become involved in it. And you haven't listened to a record until you've really listened to it. If you have it on the car stereo, while you're sharing road-rage with the guy in front of you, then you haven't really listened to it. What I'm trying to say is that it looks easy, what I do. James Fearnley from the Pogues said to me once, 'All you do is sling a load of swear words together.' And it's true. But I'm very good at slinging swear words together. There's an awful lot of swear words you can sling together. A thing that annoys me, too, is that people are distracted by appearances. Steve Buscemi is an actor who's been in hundreds of films. You'll find him under the same stone as James Woods, but James Woods has managed to escape from under the stone and Steve Buscemi hasn't. Because James Woods is tall and goodlooking. Steve Buscemi is short. But he steals *Reservoir Dogs* off Harvey Keitel and to steal a film from Harvey Keitel is good acting. I identify with Steve Buscemi. I think he's had it rougher than me, because he's never even had a 'Fairytale of New York'. People will always remember that he was a slimeball in his movies. Most people don't even notice that he doesn't get shot at the end of *Reservoir Dogs*, he picks up the diamonds and splits.

—Okay then, who's your favourite actor?

—The actors that had the most influence on me were Humphrey Bogart and Steve McQueen. *Casablanca* is one of my favourite films and *Treasure of the Sierra Madre*. Classic film. It's the original gringos in Mexico film. Banditos. Mexican banditos fighting it out with gold prospectors in the Sierra Madre mountains. John Huston is my favourite of the old Hollywood directors, because he's the toughest, most down to earth, realistic, violent one. He really knew how to tell a good adventure story. What I want to see when I go to see a film is a good adventure story. Or a good comedy. I wouldn't say I was obsessed with violence, but my favourite type of film is a really good thriller. And a really good thriller has to have a lot of violence in it, because people have to be killed to make the situation serious, to get you on the edge of your seat. Implied violence is no good, you have to make it absolutely clear in a thriller that there is the potential for real violence. You've got to know they're not fucking around, they're not posing. That's always been a thing between the film directors and the producers, who feel that they're protecting people's morals and stuff. And the man who broke that apart was John Huston. Who was Irish. It's very important that he was Irish.

The two greatest film directors, as far as I'm concerned, are John Ford and John Huston and they're both Irish. John Ford had morals in his films, but there's no morality in John Huston's films, they're amoral. And I don't believe in morality. I believe in good and evil, but morality is just a code that society tries to impose on people, in order to get them to behave themselves. John Huston was always getting into trouble for his sex scenes being too sexy and his violent scenes being too violent. He was a really brilliant, realistic, romantic film director. I love realism mixed with romance. I've been called a romantic of the urban brutalist school, which is a ridiculously pretentious statement, but if I am one, then so is John Huston. And so is Sam Peckinpah.

The Wild Bunch influenced me the most, of course, after John Huston's films. It's a much more violent film than *A Clockwork Orange*. Kubrick didn't have the guts to go the whole way. It made me realize that under the thin veneer of civilization we're all fucking animals. That's what the film's about, about how low people can sink, for money. You don't get many English films where they admit that. The Americans have always been better at admitting things. The English seem to live in a dream world of good sportsmanship and stuff. Huston and Peckinpah are the film equivalents of writers like Hemingway and Steinbeck, to me. They got the message across that just because you're right doesn't mean you're going to be all right. You have more chance of getting your head caved in if you're on the side of good than if you're on the side of evil. And *The Wild Bunch* is a film about that. Also it's got a couple of brilliant massacres in it which didn't influence me at all!!!

Shane snorts, vehemently.

—That was the film that got me hooked on movie violence. I watch a lot of movies, as you know, two or three a day and I've yet to see *The Wild Bunch* outdone. Certain films, like *Once Upon a Time in America* and *Reservoir Dogs*, I watched seventy or eighty times in a row. *The Getaway* I can watch any time. If you put it on right now, I'll watch it.

That's got the magic combination of Peckinpah and Steve McQueen and Walter Hill wrote the fucking screenplay. It's got a pump-action shotgun as one of its main stars. There's an intensely violent pump-action shotgun scene which is worth watching for itself alone. And it shows you how to beat up your wife. It's got a particularly juicy wife-beating scene.

—You're *obsessed* **with violence, aren't you? That worries me, how obsessed you are with violence. I really think you should see a shrink about that . . .**

—Actually I don't get a kick out of real-life violence. I get a kick out of hitting something inanimate, or carving something up with a samurai sword, but not another person, because I have too much respect for other people's right to live. I don't think watching violent films encourages you to be violent in real life. If you are going to suggest that it does, then you've got to ban *War and Peace* and *Don Quixote* and the Bible.

—The Bible?

—The Bible is an extremely violent book. The Bible's got everything in it that's bannable. It's gratuitously violent, gratuitously sexual, totally sexist and racist and it does encourage people to be violent, although it does that because of its philosophy, not because of the descriptions of the battles in it. Which is why I like films that are amoral, which don't put across a philosophy. I don't think there should be any message in films.

Actually it's my mother's fault I like violent films, she made me watch *The Untouchables* every Saturday night. She was a horror movie freak and a violence freak and she liked whodunnits and thrillers. She didn't just like Hitchcock and Agatha Christie, she liked heavy violence. She revelled in it. And she encouraged me to watch it when I was a kid. My mother was a very different sort of person before her nervous breakdown. She is a strong woman now, but she was more obviously a strong woman then. There was none of this, 'Yes, darling, I'll get you anything, pet, I'll do anything for you, pet . . .' None of that. It was, 'You get your arse in gear and work. You're going to do the things that I never got the opportunity to do. You're special and you're going to be famous and I'm going to make sure you are.'

And she did that to me until she had the nervous breakdown and then she gave up. And when I did make it, she said to my father, 'Yes! Tipperary 500, Dublin 0.' She drummed into me over and over again: Don't get married. Don't get married until you're absolutely sure you've made enough money to be financially comfortable for the rest of your life and for your whole family to be that way as well. That was her rule. Or if you do get married, marry somebody strong. Don't marry somebody weak. Don't marry a wimp. Don't marry a stupid cow and don't marry a snob. Don't marry anybody who will take second best. But put yourself first. Always put yourself first. Don't worry about me. All I want is for you to make it.

—Very sensible.

—She was like that. And she made it all sound very reasonable. A conversation with me and my mother when she's drunk is something else. She always used my old man as an example of everything not to be. But she's mellowed now. I made her happy. We had a classic Oedipal situation, it was always me and my mum against my dad and my sister, Eugene O'Neill stuff. But the years have mellowed us all.

—And you didn't get married.

—I want to marry you. You don't want to marry me. Anyway, by the time I decided that I wanted to marry you, I had already made a packet.

I got my taste for violent films from her, though. She'd be watching a violent movie and she'd be going, 'Right, you bastard', when the guy got shot. Like the way I breathe a sigh of satisfaction when somebody gets blown away in a movie, I inherited that from her. She's hard as nails inside. She's not actually violent, but my violence comes from her. We were a violent family. We were involved in local feuds and we always won. We invented lynching and it still runs in our blood. Apart from passing on to me her love of Irish music, my mother also passed on her love of violence, because she came from an IRA family. It sank in with me, they were very rabid. Two or three times she sent me screaming to my bed in terror, because of the films that she made me watch. My mum hates normality. What she dreaded was me or Siobhan being normal.

—That's all right then.

—And that's probably why she likes my old man. Because if there's one thing about him, he's not normal. My parents are a right couple of crazies.

The beginning of *Psycho*, where it begins with a dead eye staring at the camera and then it pans out to a body in a bathtub, having been brutally murdered, it was like Christmas for her, watching that. She used to go, 'Oh, great, *Psycho*! I mustn't miss the first scene. I love the first scene, it's so well done.'

Any of the films I watch, I can watch with my mum and she really goes for them. John Turturro massacring an entire Italian restaurant, in *Men of Respect*. And she's a real Queen Elizabeth freak. She likes period drama, but not for the dresses. She's really into

Thomas Hardy. Murder, rape, disease, the works. My mum is a realistic romantic, like me.

The only acting part she ever got, she gave up, when she married my dad, I know it must have haunted her over the years, what she'd given up, I know it did, because they were always at each other's throats, and I reckon she must have thought, 'Right, if I'm giving it up for a screaming brat, that screaming brat's going to do something.'

So I was very much shoved on to the stage. She's a fascinating character, my mother, and I've got an incredible amount of respect for her. But like I say, she's got this almost childish addiction to gore and nastiness. I think she got it from the stories around the fireside. Irish bedtime stories aren't about cute little bunny rabbits. The little people are complete bastards. And then there were all the stories of the Troubles. So there's something homely about it, to me, and there's something homely about it to her.

—You could easily make films. You know enough about them and you write songs that are like miniature films, like 'Body of an American'.

—I'm not in the film business because I'm a musician, even if I just wrote soundtracks I'd get frustrated, because I'd want to rewrite the whole bloody film. But making films is a very technical process, it's like you can't just suddenly decide you want to be a lead guitarist, it takes skill. Maybe I'm wrong, maybe directing a film is just a question of having a vision and if it is, then perhaps I would like to write and direct a film myself. It would be a very violent film, a thriller.

—Obviously. What was the first film you saw?

—The first film I can really remember seeing is *Ferry Across the Mersey* with Gerry and the Pacemakers, which was as bad as you might imagine. But I did get a glimpse of a nude woman in it and this was in Cloughjordan, in Ireland, in 1964. I was six or seven. They had a cinema in Cloughjordan in those days. My Uncle Mick took me. You just saw a quick shot of a nude girl's back and you see the back of the canvas, so you can't see any tits or anything. But for me it was incredibly exciting. I was a highly sexed child.

—Right. So you said. Sex and drugs and rock and roll. You're such a cliché.

—Do you want another drink?

—Yes, I'll have a Diet Pepsi. Shane . . . if you were alone in a room with a drink, could you not drink it?

—Yeah.

—For how long?

—If I had some water, for ever.

—Why do you reckon that is?

—Well, you haven't specified the drink but I . . .

—Okay, martini.

—Easy. I could easily do without drinking that shit.

—Why?

—Cause I don't like the stuff.

—Wine?

—Don't like that much, either.

—You drink it all day!

—I hardly ever drink wine. I drink wine with my food.

—You drink it every day! You drink at least two bottles every day.

—I eat every day!

—So, if you were being given food, and there was a bottle of wine sitting there . . .

—Yeah . . . ?

—. . . would you have to drink the wine, in order to be able to eat the food? Or could you eat the food without drinking the wine?

—If I had a glass of water, I could do it with the water.

—And supposing there was a line of coke . . .

—Yeah . . . ?

—. . . could you survive without doing the coke?

—Yeah.

—For how long?

—As long as I stayed there.

—So, is there any drug that you couldn't sit in a room with, without taking it?

—No.

—There's no drug?!?

—No.

—So, you're not addicted? You're not compulsively addicted to anything?

—Possibly a cigarette.

—Cigarettes?

—There's a possibility that . . . No . . . I think that if I was determined . . . No I . . .

—What if there was a million quid riding on it?

—If there was a million quid riding on it I could do it with a cigarette as well as I could do it with anything.

—Supposing it was only five hundred quid?

—Then I'd think, 'Fuck it', and take the thing.

—Right. Supposing it was a grand?

—Same thing.

—Ten grand?

—Same thing.

—Twenty?

—Same thing.

—Fifty?

—Same thing.

—Fifty?!?!

—Yeah.

—For fifty grand?! You'd rather have a cigarette?!

—Hmm.

—Wow.

—Come on . . . think of the magic figure.

—A hundred grand?

—That's not a magic figure.

—It isn't?

—No.

—Five hundred grand?

—That's a magic figure.

—So it would have to be five hundred grand.

—Yeah.

—To motivate you.

—Yeah.

—Nothing less.

—No.

—So money motivates you more than anything else?!

—Yeah.

Shane laughs, impishly.

—What about me, or . . . me or five hundred grand?

—I'll take you.

—Me or a million?

—I'll take you.

—Me or ten million?

—I'll take you.

—Twenty million?

—I'll take you.

—Fifty?

—I'll take you.

—A hundred million?!?

—Once you've gone over a million it doesn't matter how many millions there are.

—Really?

—Uh-huh.

—That's very complimentary. We haven't had me in the book at all. Are we going to have me in it?

—Yeah, sure, not today.

—You always say that. Are you reluctant to talk about me?

—This is all going down on tape.

—Oh, okay . . . Ehm . . . so you don't think you're addicted, possibly, to anything?

—I told you I'd have the cigarette rather than a hundred grand, know what I mean. In the end I'd really want a cigarette. And that probably applies to all the other things as well. But if there was five hundred grand riding on it – then, whatever it was, I wouldn't touch it.

—Yeah. Neither would I. Unless it was a million quid. Do you want to go yet? I think they're trying to get rid of us, that's the third time the waiter's picked up the bill to see if we've paid it yet.

In the backgroud, the etiolated waiter, fresh from doing battle with the Versace lady, hovers, menacingly. Shane leers at him, jovially.

—They're wankers in here. I don't know why you always want to go to such poncey places.

—I don't know. I like a bit of glamour. We're supposed to be having a glamorous life, aren't we? You're a rock star, so I want us to act like a rock couple.

—You're really fucked up. Okay, let's go.

Shane tips the waiter, outrageously, and the glamorous couple leave the restaurant, charismatically, as Madonna is turned away, unhappily.

Scene Two

A black taxi, London, night. As the vehicle speeds through the metropolis, precipitately, Shane smokes, industriously, and Victoria watches, devotedly.

—You were run over by a black cab once, weren't you? Aren't you afraid of them now?

—No. Why should I be?

—I don't know. I would be. You were meant to be meeting me that night. If you hadn't stood me up, you wouldn't have got run over. Why did you stand me up?

—I forgot.

—And you broke an arm and a leg. That's karma.

—Well, people used to come in and see me in hospital with bottles and cigarettes, drugs and everything and stay there until twelve or one o'clock in the morning partying until they had to be thrown out by the nurse. So that wasn't too bad. And you did come to see me, too, so you can't have been that pissed off. And I voluntarily discharged myself and I came to meet you in the pub. I made up for it by taking you out that night. Anyway, I want to tell the story of the 'The Chair' now, so shut up.

Victoria sulks, charmingly.

—Okay, I will shut up. You go ahead. I don't care.

—All right, I will. I was living in a squat at the time, with my girlfriend Shanne and John Murphy. And if you want to know all the details, the Nips drummer at the time, Grinny, who was originally in a band called Screwdriver, and he was from Manchester. And he had his girlfriend with him, and she had a cat that shat all over the place. It shat on my pillow regularly, and it shat on my records, and it

111

wasn't a popular cat. Me and Shanne were always hoping John would kill it, but he wouldn't do anything useful like that, would he? Instead he did things like skulk around in the basement, just like banging around in there. We didn't really talk. I didn't talk to Shanne much, and I didn't talk to John much. I just kept myself to myself.

But me and John were in the pub one night, and we got arseholed, right. And it was just one of those things . . . it occurred to me at the time – 'Don't let this happen . . . You can avoid disaster now, if you just pull yourself together for a few seconds . . .' – But I didn't. I saw him pick up the chair. I saw him hoist it on to his shoulder, and walk out of the pub with it. All I had to do was get it. Take the chair off him, and a whole lot of aggro would never have happened, right. So much aggro. But I was drunk, and I thought, 'Good ol' John, he's having a good time', y'know what I mean. I was really drunk, and I was in a good mood cause I was meeting Shanne for a meal across the road. We had just broken up, so this was an attempt at a reconciliation. So Shanne, of course, noticed, and said, 'Did you see John nick the chair?!?' And I said, 'Yeah, so what . . . it's no big deal, is it?' And she said, 'What if the police come?' and all that. And I said, 'The police won't come.' I didn't want to . . . y'know . . . fight . . .
Victoria smiles, reluctantly.
—**You were eating.**
—Yeah, I was eating. We were eating. We went home, and we slept together. We didn't screw, but we slept together, and fondled, and you know . . . we did everything except fuck.
—**Why?**
—Cause she asked me to sleep with her.
—**No, why didn't you fuck?**
—Cause she was keeping me on a long leash. She was making me work for it. At that stage it was still possible that we would've got back together. But that's exactly when EVERYTHING WENT WRONG.

The doorbell rang, and I went downstairs and opened the door, and it was the coppers. And they said, 'Do you mind if we search these premises?' And I said, 'Have you got a search warrant?' And they said, 'Well, if you insist on us having a search warrant, then we're going to be suspicious that you've got something in there, aren't we? It would be better if you just let us search the place, if you've got nothing to hide.'

I said, 'Well, I've got nothing to hide, search the place.' I'd totally forgotten about the chair. I didn't know what was going on, y'know, but I was confident. I was guiltless. I'd just spent the night with Shanne. It was great. I was just about to make her breakfast. So they walked into the kitchen and said, 'What's that?' And I said, 'I don't fucking know'! And then I looked at it again and said, 'OOHHHH!!!' And I remembered, y'know. And then I had to think really quickly, right. What the fuck am I supposed to say now?! And I said the wrong thing.

—What?

—I didn't check my law computer properly. I said, 'I found that in the street last night, on the way home.' And they said, 'Well, that's theft by finding.' And I said, 'Is it?', and they said, 'Yeah.' And I said, 'Oh. I thought you could just pick something up out of the street and take it.' And they said, 'Well, I'm sorry, you can't, so, can you accompany us down to the station please.' So down I went to the station, y'know. Cause what I should've said was, 'I don't know where that came from. I've never seen it before. But there are four other people living in this house, so you'd have to talk to all of them, really. But I don't know anything about it.' Then it would simply be a matter of them asking all the other people, and John would've owned up in the end. And like, they wouldn't have put him away again for nicking a chair when he was drunk, know what I mean, they're not that bad. And everything would've been all right.

But this started a really confusing set of circumstances, right, cause I got nicked. And Shanne was freaking, going, 'What's happening?!?!' And I said, 'They're nicking me, for nicking this chair.' And she said, 'But John nicked it!!', and I said, 'No no no no . . . I found it in the street.' And she looked at me really angrily. I'd done the wrong thing in Shanne's book. In Shanne's book you shop people. In Shanne's book you put the blame on the person who did it, you don't try and help them out, y'know. In other words I'd been a fool. I'd been all the things that she hated about me. I'd lied, I'd been stupid, I'd been all the rest of it. And now I was getting nicked. But on the other hand she was really worried about me. And it was awful, after the night before, and waking up all happy, with a lot of hope in my mind, and in her mind, about whether we were gonna make a move and all that; next thing I know I'm getting carted down to the nick. And just my luck, right?

Now I knew they couldn't hold me, I knew they didn't have enough to hold me. But it was just my luck that there was a sixty-year-old, absolute psychopath of a detective inspector at the station that day. So after they've interviewed me in the cell – the normal interview, yeah – they go out, and I can hear them talking. I can hear the desk sergeant saying, 'You haven't got enough to hold him. You're gonna have to let him go.' And while they were doing all that, this guy comes in . . .

Apart from his horrible English face, he looked like a Paddy, y'know. He was big, red-faced, grey-haired, and his body was like an old Paddy. He was wearing a maroon suit I think. He almost looked like he was imitating a Paddy in his maroon suit. He could've been London-Irish, I don't know. Anyway, he was a bastard. You could tell just by looking at him that he was a bastard. He said, 'Well, is that all you have to do with yourself? Make an old lady unhappy by taking one of her prize set of chairs that she managed to keep through the war?' 'Cause the story came out that the woman who ran the pub, the reason she was upset – the only reason why she was upset and then called the police – was because the chairs were all matched in the pub, and they'd been in her family for generations, and she'd had a lot of trouble getting them out of fucking Switzerland, getting them through the war, know what I mean. It wasn't the money, it was that she wanted her complete set of chairs. And she was quite satisfied for John, or whoever . . . me, in this case . . . to go in, hand over the chair, and say, 'Oh, I'm very sorry. We were drunk.' Because we were good customers, and she liked us, y'know. But the police wanted to press charges, so there was nothing she could do. So anyway, this guy comes in and gradually works himself up into a fury about how I didn't fight during the war, and how I'm probably a druggie, and how I'm a waste of space, and what do I do for a living, nothing, and I'm scum, and all the rest of it . . . you know, up to a fever pitch. And then he said, 'Now fucking tell me what happened!' Cause I had changed my plea by then to 'Not Guilty'.

—Why?

—Cause I wasn't guilty! And my story now was that I was confused and I didn't know where it had come from, and so I just made it up on the spot, y'know. I didn't really know it was stolen, I had never seen it before. So he beat me seven shades of shit round the cell. Twenty minutes of solid beating. Really heavy. And going, 'And now you're going to have assaulting a police officer added to your charge!' It was a really heavy kicking . . . the heaviest kicking I'd ever had in a police cell and it was about a bloody chair! And this wasn't even his case.

—Why didn't you just say that you'd stolen the chair?

—After a while, the desk sergeant walked in really quickly, and said, to the detective, 'Come here please. This isn't your case. It's about time you went home.' And the guy dropped me, spat on me and walked out. The desk sergeant just sort of went, 'You won't do yourself any favours telling anybody about that. Okay.' And he went out again. Cause he obviously knew what that guy was like. And after a while, I got released. So then, to me it was simple, John should go down to the nick – I was meant to go back to the nick in two weeks, right . . .

—For what?

—So that they could review the case, and decide what to charge me with and all the rest of it, y'know. John should go down to the police station, and admit to the theft. We should go in and apologize to the landlady. So, we went and did that, and it was fine with her, but she said, 'There's nothing I can do. The police are pressing charges, not me.' So, that was that . . . she couldn't help us.

—I thought the police couldn't press charges unless . . .

—They can if they want, yeah. And we were squatters, so when they looked round the flat they weren't impressed with the condition of it, know what I mean. And they were annoyed that they didn't find lots of drugs. But I thought at least John should go down to the police station . . . it took him five days to do it!! I was saying, 'So are you gonna go down, John?!?!' And he was going, 'It's your fault I'm in this trouble!' And I said, 'Look, what the fuck was I supposed to say!?!? I said the first thing that came to my mind! I didn't want to drop you in it.' And he goes, 'Well, you fucked me up now, you know!!' So he went down and admitted to it, right. And so it was all set up that I'd plead 'Not Guilty' to theft, John would plead 'Guilty', and the cases would be heard together. Then John's solicitor told him to plead 'Not Guilty', on the grounds that he was drunk at the time – diminished responsibility. So when the cops heard that he was pleading 'Not Guilty', they changed the charge on me to handling stolen property. So now I was going down for a tougher offence than John! So anyway, we were both found Guilty, and I was given a bigger fine than him.

—Wow. How much?

—Around three hundred and fifty quid, or something.

—That's a lot. That's an awful lot for having a chair in your house that wasn't yours.

—Well, being booked as 'receiving stolen property', implies that you do it regularly, you know, like you're a fence. And you can quite easily go down for that, so I was lucky. I was fucking lucky!

—Gosh! That's unbelievable, that is.

—What?

—Well, that you could be fined more than him, because he stole a chair and brought it back to the flat.

—I might've gone to jail!!!

—Wow.

—It's not unbelievable.

—Yes it is.

—The law is ridiculous. Are we home?

—Yeah.

INTERVAL.

Coffee and biscuits will be served in the church hall, next door, presently.

Act Four

Luxurious house in Hampstead, early winter morning. A weak and palely loitering sun creeps across a grey and chilly December sky, hesitantly. A smattering of cigarette butts is sprinkled over the white shag-pile carpet, seductively. Record sleeves and burger-wrappers are likewise strewn, creatively. Empty wine bottles vie for space with general rock and roll paraphernalia. Shane MacGowan hovers over an antiquated hi-fi, dangerously.

—Should I put Oasis on?

—**Yeah go on then.**

—No, the Beatles.

—**Oh come on, Shane.**

—THE BEATLES!! This is a shit-hot album. I mean when you listen to this, it's real . . . with Oasis, I don't see what the bother's about. He can't sing! He can't. It's just a nasal whine. Noel can sing better than Liam does. It's true, isn't it!?

—**I don't know.**

—The guitarist. He sings on, 'Don't Look Back in Anger'. He sings better then the lead singer, Liam.

—**Oh right, yeah.**

—Don't you think?

—**Shane, the tape's running.**

—Oh, yeah.

—**What was the first song you ever wrote?**

—'Instrument of Death' was the first song I ever wrote. When I was seventeen, I had a band called Hot Dogs with Everything. Hot Dogs with Everything was managed by Dozy. Dozy . . . although he was the youngest of us all, was a most self-confident brat. And the best dressed of all of us. And he wore things like Aquascutum macs, and bottle-green velvet brothel creepers. We used to go on shopping expeditions at Biba's . . . or rather, nicking expeditions at Biba's. And we used to go up to the roof garden, where the giant toadstools were, after getting legless in the pub on Lamot, which is a very strong Belgian lager. Very strong. And although we were meant to be at college, we used to just go into college every day, and make an appearance and then go straight to the pub, and then later go off to Biba's, when we were legless, or go off to our jobs. We all had part-time jobs . . . things like painting and decorating and stuff. And we all followed Dozy, Dozy was the man. Dozy called acid 'Zen'.

—Zen?

—Yeah. 'Put some Zen on me.' He had his room decked out so that he could just like, roll over in the morning and press a switch, and the record would flop on to the turntable, and the needle would go down, know what I mean, it would be a record that he had put on there the night before.

The group was me, Bernie, and Charlie, who never went anywhere without an Arab sword tucked into his belt. We used to use our old record players as amplifiers. Stacked them up and used them as amplifiers until they blew up. We were ahead of our time, because we were playing Sex Pistols type music, know what I mean, loud, rock and roll . . . old Them numbers and stuff like that. And we had a photo of ourselves; me, Charlie, and Bernie, taken in a photo booth, and Charlie, who was an expert graphic artist, turned it into a poster of Hot Dogs with Everything. We had all our graphics together . . . we had everything together, know what I mean. The image and all that.

—What was the image?

—Well, we had long hair . . . it was very much a Jesus and Mary Chain type image, y'know, backs to the audience, and loads of feedback, and all the rest of it.

—That sounds good.

—Yeah, it was ahead of its time.

—Did you play gigs?

—We never got around to playing a gig.

—So what did you do?

—We just rehearsed a lot. Our drummers kept OD'ing, y'know (joke). Whenever we had a gig the drummer OD'ed.

—Oh yeah? How many drummers did you have?

—Oh God . . . we went through about ten or something (joke).

—Did you make any records?

—No, we didn't.

—Well that's a pity, isn't it?

—Yeah. We had everything but the records and the gigs.

—Right.

—And the deal.

—Right. What happened to John? Wasn't he in the band?

—Well, after the chair, we got on really badly, and one day he decked me.

—Yeah? Why?

—Cause I hadn't done the washing up. So after that, I didn't really talk to him, y'know.

—Did he hit you very hard?

—Well, no, but he didn't have to. Obviously he felt really guilty afterwards, cause I just stood there looking at him like, 'John, how could you?', you know. I wasn't hurt or anything. I was just hurt emotionally, and I looked at him, and he looked really guilty, know what I mean. And then he couldn't stand to look at me. He felt too guilty to look at me. And we grew apart. It was the system that did it to him though, and that's a really horrible thing to see. That is one of the most horrible things I've seen in my life. An individual . . . transformed like that – Aahhh . . . Don't turn it down any more!!! – I don't know what that riff is . . . I recognize it. I think it's an Earth, Wind and Fire thing.

—It's nice.

—Oh . . . they're actually doing the original track of 'Only the Strong Survive'. But they've remixed it and put a new vocal on it. They build the tension by leaving out the riff, and then suddenly bringing you in, y'know . . . it's really effective. That's something they never do on rave records. You know what I mean, on rave records they're just bleeping all the way through, they haven't got any kind of hook or anything, it's just the same thing, played all the way through. Well, this is the kind of soul that I got into . . . that me and Bernie and people were into. And eventually, when we got bored being freaks, we became soul boys. I had always been into soul, but I hadn't been particularly into going to the discos, know what I mean.

—Why not?

—Because! . . . Like I said before . . . the lads used to fuck up the discos. They'd go along and have a few pints, pull a chick, then have a row about her with a bloke, and somebody always ended up getting bottled. And it could be you, without you even knowing it. To be a soul boy, you needed to be on top of it. You needed to be cool. Cause the lads aren't cool, y'know, so you had to be sure that you didn't give them any excuse to start a fight with you. Cause you were there to dance, and maybe pick up a woman, but that was only secondary.

—Yeah? Why?

—Cause us soul boys were there to dance. We were into the music.

—Oh, right.

—And the whole scene, y'know, looking sharp, and . . . short haircuts, and all that. It's like when you have long hair and a beard, and you shave it all off . . . and when you were wearing like, a bearskin, and you take that off, and you change into a Savile Row suit, and you have a really good haircut, and you go and live on a yacht in Florida, and all the rest of it. Know what I mean? Your whole attitude towards everything changes, obviously. When you're a teenager, your physical appearance and the music you like are usually reflections of what's going on in your head. Yes?!

—Yes.

—I'd just come out of the loony bin, so for me it was like, a farewell to heavy downer abuse, know what I mean. I wanted to just drink and take speed, and like . . . dance.

The telephone begins to ring, annoyingly.

—And do my job, and be a barman, y'know, be an adult. I was sick of being poor.

The telephone continues to ring, intrusively.

—And it was great, having a job that I knew was going on and on and on, rather than just some fucking . . . having a job that wasn't . . . PICK IT UP!!!!!

Victoria answers the phone, graciously.

—Hello? Hi, we're still in the middle of doing the inter . . .

—WHO IS IT?!?!

—. . . view. Yeah . . .

—WHO IS IT?!?!

—Yeah . . .

—WHO IS IT?!?!

—I don't know, it's probably going to be another couple of hours. Yeah.

—Let me talk to them . . . IS THIS SOMETHING URGENT!?!?

Shane unplugs the telephone, briskly.

—. . . So, I had a whole new attitude. I wasn't a wasted druggie zombie, and I wasn't constantly having rows with my parents, and generally being in a state, like I used to be . . . I felt sharp, alive. I had money in my pocket, y'know, I was into looking good. I've always been into my appearance . . .

—Have you???

—. . . and it was time for a change in my appearance. And I was into the music, anyway. And there weren't any good gigs on any more, really, so I got into dancing . . . going to discos, and listening to soul.

—So what year would this be, about? How old would you be?

—1976. Eighteen.

—So what happened to the punk gigs? If there weren't any good gigs?

—That came later.

—Oh, right. Of course.

—Most of the punks were soul boys.

—Oh right, first.

—First, yeah.

—I get it. And having a job meant what?

—Being a barman, for me, meant cleaning myself up, anyway.

—Did it?

—Yeah.

—Tell me about being a barman. That's interesting.

—Well, this was in a big pub in the West End. It was an Irish pub, but it had three bars. There was a whole mixture of clientele. There was a lot of business trade, commuters, travellers, a whole lot of Cork builders from down the road. A huge gang of them were always causing trouble, and there were loads of fights in there. A lot of fighting . . . with Paddys, and there were also guys from up North on the buildings. There was a lot of building going on. It was right next to Charing Cross station so it was always busy.

—So what was it like, working in a bar?

—Well, all bars are different. You mean, what was it like for ME working in THIS bar, is that what you're asking?

—Yeah.

—It was hard work. It wasn't bad. When it was busy, it was hell. What? Do you want some of the characters and stuff?

—Yeah, go on.

—Well, the head barman was a queer.

—Yeah?

—And he was after my arse. And I used to have to help him out in the dive bar. There was a dive bar, a food bar . . .

—A dive bar?

—It's a downstairs bar where you have really loud music, and people drinking doubles and . . . a dive bar! A bar for partying in. A bar for drinking in, and . . . for getting off with women in, and listening to music in, as opposed to a pub bar, where you'd just sit around and chat and stuff . . . it's where people go after work, and at the weekends, to unwind. A dive bar. A sleazy sort of place where everybody gets really drunk and the music's really loud, and it's busy and sweaty and hot, y'know.

—That sounds unpleasant.

—You don't know what a dive bar is?!?!

—No.

—With special lights, and you know, soft lighting and all that . . . where all the soul kids and lads, and office workers, and people like that, go to get pissed and maybe pick up a shag after work, yeah? And get really disgustingly drunk.

—Right, yeah.

—It's also where genuine alkies go. They just sit at the bar and drink and drink and drink. They do have them in England, but they're more common in America.

—Yeah.

—You must have seen them in American films.

—Yeah.

—You know, when the cops go into those really packed bars? Know what I mean? . . .

—Yeah.

—. . . and look for some pimp or something, yeah. Yeah? Anyway. There was loads of regulars, and you never gave a pint of slops to a regular. We kept all the slops and put them back in the barrel, right, so the first few pints out in the morning would be pretty dodgy. We'd have mixed in Guinness, and lager, and bitter. You'd drain it off a bit, but you'd leave what you drained off and give it to some non-regular costumers, you know, particularly hippies, blacks . . .

—Oh no!!! Are you serious?

—. . . students, uh, who else . . . people you didn't really like the look of.

—Like black people?

—I just said that to wind you up. But some people might have done it to black people. And Yanks. And at the time there was a paranoia going around about Arabs, cause the *Sun* got an Arab to go round all these pubs in London and ask for a glass of water. And the least he got charged was twenty pence.

—Wow!

—And he got charged up to ten pounds.

—Ten pounds?

—For a glass of water. Which is free. In all the pubs he went in, he was charged. And there had also been a recent case where a guy got chipped . . . got his mouth cut from a chipped glass – sued the pub and made a fucking fortune. So we were told we had to be extra careful about chipped glass. I still notice when there's a chip in my glass, but I can't be bothered to sue anybody. I should do it, really, you know, in a pub where I'm not known. Obviously I wouldn't do it in Filthy's.

Anyway, it was a twelve-hour job. Eight in the morning, get in, bottle up, do a lot of set-up work, pushing barrels.

—**Pushing barrels?**

—Yeah. And putting all the empties away in the right boxes, things like that. Really boring work that was. And dirty. It was a nice pub to work in, but you got dirty, so then you had to clean up and go upstairs and serve. And your day wouldn't be over until twelve o'clock.

—**That's an awfully long day.**

—You had a break between half-three – no, four o'clock – cause it would take you half an hour to clear up; so, between four o'clock and half-five. So I used to dash home and drink a bottle of vodka.

—**Drink a bottle of vodka?!?!**

—Yeah, or just under a bottle of vodka.

—**Yeah?**

—Yeah, and I would come back and I'd be dropping glasses all over the place.

—**How did you keep the job?**

—I could handle a bottle of vodka. I could handle it . . . I could work on a bottle of vodka.

—**Could you?**

—Yeah.

—**But you'd drop glasses.**

—Well, when I first got back I'd be so pissed that I dropped a few glasses, but I'd soon get in the swing of it.

—**And did nobody notice?**

—Nah.

—**Nobody noticed you had drunk a bottle of vodka?**

—No.

—**How come?**

—Because it's not a lot to me, a bottle of vodka, you know. You know it isn't.

—**Yeah but . . . you were only eighteen and you drank a bottle of vodka in your lunch break?**

—Yeah. An hour and a half is plenty of time.

—**What, you would just go home and sit and drink a bottle of vodka?**

—And watch the telly. And I'd buy my sister her dinner. She'd be home from school, and she'd be hungry, so I'd go across the road to the café and get her a sandwich.

—**A sandwich.**

—Yeah.

—**That's all she had for dinner?**

—Well, yeah, unless my dad decided to cook something that night, or I did. It was me, my dad, and her living there. So, it was basically whoever could be bothered to cook something.

—**So, did she not get fed much?**

—Well, she didn't get fed much, no.

—**Awhhh. How old was she?**

—She was pretty helpless. She couldn't really cook a lot of food for herself. How old was she, did you ask?

—**Yeah.**

—I was eighteen, so she was thirteen.

—**So she was old enough to know how to cook.**

—Yes, she was, yeah. If she was desperate she knew how to cook herself a tin of beans or something. There was always something like that, you know, we didn't starve. But my dad . . . let's just say that my dad isn't one of the most – he doesn't go mad when he goes to the supermarket, know what I mean.

Shane laughs, bitterly.

—Just gets a few tins, and chucks them on the shelf and says, 'There's beans there, and mushrooms, and new potatoes.' They were all in tins.

—No wonder you're such a . . .

—I sold him a tin of beans!! One of the tins of beans that I'd nicked.

—Really?!

—Yeah!

—Sold it to your own father!?

—Yeah. I sold him a big can of beans.

—How much did you sell it to him for?

—A fiver.

—The same price you would sell it to other people for?

—Yeah.

—So, you sold your own father a tin of beans for five pounds.

—Bloody right! I should have doubled the price, the cunt.

—Shane. I'd better not ask you why.

—WELL, HE PUT ME IN A FUCKING LOONY BIN, DIDN'T HE!!!!!!

—I guess so . . . maybe you were mad.

—I wasn't mad. That's the first thing that became obvious when I went in. Nobody in that place was . . . well, there were mad people in there, but there weren't any there when I got there. Some arrived, after I'd been there a while, but it was a drug ward, so most of the people were sane. Anyway, it was good living in London. My mother had moved out to the country.

—When did that happen? When you were eighteen?

—While I was in the bin.

—While you were in the bin.

—Yeah.

—Not before it?

—No, while I was in the bin. But it was building up to it, before it. I was gradually going more over the top . . . cracking up. Let's say it was a contributing factor. I mean the household was ridiculous. There was my sister who . . . like just didn't know what was going on. She was completely confused. There was me, constantly zombified. And there was my old man, worried all the time, and my old lady sitting up in the bedroom pilled out of her tiny little mind, white as a sheet, covered in sweat, looking like she was about to pop any minute. So, Siobhan would be . . . she'd just sit and watch the telly, and me and my old man would shout obscenities at each other across the room. You know what I mean, have arguments about anything. Vegetarianism was a regular one. And that used to turn into a fight.

—**Really?**

—Yeah.

—**Why?**

—You know he's a vegetarian now.

—**Yeah.**

—But he was a dedicated carnivore then, and he was always taking the piss out of me because I was a vegetarian.

—**So why were you a vegetarian?**

—I had become a vegetarian because this girl Sarah was a vegetarian, that I was really into.

—**Are you serious?!?**

—Yes.

—**You became a vegetarian because you fancied somebody who was a vegetarian?**

—Yes.

—**That's pathetic!!!! And you stayed a vegetarian?**

—What's more, I un-became one because I fancied someone who liked hamburgers, called Shanne. And then I became a vegetarian again because I wanted to, so.

—**So why did you have those arguments?**

—Well, my dad would say that there was nothing wrong with factory farming, and all this.

—**Yeah?**

—Yeah. And I would rant and rave and give the other line, right. And then if he wanted a really good one, he'd start calling black people jungle bunnies and say that they weren't as developed as us, and that they couldn't rule themselves, you know, and that's why Africa's such a mess. But he was only winding me up there, cause he knew that would get me going.

When I was a freak, I used to bring friends home and we used to sit around on the floor, you know, stoned. There wouldn't be anybody there, except my sister, and my old man would be popping in and out on his way to a pub, or whatever, and my mum would be upstairs. So we used to sit around watching telly, cross-legged, in a circle, you know, passing joints.

—Cross-legged in a circle watching telly?

—Yeah.

—Yeah?

—Passing joints. Yeah.

—How can you sit cross-legged in a circle and watch the telly?

—Well, we weren't really sitting cross-legged in a circle, he made out we were.

—Ah, right.

—We were just on the floor watching telly. Some of us were sitting cross-legged, some of us . . . just lounging around out of it, you know.

—Yeah.

—He used to call us the Druids. He knew that would annoy me.

—Why?

—He said we were like druids with long hair, sitting around in a circle.

—Why did that annoy you?

—Because we didn't look like druids.

—But why would it bother you?

—Because it meant he was saying we looked like hippies, you know, with long hair, and beards and silly clothes. We didn't. We weren't hippies. We were young guys. We were freaks, you know. He knew how to get to me. He knew I hated hippies, and he knew that any implication that I was a hippy would get me.

—Your father used to call you a hippy.

—My father used to get at me by implying I was a hippy, you know, which was really annoying.

—Why was that so bad, being a hippy?

—Cause I loathed hippies. Cause I loathed all that peace and love, afghan, flowers and communes shit.

—Yeah, although you smoked dope, and you sat around . . .

—I was into drugs and rock music, you know.

—But you sat around cross-legged, smoking dope.

—No, we would just be staring blankly at the telly and passing a joint, you know, cause we'd be out of the other stuff. The only thing we did like hippies was smoke a bit of dope. But everybody smokes dope. We were into pills, you know. And he knew that I didn't regard myself as a hippy.

—Right, so he did it on purpose.

—He constantly tried to make me feel like a hippy. And it was bad because I had a friend who was a hippy. A real hippy. The only real hippy I ever had as a friend. And I don't know why he was my friend . . . we were friends for some reason although we were completely incompatible in most ways. But for some reason it worked.

We were good at thinking up ways of making money. We were good partners in crime. Good at getting drugs, making money, thieving, you know, and all the rest of it. But like, he was heavily into space rock, and all that space stuff, and it got worse and worse, till in the end he didn't need to take acid any more, he was on one permanent acid trip. And he had this afghan that he never fucking took off. So my dad loved him cause he could say like, 'So what are you two hippies up to tonight then?' And I couldn't say anything. I couldn't say, 'I'm not a fucking hippy!', cause I would've insulted my hippy friend. But he did get on my tits with his afghan coat, his boring spaced-out crap talk, you know. We were on a completely different wavelength, you know what I mean . . . he was into long space-guitar rock solos, he was into that sort of trip – psychedelic music, and getting it together. And he called women 'chicks'. He was a really feminine person, he had no male aggression in him.

—Well, that's nice.

—I was the one with all the male aggression. I'd decide what we were gonna do, and then he'd work out how we were gonna do it.

—So he was like a girlfriend.

—He wasn't like a girlfriend. He was like a friend who just happened to be a girl. And a very mad girl. No! He was a hippy! But he was the same age as me. I can't understand how he could be a hippy at the same age as me, but he was. Because hippy days were over, y'know. But he'd just taken too much acid, basically. And the afghan! I was really embarrassed walking around with a guy in an afghan. But my dad liked him so much, he bailed him out when he got nicked at Victoria station for having an offensive weapon.

—He had an offensive weapon and he was a hippy?

—All he had was a steel comb, but they call that an offensive weapon – a steel comb. The Victoria police were bastards, right. I'd been roughed up by them a couple of times, in those days. So they nicked him for it, yeah, and his old man said, 'Serves him right. I'm not getting him out.' And I told my old man about it, just in passing, cause he said, 'How's your hippy friend?' and I just said it in passing. I couldn't even give a shit about him, y'know, I wasn't in jail, I couldn't give a fuck. That's what I'm like. He could've rotted there for all I cared. But my old man went, 'If his own father won't get him out, that's disgraceful, I'll get him out.' And he went down and bailed him out! Inside I was going, 'Oh Dad, no!' I thought he was doing it just to get at me.

—Are you sure it was to annoy you?

—No, my dad is a stickler for justice. He'll stand up for anybody who he feels is being injustly treated. He's always stood up for me against the police. I've seen him . . . well, one time, me and him got in a fight in a bar with a couple of coppers, because he was telling them what a bunch of corrupt bastards they were. It could've got nasty, that. But luckily the governor – it was his local – the governor sorted it out. He said, 'These are regulars, so don't abuse these men', y'know.

—So you used to go drinking with your dad?

—After I left home, if I went to visit him, I'd go drinking with my dad quite a lot, yeah. After I left home everything cleared up, it was all fine, we had a great relationship. After I left home. And when he said he liked my records that was good, cause he'd be the first to criticize them if they were bad.

—Yeah?

—Yeah, cause he always liked to criticize what I did.

—**Really?**

—Yeah, it was a way of getting to me . . . in a humorous way, you know. But he quite seriously said that he thought the third album was an amazing record. And he's a man with good musical tastes, you know. He likes jazz, country, rock and roll, and likes a bit of punk. And of course he loves Irish music, so like . . . I mean, I knew my mum would say it was wonderful.

The minute I moved out of home that was the end of all the trouble. I would go and visit occasionally, and we'd go for a drink. Well, a few drinks . . . in fact we'd get fucking arseholed. And I introduced him to Southern Comfort and he got hooked on that. He used to drink loads of Southern Comforts and get up completely rat-arsed, and that's when he started the fight with that copper. And I came in with him, and the next thing we knew we were fucking having a fight with two plain-clothes coppers.

—**In a pub?**

—Luckily the pub was his regular, and like, the landlord is a big man who could sort anything out, y'know. Was. And he told the coppers, 'Look, you started this', you know, which they did, 'and these are regulars, right. So let's just leave it at that.' And we left it at that. Anyhow, that's enough about my dad.

—**That's enough about your dad?**

—For the time being.

—**So anyway, what happened after your job in the pub? Was there anything else about the job in the pub? Any funny stories about it?**

—Hmmmmmm, it was . . . it was very hard work, you know. When it was quiet it was fun. I'm not really cut out to be a barman, because I'm not very good at making small talk.

—**You're not good at making small talk?**

—I had fun ripping off Americans.

—**How?**

—Well, rich American tourists are so dumb they don't know the value of anything, right. And they know that you don't have to tip over here, and they're mean. So, you take advantage of that because you know

they'll never buy you a drink. You know what I mean? And so, if you've got a load of Americans, and they're all drinking doubles, right, just ring it up and then double it. I'm serious. They pay it without a word. It doesn't even occur to them that you're ripping them off.
—**Of course not.**
—And so you get half, and the pub gets half.
—**Did you do that to other people or just Americans?**
—Americans are the only people you can do it to.
—**Why? Why not Japanese, or . . .**
—Japanese aren't as stupid. Japanese know what they're doing. They get the fucking value of their money sorted out, the minute they get here, you know, what everything costs and that. You can't rip off a Jap. Who's gonna try and rip off a fucking Jap? But Americans, y'know . . .
—**Uhmmm . . . do you think you're going to be upsetting your American fans?**
—I'm talking about well-off Americans, buying rounds of double whiskies, and gins, not simple . . . I mean, I'm not talking about ripping off a couple of normal Joes . . . normal American tourists who are just having a pint. I'm talking about gangs of businessmen. They're very rude, because, of course, that's the way they are in America. People are rude in bars. But it stands out, over here.

And all our scotch bottles had the same scotch in them. You know, the cheapest shit you can buy. And you'd get these old farts who'd go, 'I'll have a Bells, please.' Or, 'I'll have a Teachers, please.' For a start, it's all blended Scotch, so it's all shit, right? I mean, there's no difference till you get to the malt whiskies and things like that. The difference between Bells and Teachers is like the difference between shit and shit. One sort of shit and another sort of shit. And anybody who drinks that shit deserves all they get. So it all had the same old shit in it.

So you'd get this guy, very proper, 'Make sure it's Bells, please.' And you'd give him a double Bells and he'd drink it, and he wouldn't say a word. And these are the kind of guys who would tell you that they could tell from the smell of it what brand it is. A very pompous

breed, people who drink blended scotch and actually think there's any difference between them. I mean they all taste like gut rot.
—**Did you do it with any Irish whiskies? Were they all the same too?**
—NOOOOOOO!!! You can't do it with an Irish whiskey.
—**Why?**
—Irish Whiskey is malt. It's good whiskey, yeah?!?!
—**Okay.**
—You can't do it with Scottish malt either. You can't do it with Glenfiddich or anything like that. But Teachers, Bells, all them . . . just put the same cheap rubbish into all the bottles. And I told you about the slops, and how they all go back into the tank at the end of the evening.
—**Hmmm. That's pretty nasty. What other nasty things do they do in pubs?**
—Uhmmmm. Just serving slops is pretty nasty.
—**It is.**
—But they do that.
Shane gets up suddenly and lurches towards the hi-fi, urgently. Scouring the pile of records on the floor, he selects one, triumphantly, and plays it, loudly.
—This is the first 'Wailers' album on Studio One!!! *Simmer Down.*
Shane sings, cheerily.
—'Simmer down . . .' Listen to that ska beat! 'Boom boom boom boom'. There's an Irish tune that has a ska beat.
—**Is there?**
—'The Sport of the Chase'. You know it, it goes, 'Dit de di de di, de dit de dee de . . .'
—**Yeah.**
—'De di de de, di de di de . . .'
Victoria yawns, impolitely.
—**Yeah.**
—'De dit de di de, dit de di de . . .'
—**Yeah.**
Shane warms to the task at hand and raises his voice, vociferously.
—'Di di di dit, di di di dit diddle de dit . . .' Yeah? Uhhh, in the

evening . . . after hours, the coppers would come round and have a few drinks.

—**And you'd beat them up.**

—No no no . . . I'd lick their arses. They'd take a bit of money. Just so that . . . just so. Just. To keep . . .

—**Just to keep what?**

—To be cool. One fight we had in there was with the Cork builders. About eight of them went out through a plate-glass window. A whole plate-glass window. And they all went crashing out through it, to the street. There was four of us barmen against fucking ten of these bastards, you know, and we were in trouble. We had a crowbar, but we were . . . it was pretty hairy. Luckily they were really really drunk cause they were big guys.

—**Why did you have a fight?**

—We had decided to throw them out.

—**Oh right.**

—They were being really obstreperous. They were tickling girls' fannies. It's the sort of thing you come to expect from those cultured, sophisticated Cork people. Ireland's second city. Fuck off! City of cathedrals and bridges. Nah, I mean they were the worst type of Cork guys. Fat, violent . . . I don't know when they did any work, they spent the whole day in the fucking pub.

There was this bunch of Northern guys who were really nice guys; they used to come in and drink a lot. And one day one of them came in and he had a letter in his hand, and he looked really upset. And his mate was with him, and his mate kind of . . . seemed to be consoling him. And he said, 'Give me a pint and a straight gin.' So I gave him a pint and a straight gin. And then he said, 'Another straight gin!', y'know. So he'd obviously gotten bad news from home, I don't know what. I put up another straight gin . . . and in the end everybody was looking at him, and he had me counting, he wanted me to count the gins. He drank seven pints, yeah, with twenty-six straight gins in between. In two hours. Between nine o'clock and eleven.

—**Cool.**

—Walked out of the pub, and the minute he hit the air he fell face first on to the pavement. But he walked out of the pub. People were clapping, y'know.

—Did he pay?

—Of course he paid. He slung a load of money on the bar and said, 'Just keep 'em coming. But you keep count, kid', y'know, 'you keep count'. So I did. And people were going, 'Twenty-one!!', you know what it's like, 'Twenty-two!!!' You know what I mean, it was like something out of a film.

—And did you ever find out why?

—No. I presume it was his mother, or something. Either his girlfriend left him or his mother died. Something. I never... I wasn't nosey enough to ask.

—Did you never have those kinds of conversations with people? You know, people have the barman when there's no one.

—Yeah, I did. A couple. Not very often, you know. Cause I don't...

—Make small talk.

—Well, I could've made small talk, but I wasn't gonna say to him, 'What's the matter with you!? Is your mother dead!?' You know what I mean?! I'm not that sort of person.

—No.

—If the guy wants to drink twenty-six gins and seven pints it's his business, as far as I'm concerned. As long as he could stand.

—Did you never throw people out because they were drunk?

—Just for being drunk?

—Yeah.

—No. Only for causing trouble.

—Did you ever refuse to serve people for being drunk?

—I think a couple of times, yeah. Real drunk. But I'd never do what a lot of publicans do, take one look at you and just guess that you're drunk, they way they do it to me all the time. They'd have to be really obviously drunk for me not to serve them. Yeah, but throwing people out was fun. A bit of violence... Oh yeah, while I was at the bar...

—Yes...?

—I went to see the Ramones for the first time, at the Roundhouse. I was working at the bar. And that was a great night. I put on my white t-shirt, jeans, and white plimsolls; which is just white tennis shoes; which is what the Ramones wore.

—Was it?

—Yeah. It's what they wore with leather jackets.

—Oh yeah.

—And all the other kids there were my age, and were wearing white t-shirts, jeans, and plimsolls.

—Yeah?! Everybody had the same clothes on?

—YES!!

—Really?

—And there was a whole army of us up at the Roundhouse.

—I thought you were an individualist.

—I wasn't a punk yet!

—Oh, right.

—I was in the process of becoming a punk. I was still a soul boy.

—Oh, right.

—There was a Scottish guy who used to come in a lot, and I'm pretty certain that he was homosexual.

—You've got a thing about homosexuals, Shane! Have you ever ...

—He was a body-builder, and he had a moustache.

—Shane, I think you might want to ...

—And he was very talkative and he bought me drinks a lot, y'know. And when my friend Pete came in, he got very interested in Pete and bought him loads of drinks.

—Yeah?

—In fact, that was the night of the brick. Pete got pissed on whiskey with this guy. This guy kept saying we should go down to his gym, you know, and work out. And uh, like ... I think he was a bender, yeah.

—Are you sure you ...?

—He was a sort of character, you know.

—Are you ever ...?

—You know he's a bender, but he wouldn't pressure you. He

Threshing at the farm in the 1930s. Auntie Nora (left) and Granny (middle) are gathered with their neighbours. Uncle Jim and Uncle John are on the steam engine and tractor at the back.

Uncle Willie and his daughter, Auntie Monica.

The farm where Shane spent his childhood.

Uncle Sean.

Shane's parents at the beach in the 1950s, before they were married.

Shane's mother modelling in the early 1950s.

Shane's parents signing the register with Canon Donaghue, on their wedding day, 1 August 1956.

Shane's mother as Irish Colleen, St Patrick's Day Girl 1954.

Top: Herding geese with Uncle Willie.

Right: Auntie Ellen, Uncle John and Uncle Willie and Shane, aged three.

Below: Threshing day in the early sixties. Auntie Nora and Uncle John are on the tractor.

Threshing with Uncle Willie *(left)* and
Auntie Ellen *(right)*.

Shane aged four.

Shane's mother at
her dressing table
in the early 70s.

The family. *Left to right:* back row, Uncle Willie, Auntie
Nora, Auntie Ellen, Grannie, a neighbour and Auntie
Bridget. Front row, Shane, Auntie Monica and a friend.

Siobhan aged two.

At the farm, aged five,
with Cousin Puppe.

Shane with Siobhan and Auntie Nora.

Shane aged six, with his parents
and Siobhan.

Siobhan aged five.

Shane in the late 70s.

Right: Granny and
Grandad MacGowan.

Shane's mother in
the early 80s.

Shane, Siobhan and her friend Mary
in Connemara in the early 80s.

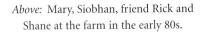

Above: Mary, Siobhan, friend Rick and
Shane at the farm in the early 80s.

Top right: Cutting his birthday cake
on Christmas Day, 1986.

Right: Siobhan standing with the remains
of the steam engine still at The Commons.

Shane and Siobhan outside the Town & Country Club after a performance.

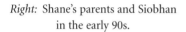

Above: Shane's dad in the parlour at
The Commons in the late 80s.

Right: Shane's parents and Siobhan
in the early 90s.

Shane and his mother in Tipperary around 1993.

wouldn't try to ball me or anything. Saying like, 'We've got a gym, and we're into having young men . . . young guys around.' You know what I mean. 'Come down, y'know, and hang around. Put on a bit of muscle. If you want a fist fuck, it's up to you.'

—No! He didn't say that.

—Well . . . no. It's what he was implying, you know.

—It is?

—So. Of course he could've been a fucking serial killer! I could've gone down there and got fucking chopped up into bits.

—Yeah. You should have gone.

—But he was a really cool guy. He wore black, you know. And he had a moustache. He looked like a sort of martial arts hero. You know, he looked like a genuinely tough guy. He looked like a hero from a . . . like Jean Claude Van Damme, or Chuck Norris, or Charles Bronson sort of thing. You know what I mean, he was very macho, but friendly . . . and Scottish. He's just someone I remember.

—Are you anti-gay?

—No. How could I be anti-gay? You know what I mean, I've known so many gays over the years . . .

—Yeah?

—What's more, the soul singers always had lots of gays into them.

—So why do you say things like that, about how you think he was a homosexual, or a bender, or . . .

—I think he was a bisexual. No, I've got a definite homosexual vibe. But he just talked about the gym, and all that – and came in every night, bought me drinks. We chatted about all sorts of things. He was a cool guy. The kind of guy I could talk with, you know. Who wasn't small talking, he talked about interesting things. He was an intelligent Scot, you know, like Jock.

But he had a heaviness about him which was sort of like, tangible, you know what I mean, you wouldn't mess with him. Perhaps he was a black belt in karate or something or other. Perhaps he was a mercenary. You never know. That was at the time Angola was going on.

—Angola?

—Just to slip it in. That was an interesting period.

—Why?

—Well, all these British mercenaries got arrested in Angola by the revolutionaries.

—Yeah? Why?

—Well, they were fighting for the fascist government. All these British mercenaries and the British government had to try and get them out or they were going to be executed. It was the big thing at the time. And I used to go around saying, 'I got a my hole-a in Angola.' *Shane laughs, amusedly. Victoria frowns, bemusedly.*

—**You what? Said what?**

—I got a my hole-a in Angola.

—**Oh right.**

—That was the sort of sense of humour I had at the time.

—**Oh yeah?**

—That was what the Italian mercenaries used to say, [mock Italian accent] 'I gotta my hole-a in Angola.' Nah, you know, it was just one of those things, I was always . . . I was fascinated with Angola.

—**I don't even know what it is, or where it is.**

—It's in Africa.

—**Oh.**

—And uh, did you see *Mountains of the Moon*?

—**No.**

—You bloody have!! With fucking . . . with Patrick Bergin and another guy exploring through the Nile.

—**Oh yeah.**

—Remember it?!?

—**Vaguely.**

—Do you remember the really cruel tribe that took loads of drugs? Well, that was Angola. But anyway, it became a British colony, and obviously when the Brits left, they left them there to get taken over by a bunch of murdering bastards, right. And there was a people's revolution. A bunch of ex-army British mercenaries went over there to fight for the government, and the government lost, and they got captured. And they were gonna be executed, and the British government was trying to get them out. I just thought it was interesting. The MPLA were in Angola. The MPLA was the name of the revolutionaries. The MPLA, yeah. And the MPLA boys had one of the big toasting records around at the time. Cause I was into reggae, and reggae was very political. Johnny Rotten was heavily into reggae as well. It was a great period for reggae. I listened to a hell of a lot of reggae at the time. Cause it was the golden age of toasting. Do you know what toasting is?

—**Yeah, kind of.**

—It's dub. You don't know what toasting is?!?

—**I do have an idea.**

—OH COME ON!!!

—**Oh no!**

—No, you gotta know what toasting is if you want to know what I'm on about!! Do you know what dub is?!?!

Victoria sighs, noisily.

—**Yeah.**

—You sure?!?!

—**That's sort of heavy like, boom boom boom?**

—Yeah. It was the golden age of dub and toasting, yeah. And uh . . .

—**I'm quite sleepy now . . .**

Shane ignores Victoria, dismissively.

—I was heavily into that stuff, yeah. So I had a lot of different musical influences going on in my head at the time.

—**Uh-huh.**

Shane selects another record, eagerly.

—This has got toasting and dub on it so you can hear it.

—**Is this some sort of test . . . ? I have heard it, Shane, obviously, I just couldn't define it.**

—But listen. At the time I'm talking about, it was a specific type of toasting.

—**Yeah. It's just some bloke talking over the . . . well, rap.**

—Listen to that, yeah!?!

—**Yeah.**

—Now that's toasting.

—**Yeah. That's brilliant.**

—And the greatest dub album ever came out at that time, *King Tubby meets the Rockers Uptown* by Augustus Pablo. And it's dub. DUB!!! This is one of the most, this was one of the biggest albums at the time.

—**Yeah.**

—And it was a really heavy year for toasting. Do you like this?

—**Yeah.**

—Well, the soul boys who had a wider range of tastes listened to a lot of reggae, that included Johnny Rotten.

—**Was he a soul boy?**

—Well, seeing as there was no punk records.

—**What!? Johnny Rotten was a soul boy?**

—Well actually, Johnny was a freak, I think. Johnny was a freak. I don't think he went through a soul boy phase. But he was always an individualist as a dresser. He had really long hair for a while and he was quite fat. Then he cut his hair off, bought a suit down the King's Road, tore it to bits and safety-pinned it together again. And that's how that started, you know. So, the music the punks listened to was soul, the latest soul imports, and reggae imports, yeah.

—**Yeah.**

—That was what they listened to. That's was what they danced to in the clubs. There were no punk records. So reggae was very big, yeah.

—**Yeah.**

—And Louise's was a lesbian disco in Poland Street. And all the other discos wouldn't let the punks in.

—**Why?**

—Cause of the way they looked.

—**Hmmmm.**

—But this lesbian disco, Louise's, would. Boy and girl punks. So that became the first punk club. And downstairs was the best disco in town. That's where I first heard 'Cocaine in My Brain' by Dillinger. Where I first heard *Low*. They'd got hold of a pre-release copy of *Low* by David Bowie.

And upstairs there was a bar, where drinks were really expensive, but . . . BUT, people wanted to talk to you if you were a punk, to find out what you were about, so they'd buy you drinks. So you'd sit around getting bought drinks by these people, and they'd just be sort of getting off on drinking with punks, you know. And sort of saying, 'What are you guys into? What drugs do you do? What sex are you into?' and all that. Me and Shanne used to lead each other around on a dog-chain.

—Oh yeah? Who was leading who?

—I used to lead her, and I used to let her lead me. It was mutual, it wasn't sexist.

—And where would you go? Into bars?

—Occasionally into bars, yeah.

—And what kind of reaction would you get? Would they hassle you?

—No.

—They didn't hassle you?

—No, they were too shocked.

—Yeah?

—Yeah. They were more liable to hassle you about your hairdo anyhow, and your clothes. Like my mate Claudio got beaten up for wearing pink drainpipes and winklepickers. And someone started a fight with me over Shanne. Shanne had a skunk stripe down her head. Blonde on each side and black down the middle, you know. And someone came up and hassled her, so I jumped in and we had a fight with pool cues. There was the occasional hassle, y'know. But generally people were too shocked to hassle me. The thing that started all the real trouble was the 'God Save the Queen' thing. You know, Johnny saying about how he hated the Queen, and all that. That made things bad for everyone.

—Why, what happened then?

—Well, then you got Loyalists picking on you. Before that they just thought we were a bunch of poofs, and they left us alone. But when Johnny attacked Our Majesty, know what I mean, then they got very angry.

—Did you know him?

—Johnny himself was cut up very badly in the car park of the Pelican in Stoke Newington. Paul Cook was hit with a hammer coming out of Hammersmith tube station. Did I know who? Johnny?

—Yeah.

—Yeah.

—And what's he like?

—Self-centred, arrogant, opinionated. Very much into himself. Me me me. And he always liked a lot of attention.

—Can you remember any instances involving him?

—Not really, no. He never did anything outrageous, really.

—No?

—Nah.

—Did you like him?

—Yes.

—Why did you like him?

—You couldn't help but like the guy, you know. Although with the audience, generally, it was very much a love-hate relationship. He used to tease them and heckle them . . . drive them mad, till they started fighting. But he'd always be out of the way when the fighting started.

—So tell me more. Tell me, what did you do when you left home?

—I moved into a flat with a couple of guys I had gone to school with. We were all on the dole. And we all had to stay up all night, the night before the dole cheques came, because otherwise the first person up would have all the dole cheques, forge all the signatures on them, and beat you to it. And spend all the money before anybody else was up. So, it was a tense night, Thursday night.

When I got my dole cheque, first thing I'd do, having lived on porridge and water the whole week – which is what we lived on for most of the week – I'd go out and get a box of eggs, a loaf of bread, and some butter, and have three or four fried-egg sandwiches. Then, once I wasn't hungry any more, I'd start . . . I'd go out and spend the rest of the money.

—Where would you go?

—Louise's, or the Roxy, or somewhere. Once we were out, we'd stay out all night . . . and day . . . just doing the clubs. Louise's and the Roxy were the main two places. Louise's was a private members club, but punks were allowed in.

—What did you want to do with your life? I mean, did you enjoy just like, going to clubs, or was there something . . .

—That was what we enjoyed, yeah.

—Why did you enjoy that so much?

—Well, it was a hell of a lot of fun.

—Was it?

—Yeah. Well, in those days, clubs were really good. The things they have now which are called clubs are pathetic, you know. I'm talking about a completely different thing.

—What was different?

—Well, Louise's upstairs had a beautiful cocktail lounge where you'd drink Pernod and stuff. Drink Pernod and smoke Winstons. And . . .

—Only Pernod and Winstons? Not Bacardi and Marlboro?

—Yeah.

—Why?

—Because the right cigarettes were Winstons, and the right drink was Pernod. The right dress was what was the most individualistic dress there, y'know.

—Well, why was the right cigarette Winstons? And why was there a right cigarette? I mean . . .

—Because it was a bit like mods, it was elitist. A lot of really clever little London teenagers. And we would never dream of calling ourselves a movement. We were individualists.

—If you were individualists, why did you all smoke the same cigarette?

—Well exactly, yeah. There were just some things which were classic punk style. Winstons were the obvious cigarette, cause uhm . . . where's my fags?

—Over there. Wasn't Sid Vicious at the same college as you?

—No. He was at the same college I applied for.

—Oh right.

—Him and Rotten got in . . . but they wouldn't let me in. I was regarded as too much of a scumbag, but they let Rotten and Vicious in. I went to Brook Green, the bottom of the pile, with Bernie and Moisey. Charlie didn't go to college, himself.

—So what was Sid really like?

—Well, Sid was a very shy guy, know what I mean. Quiet. I'd have a drink with him, whenever we met. And then he joined the Sex Pistols and became above it all. And I didn't really see much of him after he joined the Sex Pistols, cause he kept himself to himself. He didn't used to, in the early days, but once they signed their deal, they didn't hang around with the old crew.

The last time I saw him alive was at his gig in 1978, not long before he died, at the Electric Ballroom. Promoted by Frank Murray. That was a really good gig, y'know, he was really good. And Nancy got up, that was a bit of a low point, and did some songs. He did 'No Fun' and 'I Wanna Be Your Dog', and stuff like that. And then a few months later he was dead, and nobody could believe it. Dead in America. A lot of people tried to convince him not to go to America. I was friends with a group of girls that he hung around with a lot. I was friends with them, and they told him he wasn't gonna come back, but it didn't work. And true enough, he didn't come back.

—Didn't he used to call you 'Bondage'?

—Yeah.

—How did that happen?

—Well, I wrote and published *Bondage*, which was the first graphic fanzine. In other words it wasn't typewritten, it was written out by hand. And then it was covered in graphics. Like, each page was covered in safety pins and chains and stuff . . . real ones, yeah? And I photocopied it like that, for the original copy. I took the whole thing down with the chains and stuff on it, to the photcopying machine at Oxford Circus, and photocopied it once. Then I got the money to publish it by going around places like Compendium and Rock On and saying, 'I'll give you a certain amount of copies if you give me the money upfront to get it printed.' And they would give it to me.

—Wow, that's unusual, isn't it?

—Yeah. And what's more, I made a huge profit on it. Because fanzines were generally done by all the little raincoat types, who were doing it for the love of it. But I was doing it for the money. It cost about ten pence to produce a copy, right? The other fanzine writers would charge fifteen pence. I'd charge fifty pence.

—Fifty pence?!

—Yeah.

—That was a lot in those days.

—Yeah, I know. I made a massive profit.

—Wow.

—But people bought it, y'know.

—Fifty pence was probably about the price of a single, wasn't it?

—Yeah.

—Why did they buy it?

—Because I put the Sex Pistols on the front. Simple. And it had an article about the Sex Pistols in it. There was no interview, it was just me ranting about the Sex Pistols. And I also wrote an article prophesying that the Jam would be a huge group. So my word was very important, from then on. And some people called me 'Bondage'. Sid called me 'Bondage'.

—Why did you call the magazine *Bondage*?

—Cause that was the thing with the graphic design, y'know. It was all like, chains and safety pins, and drawings of spiked gloves and stuff like that.

—Did you enjoy writing your own magazine?

—Yeah, I enjoyed it, it was fun. I just thought how pathetic the rest of them were, you know, and how much better I could do it. So I did it. Same reason I started a group.

—Uh-huh. So, how come you stopped? I mean, if you were making forty pence profit on each one, you could've made a really good living out of that.

—I could've, yeah.

—So why didn't you?

—I never got it together. I was just too lazy to get it together to do a second issue. Typical me, you know.

—Didn't you need the money?

—Not at the time, no. The first one kept selling. And I didn't look foward to a time when it would've run its run, know what I mean, and I'd need more money. So I chucked my job in, and dedicated all my energies to enjoying myself. I was intending to do a second edition, if there were other bands that I wanted to do. The first issue had a list of contents for the second issue in it, but I never got round to doing it. But I could've made some bread right then. At that stage I was being interviewed by the *Evening Standard* regularly, y'know.

—Why?

—The Face of '77, y'know.

—And why were you being interviewed?

—I was The Face of '77!

—In the *Evening Standard*?

—In everything, y'know! I mean, I was known as The Face of '77.

—How did that happen?

—Well, you know me and self publicity. I was always at the right place at the right time, you know, and with my ear getting bitten off, y'know, and putting out *Bondage* . . . And the *Evening Standard* happened to choose me to interview, and did a two-page spread on me. They asked me what it was all about and I told them it was about being blank and vacant, how we didn't give a shit about anything except having a good time. And we weren't interested in love or boring old rock stars. And Johnny Rotten was our philosopher. Things like that. I was interviewed by a lot of record companies for a job as A&R man, but my natural hatred of authority put them off. I was very rude to them, I went in and said, 'It's not what you can give me, it's what I can give you.'

The ear-biting thing was with Jane from the Modettes. What we were doing was having a kind of sado-masochistic love ritual in front of the stage with broken bottles. It felt like a good idea at the

WOTCHA ZOMBI ;
STANDING IN A CROMBIE
LOOKING FOR A TOMBOY
LIKE ~~KICKS~~ US ~~MY~~ FRIEND
TOOK HIM IN THE JACKS
AND CAME OFF ON HIS BACK
A DISTANT THANK YOU
MOUTHFUL OF ~~LOVE~~
HANDS OF THE BARMAID
~~JACKING~~ OFF THE ~~WAGE~~ WAGE SLAVES
I'M SITTING ON THE FRIDGE
I'M GETTING CLOSE TO THE ~~EDGE~~
I'M A SENSITIVE PERSON
DRUNK AND BROKE
I'M A POET OF PERVERSION
~~DYING~~ FOR A POKE
~~SHE~~ PUTS ANOTHER JAR UP
THEN SHE ~~FIRST~~ SHUTS THE BAR UP
NEARLY SMASHED THE CAR UP
WHEN SHE WAS GIVING ME A BLOWJOB

time. I got off on it, I got off on the pain, both inflicting pain and being on the receiving end. It was a kick. Some new kind of kick. It wasn't even really sexual, it was just a kick. We were carving each other up with broken bottles. She wasn't my girlfriend, or anything, she was just a bird who grabbed me in the crowd and put her tongue in my mouth and carved me up with a broken bottle. The ear thing was simply that she nicked me on the ear and it started to bleed and ears bleed a lot so there was loads of blood pumping out of my ear. We were biting each other but it wasn't on the ear, it was on the arms and shoulders and necks. We were biting each other very hard, but the photographs show the bleeding ear. In the end, security came and carted her away. An *NME* photographer took pictures and it was in the *NME* the next week.

I became a punk Face very quickly. I was respected and treated with awe by other punks. But I wasn't as cool as my mate Claudio, who was cooler than Rotten. Remember the famous Sex shirt? Which was a Ben Sherman type shirt, without buttons, with Marx and Hitler on it. Claudio was into swastikas and Italian fascism, before they ever thought of it, y'know, being an Italian. He used to march around Il Duce style. And he used to sing Italian fascist songs that he'd learned off his dad, who was a waiter in a greasy spoon Italian restaurant.

Claudio was a waiter in a very classy restaurant, where he got hundred-quid tips. But he never put his money into the bank, he kept it under the bed. He had thousands of pounds under the bed. And when he finished his shift, y'know, he would go to a club, but he couldn't party with his waiter's uniform on, so he used to safety-pin the trouser legs, to make them into drainpipes. He was the first person to wear safety pins.

Like I said, we all wore dog-chains and shirts with swastikas on, and even Union Jack t-shirts, but it was obvious that we weren't being serious about it. It was obvious we were taking the piss. I was accused by Johnny of being a Brit, because I wore a Union Jack shirt, and then of changing into an Irish republican, to be fashionable.

Well, nothing could be further from the truth. In 1975 I was walking around with 'IRA' written on my forehead.
—**Yeah?**
—Yeah. And that was during a bombing campaign, you know.
—**And you supported the bombing?**
—At that stage, yeah. I mean I've grown out of that now. I didn't think about the fact that I might get bombed myself. I just thought it was a laugh, you know, I used to hear them going off. And I'd think, 'well, that one didn't get me, but I bet it got a few Brits.'
—**Are you serious?**
—And like, they only had a few own goals where they killed Irish people, you know.
—**What about the people who weren't Irish, or English? What about those people?**
—Well, the fact is that the British government doesn't take any notice until you commit an atrocity, simple fact. After the first ceasefire they did fuck-all for eighteen months. So they had to blow up a fucking large part of London, to get their attention. And that got their attention, y'know. It got it in a big way!
—**Maybe we ought to get back to the other subject we were . . .**
—Yeah, well I mean, I'm just saying the IRA do what they have to do! You know, cause the British government only understand terrorism. They're so blind. They had a chance to fucking get round a table, right, given to them by the IRA, who want to get back to their peace-loving ways, and they declared an unconditional ceasefire, without any fucking concessions being given to them, which they kept for eighteen months, or was it two and half years? . . . I can't remember. And the Brits talked to the Unionists, but they wouldn't talk to Sinn Fein, right, so the IRA got pissed off and fucking blew something up, you know, to fucking show them that they were still there, and that was the end of the ceasefire. You can't piss them around. We're leaving that subject, all right. All right. In punk, right, we were sick of all that political shit. So we wore swastikas and we wore Union Jacks, and we wore IRA fucking written on our jackets, and 'Born to Kill', and 'No Compassion', you know like, things that were all slogans.

—Yeah.

—And like, we made up pretentious titles for ourselves, like 'conceptualist'.

—'Conceptualist'?

—Yeah, I mean, one weekend we were called 'the conceptualists'. I thought that one up. I spread it around at a couple of clubs and it caught on.

—Right.

—But it was only meant to last a week, y'know. Because it was like fashion . . . it only lasted a week. The minute somebody turned up wearing the same thing as you, which you started wearing in the first place, you trashed it, and did something else, know what I mean. Sid was really good at that, but then he got stuck in that bloody leather jacket mould. And the long spiky hair, which looked good on him, but didn't look good on most people. He had the looks and the figure for it. And it was jet black. It doesn't look good purple, or fucking green, you know. But before that . . . well, you never knew what Sid was gonna wear. There's a story about how he invented pogo-ing, because he was wearing a poncho, a leather poncho, and he couldn't move his arms, so he just jumped up and down.

—Is that a true story?

—Whether that's true or not, I don't know, because I don't know anybody who saw it. And I know a lot of people who were at the gig that it was supposed to have happened at. But like, these were all legends, like me getting my ear bitten off. So anyway, we thought up names like 'the conceptualists', and they'd be sort of hip words . . . some of them were really wanky. For instance, 'important'. For a while 'important' became a word that meant that a group was really good, like, 'I think the Clash are really *important.*' Know what I mean? It was used to describe groups like the Clash and the Jam, y'know, who had political attitudes. Nobody ever said that the Sex Pistols were 'important', right?

—Right.

—The Sex Pistols were just fucking brilliant, y'know. The worst.

—Huh?

—The worst. The Sex Pistols were the worst! Which is a pretty old-fashioned phrase, y'know, meaning the best.

—Oh, right.

—Like 'bad' means good, in nigger slang.

Victoria looks horrified, suddenly. Shane laughs, cheekily.

—. . . What?!

—You said nigger.

—Yeah, so? And uh . . . well, how many black people are gonna read this book?

Shane continues to laugh, wickedly. Victoria gasps, dumbfoundedly.

—HUH . . . A few, maybe.

—Well, Don Letts might, but he knows I'm only joking.

A very . . . very . . . long . . . silence . . . ensues. Victoria fidgets, nervously. Shane swigs a Caffreys, thirstily.

—Let's just go on . . .

Victoria stumbles towards the fridge and, finding a bottle of vodka, pours herself a swift one, shakily. Shane notices Victoria's discomfort, sensitively.

—Well, what am I supposed to call them? Coloured?!? Negro?? Spades is what I normally call them. I just let that one slip out, y'know. I'll admit I used to be a bigot.

—Yeah?!

—Even though I had loads of black friends, yeah.

—Were you racist?

—Yeah, but I don't hate anybody any more. There's just two things I hate, racists and English people.

Victoria pours another, wearily.

—English people?

—That's a joke. As old as the hills. It's an Irish joke. In other words an Irish-Irish joke, as opposed to an English-Irish joke. ANYWAY . . . so, we were walking around with swastikas, Union Jack t-shirts, ripped-up shirts with Marx and Hitler on them, right, and Lenin, and 'Pretty Vacant', 'I'm so bored with the USA', whatever. That's the best idea the Clash ever had, y'know. It was really anti-American. We wore the swastikas to shock, y'know, we wore the ripped-up shirts to shock. To show that we were nihilistic. We were completely nihilistic. That was the idea behind punk. There was no future, we lived for the moment, we lived for pleasure. We took drugs, we drank, we listened to fucking bloody awful bands. We head-banged, and slam-danced, and we just got everything out of life. We dressed the way we wanted to dress. We dressed in a way that . . . well, it doesn't seem shocking now, but it was shocking in those days, to have an earring if you were a boy, and to have spikey dyed hair. Even to wear drainpipe trousers was shocking, and to wear winklepickers, y'know. The sex thing had completely broken down. Sexism, we eliminated. We really did eliminate sexism for a while, y'know. It was perfectly all right for a girl to go around with six blokes, and none of them were really screwing her, and there was nothing unusual about that, with punk. Or for a bloke to go around with six girls and none of them were really screwing him. Or for a man and woman to go around together and not be screwing each other. Because sex was regarded as boring, y'know. If you wanted to do it, you did it . . . if it felt good you did it. But love was out of the question.

—It was?

—Having children was out of the question. Cause as Johnny put it, 'If you want a baby, go to an orphanage.' And we always had to be prepared for violence, because they were violent times. And because we chose to do exactly what we wanted, and looked exactly the way we wanted to look, we were walking targets for 'lads', you know, for straights. And this was even before the skinhead shit came into it, y'know. These were the Cortina boys, and football fans, know what I mean. Not that there weren't football fans who were punks.

So we all wore dog-chains and knives and fucking things like that, and a few fatal things happened, you know. There was a lot of blood spilled. Often we ran away, if the odds were too bad, but if the odds were all right . . . know what I mean, if the odds were sensible, we fought. We fought physically, we didn't try and fight fairly, we fought physically, know what I mean. And the women fought as well, cause we didn't give a shit. And we were speeding all the time. And violence isn't so bad, y'know. It's only if you're afraid of it that it's so bad. It's only fear that's bad. When you're actually getting kicked, when you're in a fight, y'know, time stands still.

—**Does it?**

—Yeah. You don't feel the pain. The thing is, if you're in a fight . . . a fair fight, or a reasonably fair fight, you know, like three against one . . .

—**Three to one?!**

—That's about as fair as it gets, know what I mean.

—**What, three against you?**

—Yeah. I can take three people out.

—**Yeah?**

—Yeah. If I'm angry enough. Or all you really have to do is take one of them out. Concentrate on one person, y'know, and the others will leg it. If you really make a mess of him.

—**Yeah.**

—I'm not saying I'm a great fighter, or anything like that, I'm saying that I was nihilistic, know what I mean . . . ? It didn't matter to me whether I lived or died. It didn't matter to me. It really didn't. Lots of people say that, but they don't really mean it, y'know. But that's the way we thought. There was no future, anyway.

—**Why was there no future?**

—Because . . . what was there to look foward to? What was there? There was a massive recession. There were no jobs. The only way to get money was stealing. Or to think of something . . . make a fanzine or something like that. Make clothes, or fucking get a job in a sex shop. A lot of people worked in sex shops. Or record shops. Or joined a band.

That's why there were so many bands, people were trying to make money, y'know. Write a few fucking crappy songs, and fucking get up there and do it, know what I mean? Just write however you feel at the time. We didn't believe in all this shit about cool songs . . . or being a 'songwriter'. You know, the Sex Pistols could play, and they wrote great songs, but they were simple songs, you know, they were three-chord songs that anybody could get together in no time at all.

And well, it was an explosion waiting to happen. The post-hippy youth. People who didn't give a damn about peace and love or politics, or any of that shit, know what I mean. People who didn't like any of the rock music that was going around. The only music people listened to was soul and reggae, you know, imports. And the live bands, like the Pistols, and . . . well, the Pistols were the only pure punk band, with the real attitude. Any real punk will tell you that. They just didn't give a shit, they were nihilists. Which is a comical way of saying . . . it's an easy way of saying that you don't give a shit. You don't give a shit about starving people in some foreign country, you don't give about starving people in your own country. You don't give a shit about class, colour, creed, sex . . . you don't give shit about yourself, know what I mean. You don't allow yourself the arrogance of self-respect, y'know.

—Why not?

—Cause it's arrogance. Why should you respect yourself? You're just a piece of shit, you know.

—Yeah?

—Yeah, you're scum, y'know.

—**Why did you think that?**

—Cause that's what society thought we were, you know, scum. The police thought all young people were scum. The government thought all people were scum, and still do, that's the facts. Democracy doesn't exist. Nobody's ever gonna get a fair deal from protesting things, or fighting wars, life is shit. Just take what you can. Get all you can out of it. And if it involves violence, use violence, y'know. And like, don't think about tomorrow, there is no tomorrow. Tomorrow is just getting old, y'know, you die. We didn't want jobs anyway, even if there had been any.

—**You didn't?**

—No.

—**How come?**

—Who wants to work? It's just like a continuation of school, isn't it? Except you get paid for it. There are cushy jobs, though. Everybody wanted one of them. Cushy jobs, we would have taken.

—Like what?

—Working in a record shop. Working in a sex shop. Being in a band. Designing clothes . . . jobs like that. Doing what you enjoy for money, you know, then it's not a job anyway. A 'job' is something you have to do to make money. But we'd make money any way we could, apart from doing a nine-to-five job. Selling drugs, sex, petty crime, you know . . . nothing like armed robbery though, that's too fucking dangerous. We didn't pretend to be hard men, know what I mean. But we weren't gonna get pushed about.

And I'm talking about men and women, yeah? Men and women regarded each other as totally equal, you know. All that feminism business went out the window, and all that macho business went out the window. You couldn't tell the boys from the girls for a second . . . it was tricky. It's the closest it's ever been to a total overthrow of all the shit from society, y'know. If we hadn't grown up, or lost our nihilism, or if it hadn't been penetrated by police, and political activists, who misshaped the ideas . . . You know, like the Clash, they turned it into a political thing. Started people thinking politically. Old hippies cut their hair, and got into it. It was the hippies' revenge on society. The true punks weren't interested in politics. They didn't give a shit about politics. But they weren't racist, they weren't sexist . . . I mean, WE weren't racist and we weren't sexist. We weren't technically violent, but we were violent for a laugh, or for . . . because we had to be, to protect ourselves, y'know.

Which leads me round to the bondage trousers. Bondage trousers were a brilliant idea, because it sorted out the idiots from the smart ones, right? Anybody smart wouldn't strap up their bondage trousers, cause obviously somebody else is gonna come up, pissed and speeding, and just for a laugh he's gonna fucking pull you by the strap, and knock you over on to your face and kick your head in. And there's nothing you can do about it. You can't get up again . . . or anything!
Shane snorts, merrily.

—No. So whose idea were the bondage trousers in the first place?

—Well, I presume Vivienne Westwood nicked the idea off some punk.

—Right.

—All their ideas got nicked. Some punk had obviously made himself a pair of bondage trousers. I presume he hadn't strapped them up, know what I mean. The idea was that they were bondage trousers, that you could strap them up if you wanted to be . . . you know, for kinky sex or something like that. There was lots of kinky sex which was usually quite violent, y'know.

—Yeah?

—Well, there were people being razored up and stuff. It was a very popular occupation, razoring up your arse, know what I mean. Razoring up your stomach.

—Why was that?

—It's like giving yourself homemade tattoos, y'know. Drawing little pictures with a razor on your body.

—Why?

—Because there was rage in it, and it expressed itself through self-mutilation, and violence against other people. We never really started fights, but there were plenty of people who wanted to have fights with us, because they thought we were freaks. They were frightened of us because we were different. So there were plenty of stupid people ready to start fights, thinking that they'd have an easy time, know what I mean . . . thinking we were poofters, or someone they could beat up really easily. Not that you could beat up poofters really easily, cause they're usually really good fighters, know what I mean, they have to be. And of course they made the same mistake with us, and then we kicked their fucking heads in a lot of the time.

And of course they didn't realize that the girls could fight as well as the blokes. It brought out all the aggression in the women, and you know, women are good fighters if they lose that inhibition about it. Which had been drummed in . . . y'know, we broke all those inhibitions that they tried to drum into us. You know what I mean? We saw through the fucking conditioning. We were ambisexual. We were really ambisexual, not playing around like glam-rock, and Bowie and all that. You know, there were homosexuals, there were bisexuals, there were lesbians, there were asexuals, there were

straight sexuals, some of them monogamist, some of them poly-
gamists, know what I mean . . . there were no rules about sex, no
morals, we had no morals. If it feels good, do it, y'know, that was our
morals. Whether it's pulling a guy by the bondage strap, if he'd been
stupid enough to tie up his trousers, and fucking kicking his head in
– or whether it's having a scene with eight birds, or a bird obviously
with eight blokes. Gang-bangs, fucking, self-mutilation, fucking
bondage, fucking full bondage . . . y'know, the whole lot.

There was a bondage shop down the King's Road, and that's
where we got a lot of the clothes. There was a big leather and
bondage scene. It's impossible to analyse exactly all the influences
that went into punk, because it was all just fashion. We borrowed
our hairstyles, and our clothes. Some of them were completely
original, but most of them were influenced by one thing or another.
There was forties, fifties and sixties gear, and they all got mixed up
together. Then ripped up and saftey-pinned together, which was a
totally original idea. There was bondage.

There was lots of stuff borrowed from the homosexual under-
world. Like leather trousers, and leather caps, and fucking like . . .
dyed hair and earrings . . . homemade t-shirts, homemade shirts.
And Malcolm and Vivienne would study the crowd at every gig, and
if they saw a good t-shirt, or a good shirt, or a good pair of trousers,
they'd have it in Sex the next day, they'd work overnight making
them. They'd stick a hundred-quid tag on them, or a fifty-quid tag
on them, y'know.

Whoever wore the first mohair jumper to a club or to a punk gig
really got ripped off. Mohair jumpers hadn't been worn since the
early sixties, know what I mean. Somebody had picked up an early
sixties mohair jumper, and everybody thought it was really cool.

Malcolm and Vivienne, well . . . I'll give it to them that they could
spot a new fashion that was gonna take off, but I mean it wouldn't
take a genius to see that everyone was looking to get a mohair
jumper. Because it was a very distinctive thing, you know. Nobody
could remember mohair jumpers from the sixties anyway. I'd never
seen one before. Next day there were mohair jumpers in Sex, and

everybody was wearing mohair jumpers. You know, plastic macs . . . the first guy who wore a plastic mac had to take it off the next day and dump it, because the next gig he went to, everyone was wearing plastic macs, know what I mean?! It was a bit like the mod scene in that way. But it was far more elitist and intelligent.

And it was a complete mixure of class, and race, and creed. Well, there was no creed, because we had no creed. We dumped whatever creed we'd been brought up with. Although Catholic punks like Johnny Rotten and myself used lots of crucifixes and stuff, and images like that. Catholic imagery lends itself beautifully, along with bondage gear, and mod clothes and rocker clothes, and forties baggy pants . . . pink pants and stuff . . . y'know . . . the whole thing put together was just like classic punk gear. Crucifixes, and upside-down crucifixes, and rosary beads, and . . . well, I was the first one to wear rosary beads and berets, the Spanish Civil War look.

So people would see all this Catholic imagery, and whether they were Catholic or not they'd pick up on it, and it became part of the punk scene. I don't think I ever saw anybody wearing a crown of thorns, but it wouldn't have surprised me. In fact, if I was back there in those days now, I wish I'd have thought of that. I would've loved to have walked into a club or a gig with a crown of thorns on, y'know. That would've won the night, definitely. I was always winning first prize for something. But not as much as Claudio. Claudio was THE man. We were both Faces, but he was the 'Ace Face'. He was more of a Face than Johnny Rotten or Sid Vicious, you know.

—He was?

—Yeah, well, he was more original. He was more of an individualist. He was more creative, y'know. After all, Johnny and Sid just got their clothes from Sex. When it comes down to it, when it was all said and done . . . it used to be said that the Sex Pistols were simply started by Malcolm to advertise his clothes. Cause all the clothes they wore were from his shop. They got them free from his shop, y'know. Well, most of it, obviously the brothel creepers were actually probably stolen, or they bought them from Shelleys. What am I saying stolen for? The Sex Pistols never stole anything. Steve Jones is the guy who gave them their sound, y'know, their musical sound. Along with Glen Matlock. They were both great musicians, but Steve Jones was the guy that lived the life, know what I mean. He really was a fucking cunt, y'know, an obnoxious little bastard. Rotten was a total poser, know what I mean? And he'd agree, I'm sure. I mean, he admitted himself that he was a total poser.

The great thing about Rotten is that he always made his faults into his strengths. His whine, you know, his droning whine of a voice – he made it more droning than it really was, so that it became really offensive. The fact that he spoke in a whining monotone, he accentuated it. The fact that he was short, and sort of like, toothy . . . he accentuated it, know what I mean, by having spiky carrot hair, and speeding so much, his eyes were popping out of his head. The fact that he was a short little runt, he accentuated by wearing brothel creepers all the time, know what I mean, so you could see that he was short in brothel creepers.

The fact that he couldn't sing, he accentuated by not even trying. But he was a brilliant frontman, and a brilliant lyricist. Probably the best ever. In rock terms. In white rock terms, anyway. I think so, anyway. And I'm really glad I was around. It couldn't last, it was too good. Everything was going so fast, and it was so exciting. And things like that can't last, they have to burn up. It was dead by 1977, y'know, which is when most people got into it. I mean, the true punk days were like, '76, and the first half of 1977. By the second half of 1977, like I said, all these hippies had cut their hair, and they were infiltrating it.

All these people from the suburbs were coming in, with school ties on, which was one of the fashions at one stage, a really early fashion, which went out. They still thought it was hip to wear school ties and safety pins, and suit jackets, and winklepickers . . . with long hair. Dyed! I mean, talk about getting it wrong, y'know. And there were groups with long hair by then. And like, it just died on its feet. There'd been the massive backlash, and the return of the skinheads, and the teds, y'know. Decent fucking English working-class youth fought back by becoming skinheads and teds, y'know. So we didn't just have the fucking 'lads' to contend with, we had really violent bastards. Who were dedicated to killing all the punks, know what I mean. And so the punks had to go to war with them. That wasn't any fun. The occasional fight was all right, but when you fucking had to look around you all the bloody time . . . and there was armies of those bastards. And punks didn't walk around in big gangs, know what I mean, they weren't gang minded. They walked around in pairs, in twos and threes. Or on their own. So if they met a gang of teds or a gang of skinheads, they didn't have a fucking chance, y'know, however vicious they were. Or whatever weapon they were carrying.

So it became the 'Summer of Hate' they called it. It became a time of fear. And the Pistols weren't playing any more, and there was loads of crap coming out. You know, in the early days when no one had a record out, it was really exciting. The first record to come out, the Damned's first single . . . it was really exciting. Then the Clash's first single. It was all really exciting. There was the Ramones and stuff that had come out before, but I'm talking about the London punk scene. I mean we all had our Ramones albums, and our Patti Smith albums, and our Dr Feelgood albums, y'know, the sort of pre-punk people.

But by the middle of 1977, there were hundreds of fucking indie labels, putting out loads of crap. Anyone who could play three chords, and make a lot of noise, was getting on records. Some of them were making big deals, know what I mean. Cause the record companies were totally confused. All the record companies had turned down the Pistols, and they were all regretting it like fuck. And then they signed for a million quid to EMI. You know what I mean?! It was a bit like the Beatles all over again . . . the Beatles were turned down by them all, and then eventually Parlophone signed them, which is EMI again, actually. And after that, they signed every fucking group on the face of the earth, because they had missed out on another Beatles. So there was a load of crap coming out at the time.

But like I said, the hip music to listen to was reggae and soul imports. To early punks, the Clash were just a bunch of bandwagon jumpers, y'know. They were too political. And the Damned didn't take it seriously enough. They were just a comedy band. There was a few other bands that really had the idea, like Subway Sect and Siouxie and the Banshees. But there really was only the one group at the end of the day, the one English group, and that was the Pistols. And of course the Ramones, but they were American. Talking Heads didn't have a clue. They all got lumped in together, for some reason. Because people didn't understand.

Nobody listened to the Talking Heads. It was all hippy music. Cause you got infiltrated by people from the suburbs who didn't have a clue what it was all about. And not just people from the suburbs . . . anywhere, y'know. They just didn't understand. Once the elitism went, once the sort of exclusiveness went, it was destroyed. Not destroyed, but it was . . . diluted, mutated. It wasn't the same fun any more, know what I mean?

—**Right.**

Shane rummages through his extensive video collection, exhaustively.

—Do you want to watch *Bullet in the Head* now?

—**Have we done enough about punk?**

—I don't want to say any more.

—**Okay.**

As the morning sun continues to ease itself, lethargically, into noon-day position, Victoria draws the curtains of the splendid and glamorous home that the couple share, the likes of which will most certainly not be seen outside the pages of Hello! *magazine and settles down to enjoy Shane's choice of movie for what seems like the hundredth time, but in reality is only the ninety-ninth.*

INA
BLUE
VEIN

HOW MANY MILES, HOW MANY
LIES TO GO
HOW MANY TIMES I GOT TO FIX
AND BLOW
~~AND STILL BE~~ BUT PLEASE
BELIEVE ME BABY I LOVE
YOU MORE THAN YOU CAN KNOW
I KNOW YOU HATE ME WHEN I GO AM
SCORE
I KNOW YOU HATE ME WHEN I CRAWL

ACT FIVE

Lone tour-bus, desolate highway, USA. A scorching sun beats down on the grimy windows, relentlessly. Air-conditioning splutters, helplessly. Mariah Carey entertains on the CD, interminably. The Shining *repeats on VCR, repeatedly. Pizza cartons, warm lager cans, cigarette butts, copies of the* National Enquirer *and* People *magazine lounge, indolently, on the crushed velour seats and formica tabletops, typically. Shane MacGowan lights a fag, sweatily, and lurches, scarily, as the bus pulls into a truckstop. Victoria, pale and plump, emerges from the toilet, nauseously, sits down, opens a Dr Pepper and sweats, copiously.*

—**Has it been worth it?**

—Has what been worth it?

—**Rock and roll. Being in bands. Is it all it was cracked up to be?**

—Yeah. For me, when the Pogues broke, I had a good few years of just real happiness. Really fucking great. On top of the world.

—**Why was that then?**

—Cause it was non-stop excitement, know what I mean? Non-stop excitement is brilliant.

—**What do you mean? Out all the time?**

—Out all the time. Doing something all the time. Everything getting better all the time. Making loads of money, y'know. The constant creative expression. The constant outlet for creative expression. The whole scene. One minute you're in England, the next minute you're in New York and you're top of the heap. And I like being top of the heap, y'know.

—**Yeah, of course you do. It's natural.**

—Exactly. And now they're just memories.

—Time for a new scene!

—Yeah. I mean there were things after punk, there was the Specials scene. But it wasn't the same. It was good, though, I'll give it that, y'know. There were sort of mini-scenes like that. And there was the New Romantics thing, which was pretty stupid really. But it was some kind of a scene. And there was . . .

—So, basically you're a sociable guy.

—Basically I love a scene, y'know. Loads of things happening, loads of places to go, y'know, if there's a buzz around. And that was what the whole Pogues thing was about, it was fun. It was a great fucking buzz, y'know. And I'm really pissed off that it ended the way it did. Cause I honestly thought we might actually pull it off. We might actually do the biz, know what I mean. We might actually beat the business at its own game. Our momentum was so strong, y'know. But I didn't like playing Wembley. I objected to playing Wembley. And I think it was a mistake to play Wembley.

But the size of the audience, at Wembley, brought home to me how big we were. And it made me realize it was worth trying to keep it going, know what I mean. Even though I hated touring by then, and I had my reservations about the way the band was going. I thought there must be some end to this touring. I knew we weren't gonna crack America. I knew we didn't have to. We didn't have to crack America. We'd have done all right. But there was just so much ambition and greed in it, y'know. You can push a good thing too far. When it's on that level, when it's a scene, right, that's when things are really beautiful, know what I mean. There's excitement. There's a buzz in the air. There's somewhere to go, you know?

—Yeah. And you never know what's gonna happen.

—You never know what's gonna happen, but you can be pretty sure you're gonna be lying on your arse, y'know, sooner or later. Unless you do something to control the way it's going. And in both cases, punk, and the Pogues, I didn't control the way it was going. I was too busy having fun, to take a little time out to control the way my life was going.

—What could you have done?

—In the punk days I was offered jobs as an A&R man at record companies.
—**You would've hated that.**
—Yeah, well, I did it for a week, and I did hate it. I didn't HATE it, it just bored the shit out of me, you know what I mean.
—**Yeah.**
—It meant going to gigs for free, which I did anyway. And then having to talk to boring old farts about which bands I thought were good, know what I mean. And I didn't like doing that. In the case of the Pogues, I could have asserted myself more, or else split. Taken a year off, and come back with a new band, y'know. While I was still hot.
—**You did that.**
—No I didn't! I waited till the Pogues were going downhill, then we split, right, then I took at least a couple of years to get a band together, y'know, and sign a record deal. I did everything wrong, y'know. I'd been so busy having fun that I'd forgotten what a cut-throat business it is, and that you gotta watch yourself all the time, and shit. And you should never listen to advice.
—**How did you actually start the Pogues? You haven't mentioned that.**
—There was no decent live music around when the Pogues started. What I wanted to do was to go back beyond rock and roll, before rock and roll, and do Irish music but do it for a pop audience because I think Irish music is very like rock and roll, it's one of the musics that influenced rock and roll, it's one of the musics that makes up rock and roll.

A lot of Irish songs are rock and roll songs, 'The Rocky Road to Dublin', for instance, is a rock and roll song. People were doing all this World music shit at the time we started and I just found it really annoying and boring and I thought, It's there in our own backyard, Irish culture, Irish music is living and breathing here in England and all around the world. I didn't know how far around the world it spread at that stage, but wherever there are Irish people there is Irish music and they want to hear it. It was so obvious.

It wasn't really my idea to start the band, it was other people, Spider and Jem and a guy called Ollie who was the first drummer. I got swayed into it because I was mixed up with the Nips and they thought the Nips were a good band . . . I didn't ever think they were a good band but they were a very popular band, live, and if we had had the right breaks we could have had a great deal of success, we were a good pop band and we had a good following, a loyal following. I, or rather, we, created that again with the Pogues.

There was no generation gap with the Pogues, we weren't just playing to teenagers . . . we were playing to everybody. We were a bar band and we played country music and rock 'n' roll and we played stuff like 'The Green Green Grass of Home' and 'Don't It Make My Brown Eyes Blue' as well as Irish stuff. We were doing showband music, but putting a massive kick up the arse into it as well as traditional Irish music so we were taking seriously stuff that hadn't been taken seriously in pop music before. The suits, black suits with white shirts which we wore, were Brendan Behan uniform and that's why we chose them, not to look smart, but to look like as if we could have come from any decade, if you know what I mean. We could have looked like people from the fifties, sixties or seventies . . . we just looked like classic Paddys.

I was really into Brendan Behan. We were all into him but I was heavily into him. I think I identified with him because I had a massive drink problem and because I liked his writing and because he was Irish. I liked all the Irish writers but he was the most hip Irish writer, the one who was the most popular. He was the one who was a hit, who had hits. He was a bit like Irvine Welsh. He was a writer who really lived, he was in the IRA, he'd been in jail. It appealed to me that he had really been there, that he wasn't making it up. That really appeals to me in anybody.

I wanted to make pure music that could be from any time, to make time irrelevant, to make generations and decades irrelevant. I wanted not to insult people's intelligence and not to pretend to be intellectual. I wanted the music not to be about angst and how terrible it is lying in your bedroom taking heroin and all that rubbish. I didn't want it to be about how bad drinking was, I wanted to celebrate taking drugs and drinking and life. I wanted to celebrate the seedy side of life which I enjoy. I like pubs and drugs and sex. I resented the eighties trend towards apathy and towards musicians being well behaved. I wanted to stop people right where they were and take them back, back, right back before the Beatles, before Elvis and start off there.

The Pistols and the Ramones also took the music back to a stage when it was simple, but they didn't take the lyrics back to being banal. I didn't want to take the lyrics back to being banal, either, which is always a danger. Irish music doesn't have banal lyrics, so I didn't want my own songs to have banal lyrics. And they didn't.

I never intended to write as many songs as I did. I didn't want to be known as a songwriter, I wanted the group to be known as a group playing Irish music mixed with country and pop and rock 'n' roll and music to dance to and celebrate and all the rest of it, but not to insult people's intelligence. And I think I achieved that for a while, by just doing it without any bullshit. We stripped down the drumkit to one snare and cymbals and we only had one electric instrument – the bass.

We were heavily influenced, also, by the Dubliners who I thought were the band that demonstrated Irish pop music the best. So Behan wasn't actually as important an influence as the Dubliners were, because it was the music that was most important to me, always was. The fact that I wrote clever lyrics or, at least, that people thought my lyrics were clever, was irrelevant to me. I didn't want to become the one that everybody picked on to be a genius and when that started, I knew it was getting dangerous. Because once one person gets picked on and singled out, the group harmony is going to start breaking up. The rest of the group believed my press, even though I didn't believe it. And then they decided I was just a stupid drunk, after all, because they read it in the papers.

—Are you a genius?

—Whether I'm a genius or not, is something I don't want get into . . . I don't know what a genius is, anyway, it doesn't matter.

COME ALL YOU FREE STATERS
ALL STICK UP YOUR HANDS
NOW THE CELTIC TIGER
ROARS AT YOUR COMMAND
NOW EVERY MUCK SAVAGE HAS A JAP MOTOR CAR
THERE'S NOBODY SINGING
ABOUT THE BOLD IRA
SO WHO CAUSED THE FAMINE
AND WHO CAUSED THE WARS
THEY'RE ALL SAFELY BURIED
THOSE MURDERING WHORES
SUPPOSING THAT SARSFIELD
CAME TO YOU FOR A HORSE
OF COURSE YOU'D GIVE HIM A CAR
COURSE YOU WOULD, OF COURSE OF COURSE

WHO THE FUCK'S SARSFIELD
A YOUNG MAN REPLIES
A NEW STUPID EXPRESSION
IN HIS IRISH EYES
WHY BURDEN A YOUNG MAN
WITH THIS BAGGAGE OF MINE
I WAS BORN IN THE FIFTIES
IN THE RARE OLD TIMES
WE WERE POOR THEN BUT HAPPY COMES THE
                    SICKENING WHINE
ONE BAR OF "JAMES CONNOLLY"
ONE NOTE OUT OF YOU
I'LL BLOW YOU AWAY
THEN I'LL PISS OVER YOU

TELL ME HOW MANY ANGELS CAN DANCE ON MY
                    TONGUE

Whichever, for a while, things worked out and then it all went horribly wrong. But in the early days it was brilliant and I think we got better, in those days, as we went on. We peaked, I think, with *If I Should Fall From Grace with God*, which was our third album and it was downhill all the way after that. We became a rock band, we became what we hated most, what we were rebelling against, what we most tried to avoid becoming.

—**Didn't you want to make money?**

—I wanted to make money out of playing music, when we started the Pogues. The Nips had broken up and the Chainsaws were never going to make any money. So I wanted to make enough money to live on. In those days it was new and exciting so rehearsals were good but they were a waste of drinking time. I would rather have rehearsed in the day, but I was working and most of the other people were working. I was working in the record shop, Rocks Off, which used to be a stall but by this time it was a shop on Hanway Street on the corner of Tottenham Court Road So, we had to rehearse at night instead of going to the pub and I didn't like rehearsals, because of that.

—**You still don't like rehearsing.**

—I start to get nervous at rehearsals when I'm doing new songs, because I'm afraid that people are going to say, 'That's a load of shit, we don't want to do it.' I care about what people in the band think because there's nothing worse than playing with a bored band.

I never really came up with a bummer of my own, but there were some duff covers that we tried to do, 'Green Green Grass of Home' and stuff like that. If the band didn't like something, I'd just have to carry on and say, 'Oh well, we'll do it some other time.' That did happen in the later part of the Pogues, Jem used to say, 'I think this is one for your solo album.' Did I ever tell you about Phil Chevron and Cliff Richard?

—**No.**

—One time we were staying in the same hotel as Cliff Richard. And Phil and Cliff stayed up all night drinking. I don't think Cliff drinks, but Cliff was drinking whatever it is he drinks, you know, St

Clements, or whatever. And he was up till the early hours of the morning talking to Phil. Nobody knows what happened then.

—That's an exciting story. You should tell the tabloids. So, was it as exciting as that always, going on tour?

—Yeah, our first tour was tremendously exciting, the idea of going to bed in a different place every night, staying up having drinks after the gig, groupies. You know, staying in hotels. That was all very exciting for me, I'd never done any of that before. I thought it was amazing and I really enjoyed the first couple of years. Our first tour was supporting Elvis Costello. He befriended the group, basically because he was after Cait, our bass player. He wanted to be our buddy, he wanted our bass player badly. We knew he fancied her.

At the beginning, even Jem – who was always the most sensible one, the least into the rock 'n' roll madness, although he enjoyed touring in his own way; Jem was the sort of guy who would go and see all the sights and take pictures and all that stuff – even Jem, at the beginning, threw his cares out of the window and we all went drinking together every night and pulling birds, although Jem didn't pull birds, he was married.

For a couple of years, you could say, that was what was happening and we were all very happy and we were intensely loyal to each other, to the band, to the organization. We were intensely loyal, we thought we were doing something special, like we were bringing something to the people. We were bringing the wonder of Irish music to people, bringing it to the newly converted, the unconverted, the already converted.

One great thing about it was all the people that used to hang around, the gangs of fans who used to go to all the gigs. People like John McGovern, for instance. John would always cheer me up if I was feeling down because he's such a funny little geezer. He's always optimistic. Some people would say he was incredibly boring, I don't know why, maybe it's the way he talks about Aston Villa Football Club, but he is actually very knowledgeable, he's a very clever guy and he's always got it sussed out, how to get places. He's been round the world loads of times. He's been going around seeing groups since he was a kid and that was years ago. He'd been to places like Amsterdam in the sixties, but he still goes on about Aston Villa Football Club and 'Look at the pair of knockers on that bird there' and grumbles about the Guinness, and tells you what the Guinness was like in certain places and generally bores you to death, but I find that really homely. He kept my feet on the ground. He was great for keeping your feet on the ground, he never acted like a psychopath, the way some of them do, which can, of course, be entertaining too.

Then you got other fans who wanted to give you their girlfriend. I wouldn't take them. They'd say, 'Here you go, you can have her for the night', the girlfriends never minded. They were usually into it. That was a very strange scene, it was one of the first really mad things I noticed, you know, people giving you their girlfriend. I'd never dream of giving anybody my girlfriend, I don't care who the fucker is.

—That's reassuring, Sweet Pea.

—It wasn't just Spider and me who were party animals, I should point out, we all were. To start off, there was a much smaller travelling unit in the early days. Darryl driving and tour managing and roadie-ing. Paul Scully doing the sound and the group, was really all there was. Then gradually, over the months and years we added roadies, drivers, we had two engineers out front and on stage and all the rest of it.

Back to the first tour. I thought Costello was fat and boring and I wasn't a fan of his. Me and Spider used to take the piss out of him. I mean we quite liked him but we thought he was a silly old bore. We were very arrogant, as far as we were concerned it was our tour and for some mad reason people wanted to see Elvis Costello as well, but there were always loads of people at the gigs who'd come just to see us. So we blew him off the stage every night and we used to go into their dressing room when our gig was over, and we'd have a crate of beer on our rider and they'd have bottles of blue label Smirnoff, champagne and all the rest of it, so we'd go in and drink it when they were on stage and then they'd get really annoyed and we kept doing it and they kept getting annoyed and we kept doing it and they'd get really annoyed and we kept getting really drunk.

We got three warnings, three times we were nearly kicked off the tour. I'd get really annoyed if somebody drank our rider, we'd kick the shit out of them. I don't know why they put up with it, I think they were intimidated. We seemed to intimidate them and our fans seemed to intimidate their fans. Well, I suppose we should have intimidated them, we were going to have that drink whatever anybody said. There was no way we were going to stay in our dressing room without a drink when there was a dressing room full of it next door.

Gary Barnacle was on saxophone with Elvis on that tour and one night he started a fight with me which he then wimped out of and called security. He started a fight with me for talking to Kim Wilde who I think he was married to. I was just being nice. I was a fan of Kim Wilde, but she wasn't my type, I wasn't trying to chat her up or anything. I liked her, I liked her better than Elvis Costello. I always thought she looked a bit nervous and lonely so I went up to her one night and sort of said, 'How are you doing? How's life treating you?' She was really pleased to be getting treated like a human. Gary Barnacle said, 'Oi mate, what are you doing chatting up my missus? . . . I'm going to fucking have you.' And he called, 'Paddy!! Paddy!' Their main security was a big old London-Irish guy called Paddy. He loved us, and hated Costello . . . and the band, who were all prima donnas, all wankers, and treated him like a piece of shit. And he was big tough guy whose family were from Kerry. He had hands like shovels. Paddy came and said, 'What's the matter?' 'Paddy! Beat this son of a bitch up, and throw him off the tour!' And Paddy said, 'Oh, I don't think I've got any authority to do anything like that. What was he doing? Shane's always well behaved around me. Unless you've got a complaint against him, Gary, I don't know what I can do.' He was really winding Barnacle up. Barnacle said, 'He's chatting up my wife!' So Paddy said, 'Is that true, Miss Wilde?' And she said, 'No, I started the conversation. I was lonely in the dressing room, and Gary wasn't talking to me. And so I started talking to Shane. He seemed like the friendliest boy here . . . the friendliest boy around.' And Paddy said, 'Well, sorry, there's nothing I can do for you, Mr Barnacle.'

Paddy used to wander into our dressing room, having stolen a bottle of blue label vodka from their dressing room, and say, 'There you go, lads. Have a good gig tonight.' And he'd sing some rebel songs with us, and all that. He picks some security guard to keep the Irish hooligan element at bay, know what I mean!

They actually thought about kicking me off the tour, the management, but it all got quietened down and I was supposed to apologize to Gary Barnacle and I was told never to speak to Kim Wilde again. Of course, I did speak to her again and I wasn't thrown off the tour.

We used to get drunk a lot on the way to gigs. We used to be really drunk at the gigs, and we used to get really drunk on the bus on the way there and eat sausage rolls and things like that and take the piss out of Darryl, because Darryl knew all these useless facts about all the places we went to, like he always knew where the football ground was. We always had to drive past the football ground and him and Spider would have a chat about how many matches they'd won in the last hundred years, how many times they'd been relegated and Jem and me used to get really pissed off with that. We'd get really nasty with them, and the jokes would start off. 'You're so boring, who gives a flying fuck, Derby United get fucked' and then we'd all go, 'Darryl, you've missed the turn.' We knew how old Darryl was but we kept forgetting. Darryl looked about twelve, but he was, in fact, already pushing forty. He had the sort of brain power of a thirteen-year-old with all his useless football information. He was like one of those schoolboys who know everything, he could answer any question in Trivial Pursuit. Darryl, right until the end, was a gent. I was really horrible to him for a long time and then I realized what a nice guy he really was and he forgave me. But James never forgave me and I was really nasty to him. It was me and Spider, I used to egg Spider on and Spider didn't know when to stop, couldn't stop. Spider just couldn't stop basically, whatever he was doing, he'd do it until he'd done it too much, until something disastrous happened. That's what he was like. He could decide to live like a monk, he'd give all his money to the poor and be totally over the top about it, he'd give his home to the poor, he'd give everything to the poor, and then he'd be broke but he still wouldn't be able to stop. I actually think that's true. That's a character flaw.

I have character flaws, obviously, too. I really did think too much of myself, in some ways, in those days, but in other ways I didn't, I thought too little of myself. I was a sardonic, sarcastic, ironic, cynical, twisted, bitter little bastard who always picked on people's failings. I pointed them out and took the piss out of them. On the other hand, I was an easy touch, a really easy touch, sort of too easy and I didn't lead as much as I should have done. I wanted democracy but I think if I had done a bit more leading, things would have been better. A democracy can still be led, look at John Major. Well, there's an example of how not to lead a democracy. Harold Wilson knew how to lead a democracy. People do want to be told what to do, to a certain extent.

Well anyway, we all got totally locked on the road to Nottingham, once. Nottingham was the first really over-the-top night, that was where we threw a firecracker into a disabled toilet where we'd just seen a guy wheel himself in. Well, he was in there unable to get up, either having a shit or having a piss, who cares . . . He was in a vunerable position, let's put it like that. It would be bad enough if somebody was able and some bastard dropped a firecracker on top of them while they were having a dump.

Me and Spider wrote IRA and UDA all over Costello's truck which was another thing which nearly got us kicked off the tour. I was really surprised we weren't kicked off the tour for that. Spider took the rap for it.

Elvis Costello was quite tolerant, really. I think that's because he fancied Cait. We were always getting lectures like schoolboys from all these people. We were very hip, you know, it would have been good publicity for us to get kicked off the tour. It would have been 'Elvis Costello is an old bore' if he had kicked us off. I think he knew that. We were getting loads of publicity at the time, anyway, without that happening.

Then we went straight on to having our own tour, after that. I came back to find I didn't have a job left. I was told they were keeping it for me, but they didn't. So I came back to being quite broke because Frank was still working out our deal and suddenly he worked it out and he handed me a cheque for £7,000 and I opened up a bank account. It seemed like a fucking fortune to me. But it ran out quickly.

—**What did you spend it on?**

—I spent it on drink, clothes, a record player . . . I had lots of meals in restaurants – blew it all. Then we were off on tour again, around the British Isles, England, Ireland, Scotland and Wales. We did it three times that year including the Costello one. Three tours in that year and we also did Germany and Scandinavia.

That was a big hit, going to Germany for the first time, my first time being out of Britain. Except for two weeks, well, one week, in France when I was fourteen, just before I stopped going on holiday with my parents. So we did two tours of England and Ireland and Scotland and Wales that year and Germany, Finland and Norway and Sweden and I enjoyed all of it immensely.

That was when the groupie scene started raging, at that stage, and people gradually started to split into two groups. The mad group and the sensible group and me and Spider were the leaders of the mad group and then we started having rows and I actually became mad. As long as we were all mad it was fun and everything went all right. It was when we split into two groups and disagreed about whether to be mad or sensible that things got bleak and here started the root of the trouble that was going to come later on. You go mad on tour very quickly. People thought I was mad already, but I never thought I was mad, not even when people said I was. I just did what came naturally. But by the end, I was really sick of being on tour and I was very paranoid because touring used to make me paranoid. There's two very definite sides to touring and one is very paranoid and painful and nasty and the other is a lot of fun. The paranoid side is the side that drives people mad. It's just not a natural lifestyle, in any sense of the word. The roadies are fucking insane. Completely round the twist. They live harder rock and roll lives than any band.

Bands that have a reputation for being mad, they're just bands where the band keep up with the road crew, in terms of rock and roll madness. The band members are quite often ordinary, boring, domesticated sort of people. It's the road crew who don't change their underwear and take mountains of drugs and screw anything that moves and never go to bed. But I never used to sleep, either.

Anyway, quite early on, the Pogues split into two groups, on tour. Spider was in my group. Let's call it the hard style and the sensible style of touring. Doing it the sensible way, I suppose you can do it for years. But I never did it the sensible way. I've never lived the sensible way. So, on the road not being sensible can really fuck you up. It means you have a really good time, though, all the time. But if you stop having a good time even for a second, you crash into this state of depressed paranoid madness.

One of the times it came to a head was when I painted myself blue in New Zealand because I thought the Maoris were telling me to. The place we were staying in was built on a Maori graveyard. I used to go to my room when everybody else stopped drinking, but instead of going to bed, I'd stay up and write songs or listen to music or see if there was anything on the telly. I just used to pass the night quite happily.

This particular night, I started getting a very strong, totally real feeling that the Maoris were talking to me. You see, you talk to yourself in your head when you're speeding and you get turned into two people, who talk to each other in your head. Because you haven't got anybody to talk to, you talk to yourself. And I was telling myself that the Maoris were telling me that I had to show that I was one of them, that I was on their side and not a lousy Kiwi, that I was a Maori. And that the hotel walls were all wrong and they should be covered in wallpaintings. So I painted all the walls in the bedroom and then all the sheets and the furniture, every single bit of it. I used to carry paints around, on tour. I completely re-did the whole bedroom and then I went into the bathroom and re-did the bathroom. Just swirling designs and things.

I don't know why I don't do that so much now. I wish I did,

because I used to enjoy it. Anyway, it was all imaginative, interesting stuff. All over the bathroom until everything was covered. Then I painted my clothes. And then I took my clothes off because the Maoris were saying that the final proof of my allegiance to them was that I had to paint myself blue. They'd been giving me instructions all along, as to what to paint. And blue was warpaint and it showed that I was a warrior brother. And I painted myself blue from head to toe and sat there naked. In this totally painted room. And that's how Frank found me in the morning. He came to wake me up and knocked on the door and I opened it and said, 'Hello, Frank. Look what the Maoris made me do.' And his face was just a picture. He couldn't be angry. It was beyond anger. It was beyond laughing at. It was just so over the top to him. Because Frank's such a basically sensible bloke. He was completely freaked. It really hit him full on, what a fucking loony he was managing. He used to get these moments when he'd realize what a handful he'd taken on.

However much money he was making, it was just constant aggro. I was a constant source of worry and irritation and frustration for him. And he just stood there, gaping and said, 'Shane, what in God's name have you done?' And I said, 'The Maoris told me to do it, Frank.' He used to pretend to go along with stuff like this. He said, 'Oh yes, I know, the Maoris told you to do it.' And then he said, 'Could you at least leave the place with some dignity. Couldn't you at least wash yourself off. And put your clothes on.' And I said, 'I don't know if the Maoris would want me to do that.' It took him half an hour to talk me into putting my clothes on and washing my face and hands. I left the rest blue.

In America, once, we stopped outside a service station a hundred miles from Chicago. And I decided to make a break for freedom. I decided I wasn't going to be on this tour any more, even though that night was the final date. I just couldn't handle it. One more date. So I went running off into the bushes. I went scrambling through the bushes, just like in an adventure movie. *The Great Escape.* I went so far that I hit another road. And went across that road and carried on. And then I realized I was alone in the middle of this American wasteland. Nothing for miles around. And I thought, well, there's nothing for it I'll just have to keep going. So I kept going and I went round in a circle and I ended up back at the bus. They'd been waiting for an hour.

That sort of thing happened all the time. We were always losing people. It's one of the things that happens all the time. I suppose it's a bit like being in the army. That's why they have all that regimentation in the army, to stop people running away.

There was fun on the road, too. There was the girls. In the dressing room, after the gig, there would be loads of girls who all wanted to go to bed with you. I never really bothered with the ones that you had to talk to. Nobody did. People didn't really want to bother talking to them. No, some people did, actually. Spider got off on talking to them. That's all he ever did with them, talked to them.

I just used to wait to get raped. Whoever had the energy to capture me and drag me back to the hotel got the lollipop. I could afford to be selective though, some girls, there was no way I was going to go for it. I'm a fussy guy. I didn't do it for very long, anyway. It's such a hassle. It's a big hassle getting laid. You screw them and then you have to put up with them for the rest of the night. I'm not really the kind of guy who can screw a girl and kick her out of the room. A lot of people did that. I did it sometimes. But it's a bit of a hassle if you don't, because I wouldn't want to go to sleep afterwards, I'd want to do my normal thing, like paint the room or play the guitar or whatever. I liked having a lot of time to myself. I made time for myself. But on the other hand I liked going out drinking all night sometimes, too. And if you do feel like a bit of company, it's more fun to spend time with the road crew than it is to talk to some woman you don't know. Trying to be polite.

Some of them wanted to spend the night with you in particular, if you were the lead singer, they would have a hang-up on you in particular and they would have adored you from afar. That would be the big night of their life. Some of them would just want to screw whatever band was in town. Some of them would go with any member of the band, some of them would only want the drummer or the bass player, although that was rare. The lead singer is the most popular. Spider was very popular, though, even though I was the biggest pull. I gave up thinking about it. I just sort of rampaged through it. It was just an experience.

I think I've got too much time on my hands these days, which is why I have time to think about it. If I have time to think I have time to get depressed. If I have time to think, I think depressing things. I've got a leaning towards thinking depressing things. So for me, being busy is essential, even though I don't actually enjoy being busy. In fact, I need complete relaxation, and I need to be completely occupied. If I can be completely occupied all the time, I never get depressed.

But on the road, you get lots of waiting around. Fucking around in airports, on buses, backstage. Groupies, if I ever thought about it, I just think what a weird situation, what weird people they are. Some of them were very nice, I liked them, some of them were completely mad. Real pains in the arse. Neurotic. Like Dusty Hope. Dusty Hope scared me, just from reading her letters. Mind you, anyone who can get it together to write letters is really scary, writing to a complete stranger. Anybody who you don't actually know, who writes you letters, I think is weird. I've hardly ever written to anybody I did know. I don't like phone calls much, either.

—You've never written to anyone you do know, have you?

—No.

—Never?

—No.

—Not even when you were a kid, didn't you have to write thank-you letters?

—Who did I have to thank?

—People who sent you birthday presents.

—What do you mean? I was born on Christmas Day, nobody ever remembered it was my birthday.

—That's terrible.

—I did like the amazing places we went to, but I intensely disliked the fact that I never got to spend any time in them. The places I really liked were the places where I got to spend some time. Finland, Norway, Germany, I really enjoyed Australia the first time we went there. Not so much the second time.

The first time we toured America, we spent most of our time in New York. We spent a whole week in New York. We played about four dates in New York. And did three days of solid press. I'm talking about solid press, from ten in the morning till eight at night. Just one paper after another. I remember being impressed by American journalists, and how they knew what they were on about, you know what I mean. Like, they knew who Charlie Parker was.

—**They went to college, didn't they?**

—And they were interested in other things apart from getting pissed. And, they'd done their homework. I mean it's so obvious with English rock journalists, that they haven't done their homework, they don't know anything about you. They just know what other rock journalists have said about you, so they ask you the same questions. It's very annoying. So I realized we were being interviewed by real journalists, not by rock journalists. They were writers who had chosen to write about music, rather than failed musicians. You know, fans . . . actual fans of music.

And it was such a relief, although it was a very heavy schedule that the time seemed to fly by, compared to just one interview with an English rock journalist. Which is just this constant flow of defensive shit . . . defending the fact that I drink, know what I mean? Why me? Why pick on me? You know, Tom Waits drinks, Dr Feelgood drank, Miles Davis drank, you know what I mean, it's not unknown for people to drink. And I'm not even the piss artist that people think I am anyway.

But in America, they're genuinely interested in finding out about Ireland, and the music, and what Irish people thought of the music, and what it was to be London-Irish . . . etc. And then they'd ask you about politics, and they'd ask you technical stuff about music. Interesting stuff to ask in an interview, you know. You wouldn't feel as if they were trying to read your diary, when they asked about your lyrics, know what I mean? You'd always feel that the English rock journalists were trying to read your own personal diary. You know, my lyrics don't tell you what's going down in my private life. What I'm saying is, lyrics are like words that fit with music. They don't work . . . well, they shouldn't work without the music. The music shouldn't work without the lyrics. I mean, part of the time it will, but what I mean is, it should work together. A double attack, you know what I mean. The same way a painting uses colour and light. A painting can use as much colour as it wants, but if there's no light involved, then it doesn't mean anything. And vice versa. And a pile of bricks on the floor is a pile of bricks on the floor, and don't try to tell me it's anything else. How did we get on to that!? Oh, I know, it was about the English being the worst journalists in the world.

So we worked long days doing press – me and Spider, and the whole group. And the jounalists were quite prepared to talk to a couple of the other members of the group, y'know. And I always had Spider in with me on the interviews, because he'd always have an answer. He likes talking about . . . anything . . . himself, particularly. And seeing as a lot of the questions are about yourself, right, I let Spider take care of all of them.

And then we'd do a gig, maybe, and then go to the Limelight, at the time it was the place to go. The top room at the Limelight. It was a six-floor club. The top room at the Limelight was the VIP lounge. There was a cordoned-off area where you'd see William Burroughs and people like that hanging out. Debbie Harry. And like, me and Matt Dillon were in the library part, which was, sort of, not quite the cordoned-off area, but not the pleb area either, actually.

The actual cordoned-off area has a rope around it. And that's where Uncle Bill went, or Auntie Debbie. And Cait and Matt Dillon started flirting outrageously, right. And they went out on to the fire escape stairs. And it was just like a scene from one of his films, know what I mean. It was like a scene from one of his films, cause he was doing the whole sort of 'Hey, I really dig you', shit – know what I mean. And she kicked him really hard in the balls, and he went rolling down three flights of stairs.

—Why did she kick him?

—All he said was he really thought she was a groovy chick.

—She had no reason to kick him?

—No.

—I see.

—And it was the talk of New York.

—Was it?

—Yeah, for about ten minutes. It was funny. Me and Spider went down and helped him up. The guy was gasping with pain. Really ridiculous. It was only a kicking in the bollocks.

—There must have been something he said.

—He just said, y'know, 'I think you're a really groovy chick. I think you're really great. You're really wild.' You remember Cait, and that sort of behaviour.

—Tell me more about Matt Dillon.

—He's really nice.

—Tell me about the Wild Cats of Kilkenny.

—What?

—What he said about it.

—What did he say about it?

—You don't remember?

—Well, I remember what was going on.

—You told me he said that he really dug that song, and he knew all the words to it.

—Did he?!? I think that's brilliant. So cool.

—It doesn't have any words.

—I know!

—Tell me about when you made the video with him.

—Well, the first thing he said to us was like, 'You know I really dig you guys. I dig your shit. My parents dig your shit. My whole family digs your shit. I was brought up on that shit. Your shit. The Clancy Brothers, the Dubliners, I dig that shit. You know, and the Pogues, I dig that shit. I really love that shit.' And we were all saying, 'Well, we dig your shit, Matt', and he went, 'I'm glad you dig my shit because I really like to dig your shit.' That was a funny story, you know, that one that you wanted me to tell you about.

—About how he knew all the words?

—Not that! The other one. The one that you just said.

—What one? What one?

—About the video.

—The video, yeah.

—'Fairytale of New York'. Yeah. He was a cop, and I was meant to be a drunk. And he was meant to push me really hard . . .

—How did he come to be in the video?

—Peter Doherty got him.

—Oh right.

—But we met him before we met Peter Doherty, he came backstage at the first gig. That's when he said how much he dug our shit. But in the video, right, he was meant to be a cop. He was meant to violently sling me in through the door. And we were using a real police station.

—Where?

—Down on the Lower East Side, y'know. A proper, sort of – what's it called . . . ?

—What?

—That programme, you know . . .

—What *Hill Street Blues* . . . no, uh . . . *NYPD Blue*?

—Yeah, yeah. A proper nick. A real one. And Charlie was Father Christmas. And he was being nicked, as I got slung into the doors. I don't even know if he could be seen in the video or not. You might've noticed him as Father Christmas in the video.

—I didn't notice that.

—If you look carefully you'll see him. We were all really out of it, and there was a point when they were going to arrest us all for being drunk, and being under the influence of drugs, know what I mean, so we had to calm it down a bit. But Matt liked me too much to push me through the door, and to give me a kicking on the stairs. I was out of my head, I wasn't going to feel anything, he could've given me a really good kicking and I would've just laughed. He could've kicked me down the stairs and I wouldn't have given a shit. It was freezing outside. And we had to keep waiting outside till they shouted action and we would do the scene. And I said to Matt, 'Look, Matt, for God's sake, really lay into me! Don't worry about it. You're not gonna hurt me. Don't worry about it.' But he was going, 'But I like you, Shane. And I dig your shit so much. I love you, I love your shit. I can't do it to you.' And I was trying to persuade this actor to act. You know what I mean . . . to do it! To fucking push me into the doors violently, and drag me up the stairs, and kick me, y'know, in the middle of the stairs, and then throw me into a cell. Because he couldn't bring himself to do it, it took us eight takes to get a perfectly simple scene. And Peter Doherty was going mad, he was going, 'For God's sake, Matt, will you hit the guy!'

—**Tell me about Robert De Niro. You've talked about Robert De Niro.**

—Well, he never came backstage.

—**Didn't he?**

—No.

—**But he came to a gig?**

—Him and Jack.

—**Jack?**

—Jack Nicholson, and Christopher Reeves, and Steve Buscemi. Steve Buscemi lives in New York.

—**What about Bruce Springsteen?**

—Yeah, Springsteen came to a gig. Iggy Pop came to a gig. We were the toast of New York.

—**Yeah.**

—Well, I still am the toast of New York.

—**Yes, dear.**

—Now, I'm gonna give you the low-down on Frank. Among the Irish 'Murphia' who I worked for, was a man called Frank Murray, who was a character from Dublin and the group voted for him to become our manager. I voted against it, but it was useless. The Pogues were the hottest band in London, Stiff Records had picked up the single, which Stan Brennan had put out, 'Dark Streets of London'. Stan Brennan, my boss in the shop, yeah? But we were a democratic group, which is the wrong way of doing things.

Victoria swigs a Dr Pepper, distastefully.
—**Why is that?**
—Well, it was all fine while we all agreed with each other, but . . . basically it only worked as a democratic group because everybody agreed with me.
—**Right!!!!!**
—Me and Jem both booked gigs, but I did more booking of gigs than Jem, right.
—**And why's that then?**
—Cause I was more aggressive . . . I was more of a hustler . . . I was a bit of a hustler, y'know what I mean.
—**More aggressive?**
—Yeah, I'd been hustling since I was at school, I've been hustling all my life. Right in the beginning, I was forced to hustle. I've been forced to fucking fight . . . y'know, to become a good fighter. There's nothing wrong with that, I'm glad, I've become a vicious, savage fucking aggressive fighter, that would just beat the shit out of anybody who fucking looked twice at me, because of my childhood experiences. I mean later childhood experiences, when I came over here to London. Of being Paddy-bashed.

They tended to Paddy-bash, over here, so I learned how to take out four guys in one go. Using speed and technique, and absolutely dirty fighting. You know, my temper . . . it's not as bad as my sister's temper, but at the same time I've got a temper, right. Completely. I completely lose it, and I don't care if I kill all three or four of them, y'know what I mean. I used leave them lying in pools of blood. Like, I only usually had to beat up one, then the other three would fuck off.

But, on two occasions I've been beaten up. Yeah, two. That was once when I was nineteen and drunk, in a phone box, surrounded by six guys, and I knew I was gonna be beaten up, and I was so out of it I didn't really care. It was like being in a film. I was talking to Shanne on the phone, I said to her, 'I think these guys are gonna beat me up.' And I laughed. She laughed too. She thought I was joking. Next day she saw me with a head like a football. It was literally the size of a football.

—Why did they beat you up?

—I think cause I was wearing a rockabilly badge.

—Cause you were wearing a rockabilly badge?!

—They thought I was a ted, y'know.

—So what were they?

—I dunno what they were, just young yobs. They probably beat up all skins, teds, punks, blacks, Irish, you know they were a weird-looking bunch. I think they were all half-castes. And they all had blakies.

—All had what?

—They all had blakies. You know, metal tips on their boots. They all had big boots with metal caps. Designed for . . . you don't put blakies on your boots, unless . . . well, I mean Irish workmen do, to make them tougher, but a kid who doesn't work on a site has got no reason to have blakies on his boots unless he's intending to kick someone's head in. It's to make them more . . . lethal, you know what I mean. Like leather is bad enough, but metal really does the trick. It's a wanker's thing to do. Anybody with guts just uses a knuckleduster, and wears normal shoes. Once he's been punched in the stomach with a knuckleduster, it will give you time to kick him in the balls hard, harder, hard as a savage, several times, bringing him to the ground where you can kick him in the head till he's unconscious. Yeah? And all that could be done in about thirty seconds.

—Where do you hit them with the knuckleduster?

—Where would you hit them with a knuckleduster? In the stomach. Yeah, to double them up. And get them in the right position for a kick in the balls. Doubled up like that, you know, with their knees apart . . . WANG!!!! But then, not just one kick in the balls, several, you know, repeated, like a jackhammer. So they just don't get a chance to do anything. It's just concentrated pain. They're puking. They puke their way to the floor, to the ground. The minute they're on the ground you fucking start on their heads. Then if you're really mad you can kick them till they're dead. I uhm . . .

—You didn't do that.

—Well . . . I kicked them till they were nearly unconscious. I don't like taking a shot and kicking them when they're unconscious. I just make sure they're not gonna get up again. Like, if you've got four of them, you've got to select the leader. The leader is the guy who does the talking. The big guy will be watching the leader to see what he does. If you take the leader to bits in thirty seconds, then the big guy will fucking hesitate, you know what I mean. Then you go for another one, and they all move back. Cause they're worried now as well. And then you stare out the big guy. I mean, obviously if the big guy comes for you then you're in trouble . . . but you just have to repeat the process. This is where you can run into a problem. But staring out the big guy with the leader lying there fucking dying on the floor, in a pool of blood, usually . . . just screaming like, 'FUCK OFF AND LEAVE ME ALONE YOU WANKERS!' or 'COME ON TRY IT', or whatever, works ninety per cent of the time, cause it's gang mentality.

That is gang mentality. You got a smart guy . . . like say the real pyscho gang leader that I worked for, that I was friends with, who protected me for a few years at school. Somebody that gave me power for a few years at school. Not only protected me, but gave me power. He was the smart guy, the talker . . . but he didn't have much to say. So he'd basically just spit in someone's face, and then he'd start in and beat them into a pulp. And that's how he formed a loyal gang of followers who'd go, 'Yes sir, no sir', who would go and arrest anybody for him. Four guys would hold him down, and I got the job of fucking putting the dustbin lid over his head and then smashing it really hard with a hammer, y'know, with the bit of metal, like half and half. It's a Japanese prisoner of war camp torture.

Then 'Sir' would come strolling along, humming his favourite reggae tune, the latest reggae tune; and casually having a conversation with me about the new Lee Perry record. Because I was into reggae, and he was into reggae, and I knew my reggae. I knew all about reggae and he was really impressed. He was into two things, reggae and violence. And he liked the fact that I was a Paddy, right, cause his old man was a Jamaican and had lots of Irish mates. And his mother was white. His old man wasn't a rasta, you know, but he might've become one. He did become a rasta later on. He was half-caste, so he got trouble from both sides. So he had become a pyscho at an early age. And we were both big guys, and we both had a real hate in us. So we took it out on white Anglo-Saxon Protestants . . .

—**You said you'd been beaten up twice.**

—Yeah, once when I was nineteen and so drunk I could hardly stand up. I was chatting in a phone box to Shanne. She was at her mum's. And I knew they were gonna jump me when I came out of the phone box. And I came out of the phone box and they jumped me. And I just thought, 'I can't be bothered with this', but it was six of them, and whichever way I looked at it, they had me. So I just lay on the floor, crouched in an embryonic position, protecting my balls and my head and pretended to be unconscious, hours before I was. I wasn't feeling anything like pain . . . well, I was really out of it, know what I mean? I did feel the pain the next day, but nothing to write home about. I've got a high pain threshhold. But they kept on kicking me. All they'd done is broken my nose, that's all they'd done to me. They thought they were kicking me to death, so I pretended to be dead.

After about six kicks, one of which had connected with my nose and broken it and done all the damage, they sort of walked off. I stayed exactly as I was till they were out of the vicinity. And then I stood up, brushed myself off, made sure my clothes weren't too dirty, and saw that there was blood all over the place, an enormous amount of blood. I then realized I was gonna have to walk home, cause I'd spent all my money at the Nashville in Hammersmith. The Nashville was a place I went to a lot in Hammersmith cause it was a place that I'd lived, yeah. So I had no reason to expect this fucking stupidity. I mean, that gang were real pyschos. Well, they weren't really psychos, cause individually I could've taken any one of them in a second. But they would hang around in a gang of six. And they thought just because they'd spilt a bit of blood, they thought they were giving me brain damage, when all they'd done is broken my nose.

I was still really out of it, so I just started walking home. Those days I was still a big walker. And these coppers had stopped, and one of them was just leaning against the car door, and they said, 'Oi you, come here', y'know . . . I was like, 'This is all I need, I'm gonna get nicked now', and they said, 'We're taking you to hospital, you've got a broken nose!' I said, 'No I haven't got a broken nose!' I mean, I had just been jumped by a gang of fucking youths, you know, kids. I was nineteen, and they were seventeen . . . sixteen or seventeen. I was basically outside the age range, really, I was a bit old to be in an organized sort of thing. They should've been fighting people their own age, y'know. But it was because I was dressed in the style of a rocker, y'know, with a quiff, and leather, I think they just went for me, and they were undoubtedly racist, yeah. They probably wanted to be skinheads but they didn't have the guts. Or weren't allowed to be because they were half-castes. So they just hated everybody.

—So did the cops take you to hospital?

—Yeah, they were talking me into going to the hospital . . . I was so drunk, I was like . . . I'll survive, y'know. I felt my face, felt this blob, with no nose, it was completely swollen into a football shape. My eyes had completely closed. They were saying, 'Who did this to you? We wanna go and get them.' I said, 'Ahh, it was just a bunch of kids. Fuck them, they were out to get anybody. I think they were punks.' So, I didn't shop them.

—Why didn't you shop them?

—Because you don't.

—No? Why not?

—You don't ever tell the pigs about anything.

—Why not?

—Because of the street.

—If it had been me, I'd have shopped them.

—Nah, it's humiliating to have the pigs doing your fucking work for you. If you can't fucking fight your way out of a jam, then that's just bad luck. You don't fucking turn guys over to the coppers, y'know. I could easily have gotten them nicked, I mean, it was only five minutes later . . . and only down the road, that I'm running into coppers. I could've given them descriptions, and all that. Y'know, there were six guys, and I remember one guy was wearing a woolly hat, things like that. I could've easily, but I wasn't interested in going to court, I just wanted to get home. They said, 'You have to go to hospital,' and I said, 'Can't you just give me a lift home?' and they said, 'No, we have to take you to hospital, you're in a really bad shape. You've got a broken nose, it's really bad. You could have brain damage.' And I said, 'Wow, I feel all right.' And they said, 'Well, that's shock.' I felt all right cause I was drunk out of my brains. And we were having a laugh, and joking, and I said, 'Those fucking punks . . .'

I thought it was a good one to pull on cause I hated the new punks. The guys with that stupid spikey hair, y'know, the long spikey green hair and all that. Leather jackets and Doc Martens, and like, 'Sid Lives' written on their backs. You know what I mean, all that shit. They gave punk a bad name. I would never associate myself with punk at that stage. I just called myself a rocker. A drunken Irish rocker, like Vince Reardon, who was the roadie for Sham 69 and then became the bass player for the Cockney Rejects, who were the next best punk band, after the Pistols and the Subway Sect. They were like a sort of midget Pistols except for Vince Reardon, who was really big.

—Is he still alive?

—Yeah, I don't think he was a junkie, although a lot of us were speed freaks. Mickey Geggus, the singer, and his brother the guitarist were both ex-boxers. Rat Scabies was always bullying people who appeared bullyable, like he picked on women and blokes who were much smaller than him, and Mickey Geggus kicked the living shit out of him and chased him all around the Bridge House in Canning Town, which was the home of the '79 punk revival, lead by the Cockney Rejects.

Steve Walsh was Irish too, and Wobble was Irish, there was a sort of Paddy mafia within the punk scene. I used to go around singing rebel songs with Jimmy Lydon, Johnny's elder brother, and he had a glass eye which he used to take out. He was the actual obnoxious London-Irish cunt that Johnny was posing as. Me and him were peas in a pod. He went off and started 4be2 and I went off and started the Pogues. The original bass player in 4be2 was Youth and Johnny Rotten produced their first single, 'One of the Boys', which was a sort of Public Image sounding thing with a really good traditional Irish tenor banjo on it, by one of their uncles. So this was all setting the stage for Paddy beat, they did rebel songs as well and they were really obnoxious and really entertaining on stage and he was a great frontman, Jimmy, and they were managed by Jock MacDonald, who was this Scots guy who was a general entrepreneur on the London scene; that's who we should have got to manage us, actually. Jock MacDonald, under his own group's name, the Bollock Brothers, did a couple of mind-blowing records, one of which was called 'Why Don't Rangers Sign a Catholic?' and another which was called 'The Bunker', about Adolf and Eva.

Steve Walsh was a punk journalist, but he was a musician as well, he played with Sid in the Flowers of Romance. Sid was the drummer in Siouxsie and the Banshees, but he left because of differences in musical direction. Basically he just stood there and banged the drum, bang bang bang bang bang, and that wasn't arty enough for old Siouxsie, so Sid formed his own band, the Flowers of Romance, with him on vocals, because someone convinced him that he couldn't play drums, whereas in fact he could – he foresaw Poguebeat – but his musical direction was taken up by Subway Sect, who had a drummer who went bang bang bang bang bang, they were great. The most chords any of their songs had were two, which is one less than the simplest nursery rhymes. Ray Burns, a.k.a. Captain Sensible, was on bass, Steve Walsh played guitar.

At that time, a lot of blokes were getting jobs on the rags as hacks, on *NME, Melody Maker, Sounds*, the papers that mattered in those days, the comics. I was never asked to do that for some reason, neither was Claudio, I think they were afraid of us. Steve Walsh looked very cool, but he didn't look very frightening, he was a nice guy and it showed in his face. His uncle was Mr Walsh from Kilkenny that I rented a bedsit from, right next to the Arsenal ground, Stavordale Road, N5. Seven pounds a week. Which is really cheap, y'know, really cheap . . . it was a nice place too, actually, sharing a bathroom and kitchen with a queer across the other side of the corridor.

This queer used to sing in the Black Cat, in Camden. That's how he made his living, he was a drag queen. And one time he got a nose job done, and he was walking around for weeks with this plastic bandage over his nose, and when it came off he looked exactly the same. Paid thousands of pounds for it, y'know. But he used to bring home these really dodgy-looking guys, who looked like they were serial killers. You know, like fifty-year-old guys with shabby raincoats. Really big blokes. Like, they could probably strangle you in seconds. I know one of them was packing a gun.

—**How did you know?**

—Cause they were playing around with it on the stairs coming up, he's like, 'Ahhh . . . put it away, put it away!' and I saw it. It was an automatic. He's like, 'Put it away', cause I'd opened my door, and the guy put the automatic back in his pocket and looked at me. I just shut my door. But when the electricity ran out you had to have a 5p, and I didn't have any 5ps, so I had to go and knock on his door, to see if he had any 5ps. His lights were out, so he wouldn't have noticed if he had electricity or he didn't. So I listened for a while outside his door, to the humping, and he's going, 'AH OH AH OH! Fuck me harder! Fuck me harder!' and making sounds like he's in real pain, and the other guy would be grunting and drooling and going, 'Darling. Do you want me to kiss your neck?'

So anyway, to get back to my nose, the cops took me to Charing Cross Hospital, and the nurse . . . it was a Saturday night, so they had hundreds of casualties in . . . automatically assumed that I'd been just as responsible for the fight as the person who broke my nose. So she made it really painful, giving me the stitches, she didn't give me any anaesthetic. And they wouldn't do anything about the nose. So it was bent out of shape until a few days later, when it got fixed at one of Wayne County's gigs. I reckoned Wayne County really fancied me. And I used to use the booze that was laid on back stage and get in free to his gigs. Loads of big, heavy rockabillys were getting into mixing with punks, and the whole thing was getting mixed up. They were getting into mixing with the real punks. Like the Heartbreakers, and all that. They all had rockabilly fucking fifties haircuts, and all fifties style gear, and they looked like they walked out of the set of fucking *The Last Picture Show*. No, more like *American Hot Wax*, or like *The Buddy Holly Story*, know what I mean?

By the way, I went to the premiere of *The Buddy Holly Story*, which was the last place Keith Moon went before he died. I saw him the night he died. We were coming out of the premiere, we were in this downstairs stall. We got in with our mate, Jailhouse Jim, who was a rock and roll DJ, running the Hot Wax show that was based in Hammersmith at The George. Hammersmith was a big area for teds at the time. Do you remember the Adverts? Well, they were stupid enough to get a flat in fucking Hammersmith, just down the road from The George. So they found that every Tuesday night when The George was doing the Hot Wax show, they'd have to run away from teds in their own bar. They got beaten up regularly, by gangs of teds.

—So anyway, you saw Keith Moon.

—Because this was all around mid '77. Punk was dead for me by then. It was just starting for the average morons.

—What about Keith Moon?

—Well, I saw him stumbling down the stairs, being assisted by his Charlies, and Daves and Joeys. And then, on the other side of the stairs, and they weren't talking to each other deliberately, it was McCartney with Linda, looking really posh in a white suit and a tie, and a carnation, y'know, cause he owns all his publishing. You know, he bought all his publishing, so it made him another fucking . . . doubled his millions. But he not only got all the Beatles publishing, he's got all the fucking Buddy Holly publishing, y'know what I mean. That man has got millions. I think he bought Michael Jackson's publishing as well.

—Isn't that the other way around?

—I think he might have sold Buddy Holly's publishing to Michael Jackson. So anyway, they weren't talking to each other. They'd known each other for years, but, y'know, Paul McCartney is being really straight, and Keith Moon is obviously out of his brain on several different drugs and lots of alcohol. Staggering around down the stairs, with these photographers taking pictures . . . fucking hell.

It's a great movie, *The Buddy Holly Story*. It's got a great scene in it. It's got a scene where the drummer beats the shit out of him. He gets so sick of him prissying around like that, he beats the living fuck out of him, before they go on stage. Gary Busey was Buddy Holly. You know Gary Busey? Big Gary Busey. Cause Buddy Holly was a big bloke, you know. He was like six foot, and broad. He was a Texan. They were all big blokes. They were all very violent and drunken, and probably did lots of junk and lots of speed. And had loads of gang-bangs in their dressing rooms. And trashed their dressing rooms, and all that. When Buddy was on stage, he was an animal, apparently. He had these two personas, the one with the orchestra going like, [singing] 'Let's remember, baby, last September how we, da de de da da da', and that came out under the name of 'Buddy Holly', right, and then, under the name of 'The Crickets', which everyone knew was Buddy Holly and the group, The Crickets, yeah, came the real rock and roll heavy stuff like 'Brown Eyed Handsome Man', and like 'Rave On', [sings] 'Rave on, it's a crazy feeling, and I know you got me reeling . . .'

Buddy Holly was a really seminal rock and roll guitar player, same as Eddie Cochrane. Eddie had a sound that was based on distortion and using semi-acoustics. But Buddy pioneered the Telecaster. He got that sort of tinny sound. He invented that tinny rockabilly sound. Just a little bit of echo on it, in a studio. And he could do it on stage. They could both do it on stage. They were both amazing guitar players, and like, wild performers. But you expect Eddie to be a madman on stage, cause he was a bad boy, but Buddy Holly was getting the good boy sales as well, y'know. But on stage he was a complete animal. He used to wreck his equipment, and fucking start unzipping his fly. He used to get on with so much drugs and drinking, he didn't know what he was doing. They were all unprofessional like that, you know. But they used to pound out real

rock and roll, not to be equalled again until the Pistols, or Dr Feelgood. And uhh . . . how did we get on to *The Buddy Holly Story*?
—You went there. You went to the premiere and you saw Keith Moon. The broken nose was the last thing.
—Oh yeah, yeah. Wayne County. Well anyway, I reckon the guy who did it – who I knew – was out of his mind that night, cause he didn't recognize me. He reset my nose by smashing my face; smashing me full in the face, sending me tumbling down a flight of stairs. Luckily an American manager was there, who was queer and also in love with me. There were two old queens who used to hang, ageing American queens, who'd been big in rock and roll in America for years. All the Americans were coming over to London, because London was where it was happening. You know what I mean . . . Iggy came over and all that. So there was that side of it, I mean, it wasn't dead for me like that. I could still have lots of fun. I was still a Face, y'know, I never had to pay to go into gigs. And if I was seen at a gig I was photographed. And like, if the band was just a new band, I would get photographed in the article and not the band.
—How come?
—Cause I was a Face. I was spotted on the street. The first one of us in the national papers was Claudio, my mate. Chaotic Base was his alias. And Shanne used to use him as a male bodyguard/escort, y'know, you paid for him, and he fucking had to deal with any punk-bashers. So he was getting beaten up for Shanne. And one night, he walked into a fish and chipper at Highbury and Islington, in pink drainpipes, and winklepickers. And wraparound shades. He always wore them. Any time of the day or night. And Shanne was outside, waiting for him to bring her her chips. And this is around Arsenal, yeah, about four o'clock in the morning or something . . . the night was still young. And these guys started on him and he got the shit kicked out of him. And she just stood outside and watched. And when they started looking at her, and when she saw that he didn't have a chance of fucking getting up again, she just ran like fuck, you know, and left him there, for them to finish him off. But he was still around her pad the next day to bring her out.

Anyway, Claudio got picked up by the *Evening Standard*, in about July '76, and he got his picture in the paper, and they quoted him on what punk was about. He said about how the Sex Pistols were the most obnoxious group ever, and that was the whole point.

He liked it when Johnny got heckled on stage, and fucking talked back. And he always heckled Johnny on stage. He talked about that. And about how whenever a number would start, we'd all go into a mad pogo, right. And then we would pick up Claudio and throw him into the monitor. You know how the monitors are laid out front, coming to a sort of point at the top. We used to land him on his balls on the monitors. So he's in excruciating pain on his balls on the monitor. And this is all just us playing around with him. And then he'd fall off the monitor, and crack his head, and then we'd kick the shit out of him.

—And this was your best friend?

—Well, yeah, he was my best friend at the time. I mean, yes, cause Bernie wasn't interested in . . . Bernie was trying to go straight. Bernie was trying to play football on Wednesdays, and have a steady girlfriend. And, you know, he was wearing soul boy gear, and all that. Which I had been, up to very recently. And Claudio had been wearing soul boy sort of. It was like a mixture of soul boys and art students. And soul boys were the freaks.

—We had them before.

—Yeah, well, the freaks turned into soul boys. When I went into the loony bin, Bernie started being like, 'Oh, this is a loser's game. I'm getting old. I'm eighteen.' No, he was twenty by then. So he'd go out, and he'd say, 'You know I've got to work tomorrow, I'm a man. I need to make money.' Like, he had good clothes, and a car at that stage. Went to discos. You know what I mean?! Discos were the most violent places on earth in London in 1976. You know, the chances of you getting out of a disco without getting in a fight were minimal. People didn't go to a disco to dance, they went to fight.

So Bernie really wasn't pulling the right strokes at all. And I rang him up, hysterically, after I first saw the Pistols, and said, 'Listen, it's happened! It's fucking here! The ultimate rock and roll band.

They're loud, they're obnoxious, they're horrible! They make Iggy look like a wimp. The guitarist sounds like Johnny Thunders. Like a mixture of the Dolls and the Stones. And he was going, 'Nah nah . . . I'm going to play football, and then I'm going to see my girlfriend.'

But he was making up the girlfriend. Cause he had terrible acne. Girls wouldn't go near him. He kept going to discos, and kept trying to pick up a girl. And the minute he tried to pick up a girl her boyfriend would bottle him. Whereas like, I used to go to discos, when I was feeling mad enough, y'know, when I thought, Fuck it! I wanna hear some soul music. You know, it's the sort of soul they're playing now. It was rare groove. It's cool now, but it was actually happening then. It was stuff like 'Young Hearts Run Free', and the Commodores, and *Station to Station*, you know, Bowie's best period.

And it's amazing the way Bowie was still there with *Station to Station*. A lot of the Bowie crowd had gone soul boy because Bowie had gone soul boy. Then you had your actual soul boys. Then you had your soul boys who were ex-freaks. Then you had your ex-Roxy Musics, who were looking for a new sort of Roxy Music type of group. Sort of, clothes conscious, know what I mean? Elitists. Drinking cocktails. Drinking double rum and blacks. And smoking Winstons. Winstons had just come out in this country, and they were the punk brand.

—**You had them.**

—Marlboros were smoked by too many people, yeah, so we smoked Winstons. And uh . . . What?!

—**I'm just trying to remember what you were talking about before.**

—I'm gonna get round to Frank in a minute.

So like there were art students, right, who were already experimenting with dyed hair, and cutting their hair short. Cause a lot of them were fags. And the straight ones were trying not to be straight, so it's like they were fags. And the fags traded their guitar and mousse for dyed short hair. They didn't go to discos, they went to art school gigs. Which is where the Sex Pistols started out playing, art school gigs. That's the first sort of youth you hit. You know what

I mean? Converted the art students, who all proceeded to buy their clothes from Sex, and made them lots of money.

And Johnny single-handedly made digital watches the legal street-wear. Really a poser, know what I mean. Because his parents bought him one for his birthday, yeah. So, around one wrist he had a studded leather wrist band, from the leather shop in King's Road, and around the other he had a digital wristwatch; which were expensive at the time. Like a year later it was going for a fiver. And all I wanted in life, at that stage, was a fucking digital wristwatch, and a mohair jumper. But a digital wristwatch was fucking twenty-five quid or something, and a mohair jumper was fifty quid, from Sex. So I talked this French bird into buying a mohair jumper at Sex, and then told her they'd gone out of fashion, and swapped her my Union Jack shirt, which I only ever wore to Jam gigs to take the piss out of the mods. They were meant to be mods, know what I mean . . . but they weren't mods!

The Jam were incredibly un-hip, because of their mod thing, and wearing suits. Wearing Beatle suits. Not Beatle suits . . . just black suits, and white shirts, and black thin ties. And doing sixties pop numbers, but NOT fucking them up, know what I mean? Doing them reverently. Whereas the Pistols used to do like the Small Faces' 'What Ya Gonna Do About It?', but screw it up really badly. He made it into a totally different thing, know what I mean? [sings], 'I want you to know that I HATE you, baby, I want you to know I don't care! WHAT'CHA GONNA DO ABOUT IT?! WHAT'CHA GONNA DO? . . .'

Maclaren provided them with these records to fuck up. And I bet he was horrified when Johnny and Glen started writing songs, cause that meant his rodents were turning into human beings. Like Johnny started wearing things that he hadn't told him to wear. You know, Johnny went out and had a pair of bondage pants made for himself, so they had to stock bondage pants in the Sex shop. And so he got a cut out of that. A designer's cut, know what I mean? And the day that they put them on sale in the Sex shop, he previewed them . . . cause he was getting a cut out of the sales.

They stopped playing live. Before that, they played every night of the week in London. Like the Pogues did. You know, they completely conquered London. Every second night of the week, in some part of London, either at an art college, or a club. They had a residency at the 100 Club, till they had the festival there, where a girl's eye was taken out with a broken glass. And where Sid Vicious beat up Nick Kent, with a studded belt.

The other big punk dance apart from pogo-ing was pushing and shoving, you know, slamdancing they called it later. They called it slamdancing and pogo-ing, right. But it was known as pushing and shoving. There's a song, 'No Lip' by Dave Berry and the Cruisers, it goes, [sings] 'Won't get none of my sweet sweet lovin', if you don't stop pushin' and shovin', pushin' and shovin . . .', and everybody would start pushing and shoving each other, and throwing each other on to the stage, know what I mean. Then if anybody landed on the stage, one of the Pistols would boot him in the head and then try to fling him back into the audience. He'd disappear into the audience, and get trampled.

—That sounds like a lot of fun.

—He'd love every minute of it, y'know. He'd been beaten up by the Pistols.

—Who?

—The kid it happened to. And that was a news story. But back to Frank, right. You could say that Frank came in at our stage of gigging, as the Pogues, where the same thing used to happen, like, people used to get thrown on stage, and thrown off. Where we used to fight on stage, like the group used to fight on stage. Me and Jem, particularly, used to fucking hit each other with each other's guitars and banjos. All about what number to play next. Seriously fighting, yeah. And the audience loved it. And then Cait would start shrieking at us. You were there, the night of the Wag Club, when me and Cait had a row, and I threw a full beer can at her and hit her on the head, and knocked her off the stage! And she landed at the side of the stage, with her amp on top of her. And the audience had to help her up. I was a really good shot like that. You know, a full beer can is really heavy. It's got a good slap to it when it hits you in the head. But she was being intolerable, know what I mean? She was fucking screeching on about things over the microphone. And I was saying, 'Shut up, you stupid cow!' I don't know what kind of bee was in her bonnet that night. I don't know. It was too early to have been Brian. That's what we called Elvis Costello.

—**Brian?**

—Yeah, after Brian the Snail.

—**Who's Brian the Snail?**

—He's a character in the *Magic Roundabout*. A kid's programme they had over here, all through the sixties, and early seventies. They had a guy called Zebedee, who went 'Boing Boing!' And a hippy rabbit called Dylan. Which was a piss take of Bob Dylan.

—**Why was he called Brian?**

—Cause we thought he was like a snail. Anyway, I was the grumpy one and Spider was the happy one. I was the grumpy one cause I was the one with all the hate, and all the ideas. I mean it was my idea for Spider to play the beer tray. I forced him to do it. Even though he came out bruised and battered every night. Cause on 'Waxie's Dargle', for instance, he hit himself thirty-two times. And other numbers, he hit himself just that many times. And he's got metallurgy to certain kinds of metal, he can't wear a chain or a cross or anything unless it's silver or gold and it's a horrible lurgy, it was completely organic, the whole thing was organic. It was the most organic band ever, it was fucking brilliant. We'd known each other for years and we were on the same wavelength. Also, Cait was Gaelic, because she was half Scottish and half Irish, Andy was half Irish, but he was far more Irish than English, in his appearance, his manner, his drinking habits and his way of thinking. Andy and Cait were very important members.

Anyway, this democratic group was basically run by me and Jem. It was a question of like, who to side with, me or Jem. Who were you more scared of, know what I mean. Andrew was more scared of Jem, right, but me and Andrew were both good drinking buddies, so Andrew was really confused and always abstained. Cait always voted with Jem to annoy me.

—Why?

—What?

—Why?

—Cause she liked annoying me.

—Why?

—Why?! Cause she was a seventeen year old, who knew I had more charisma than her, know what I mean. And however stupidly she combed her hair, she was only ever going to be a teenybopper idol to a small gang, or crew, who were all about fifteen or sixteen. She had her own little gang of teenybopper boys, who wanted to marry her. And she dressed provocatively on stage, and was provocative towards them.

And then Spider had his own little group of screaming teeny-bopper girls, you know, who thought he was cute. Yeah? And then the rest of them . . . it was me. Well, Spider was a really popular character, but the person that they took seriously was me. And Jem was just this weird-looking little guy who played the banjo. But we were all good characters, y'know, all good characters. James had a big female following, but nothing like as big as mine. 'A Pair of Brown Eyes', y'know, and I could fuck any girl in the house. James, until he opened his mouth, was big with the girls. But then when he tried chatting up the groupies he went, 'Ello . . . are yoo doing?' and they'd go, 'Oh, sorry, I've made a mistake, I was looking for Shane.' You said he's like Dirk Bogarde. But he wasn't anything like as beautiful as Dirk Bogarde.

—I never said he was like Dirk Bogarde. I said he was like Cary Grant.

—But he had that sort of English, fucking, stiff-upper-lip hand-someness, didn't he? I never saw him as handsome but lots of women did. Lots of women did, and thought he was sexy, y'know. And also the way he managed the big accordion, which was the wrong accordion anyway, and which he couldn't play properly. He was just playing piano, and pressing the bass buttons. You know, randomly. Luckily Cait was such a tight bass player, we could turn down his bass notes on the accordion so you couldn't hear them, and all you could hear was the piano keyboard on the accordion. And he was a great piano player. So when he learned to go, 'Humm humm humm humm', which is like walking and chewing gum, he got this reputation for being a shit-hot accordion player. I really don't know why some Irish session guy didn't walk on to the stage with a box in his hands, you know, a proper Irish box, both side buttons, and blow him off the stage, know what I mean, by playing fucking . . . 'McCloud's Rule', or something.

—No one ever did it?

—Nobody ever did. James . . . I tried to teach him Irish accordion, but he never learned. But I taught him enough for him to . . . under severe coaching from me, get away with it. I also got him to listen to a lot of Cajun records. Cause I reckoned it was the only way he was going to get anything near it, was by trying to play Cajun, which is much simpler, but is a very similiar sound. But the fact is, he can't play proper Irish accordion on a big fucking German fucking piano keyboard accordion. But that's why we gave him the name 'The Maestro', you know, Maestro Jimmy Fearnley. And it was 'Country Jem Finer', cause Country Jem used to wear a cowboy hat all the time, till he started taking himself seriously. Everybody was such a laugh to begin with, and had the right attitude, know what I mean.

But it was basically Frank who bullied people into becoming professional. The only person he couldn't bully into being a professional was me. And we never played a professional gig while I was on that stage. They played loads of shit-hot type of professional gigs after I'd gone, know what I mean . . . but the audiences dwindled, and dwindled and dwindled. And the songs on the first follow-up album were awful. And the songs on the second album were absolutely pathetic.

It's like the Chieftains did with Sean O'Riada, know what I mean, I was the Sean O'Riada of the group. I was the one who actually fucking could write, compose Irish tunes, in the Irish tradition. And write lyrics in the Irish tradition but make them about modern subjects. And I could also arrange old Irish tunes, like nineteenth-century, eighteenth-century tunes, and take the 'thee's and 'thou's out, and rewrite the lyrics so that they made sense. You know, the lyrics of those songs are normally about ten verses long. And I would add a riff. A hornpipe, maybe, to introduce it. I added riffs to the tunes, which is an innovation for Irish music. Like, traditional Irish music doesn't have riffs. I mean, not introductory riffs followed by another riff, over which the song is played. You'd have a riff over which the whole thing is sung. But it's all the same riff all the way through. For instance, 'The Rocky Road to Dublin'. You could call 'De de de de de diddle de de' a riff, but it's also part of the melody. I introduced melodically related riffs.

I was bringing it into the twentieth century in the same way that O'Riada was doing it. Not in the same way, but . . . well, in the slower and mid-tempo numbers, that's where I was doing it the way O'Riada did it. By arranging. By mixing up old airs to form a new air, things like that.

I didn't realize that this was gonna fuck up my idea for the group. My idea for the group is what I'm doing now. From now on we're doing a lot more traditional stuff. We already have. We were doing 'Poor Paddy on the Railway', 'Spanish Lady' and stuff. But after Frank, traditional Irish tunes were taboo. And there was a democratic vote taken on that. Forcing all the pressure on to me to write all the music. Spider can write Irish music, and did. 'Repeal of the Licensing Laws'. And 'Jack's Heroes'. The songs that Spider wrote, while I was still in the group, were in the tradition. And Terry could as well. But the rest of them . . .

Well, I was the one who from a baby had been ingesting Irish music. Very good Irish music, you know what I mean, constantly. In the kitchen. Famous people had played in our kitchen. Paddy O'Brien played in our kitchen, because my Uncle Mikey taught him. Did a lot of teaching, my Uncle Mikey. And Paddy O'Brien is now regarded as the greatest Irish accordion player of the twentieth century. In fact, the greatest Irish accordion player of the twentieth century was my Uncle Mikey. But he didn't have any interest in playing in a ceilidh band because it was too much aggro, and he used to just have fun in our kitchen, he used to play in pubs when he was

TO LIVE AND TO DIE BY THE SIDE OF THE ROAD

SIT DOWN SIT DOWN FOR GOD'S SAKE

THE TINKERS AT THE BACK CAN'T SEE
I WON'T TAKE A DUMP INSIDE MA
SO JESUS CHRIST HELP ME
TO LIVE OR TO DIE OR TO SQUIRM LIKE A TOAD
TO LIVE OR TO DIE BY THE SIDE OF THE ROAD
LONG AGO WE WERE LORDS WHO HAD SACKS FULL OF
AND OUR LAND IT WAS TAKEN AWAY   GOLD
WITHOUT LAND WITHOUT CATTLE
WITHOUT ANY FIELDS
O'DONNELLS, O'DWYERS AND O'BRIENS AND O'NEILLS
WE SET OFF FOR NOWHERE WITHOUT SHOES ON OUR
                                        HEELS
TO LIVE OR TO DIE BY THE SIDE OF THE ROAD
WE WERE SHAT ON AND SPAT ON
SOMETIMES TREATED KIND
~~THE FINAL DISORDER~~   THE THIN ONE CAN BE YOUR ONE
~~~~ THE BIG ONE IS MINE
TILL FINALLY WE TRIUMPHED
AND THEN THERE WAS FUN
I'VE A MERCEDES BENZ
AND A BLOODY GREAT GUN
NOW BY OUR CRUCIFIED CHRIST I WILL
                        PUT DOWN MY LOAD
TO LIVE AND TO DIE BY THE SIDE OF THE ROAD
GET AWAY FROM THAT POOL TABLE
THE TINKERS WANT A GAME
AND IF YOU CAN'T FIGHT FOR YOURSELVES
                                BOYS
GO GET YOUR AUNTIE MAME
WE'RE ALL OF US IRISH, WE ALL LIKE THE BOOZE
WE ALL KNOW THAT CHRIST WAS CRUCIFIED BY JEWS
WHAT MADE YOU SEND US, ~~~~ SO LOW
TO LIVE OR TO DIE BY THE SIDE OF THE ROAD

HOW MANY YOUNG IRISHMEN AND WOMEN
                        GOT HUNG
BAD CEST TO DEMOCRACY
CRY IRELAND'S TRUE SONS
LET'S ATTEND TO HER DAUGHTERS FIRST
THEN LIVE OR DIE BY THE GUN

ITSEEMS THAT THY TEARS MIGHT CEASE
IT'S SO QUIET NOW
NO PRIESTS AND NO SOLDIERS
NO-ONE TO KILL NOW
OH CHRIST! I REMEMBER NOW
WHY I CAN'T STOP THIS PAIN
I SHOT MY OWN BROTHER
IN THE YARD IN THE RAIN

AND THEN MY MOTHER CURSED ME
ALMOST BLEW HER AWAY
WHO THE FUCK AM I TALKING TO
IN THE KITCHEN ALONE
WHAT'S THAT? THE RADIO
COMING OUT OF ATHLONE
NOW A VOCAL REQUEST NO CHRIST! NOT
THE OLD BOG ROAD

I'LL JUST HAVE A GLASS, SHE SAID
AS I THOUGHT SHE MIGHT
AND THE CIDER WE DRANK IT TURNED
INTO CHAMPAGNE THAT NIGHT
AT MY COMMAND SHE TOOK MY HAND
SHE TRIPED SO FAIR AND LIGHT
I THOUGHT WE WERE IN JERUSALEM, THOUGH
                    WE DANCED THROUGH MUCK AND
                                        SHITE
WHEN THAT WAS DONE WE LAY AS ONE ALL THROUGH
                    THAT RAINY NIGHT

younger, but he was very old by the time he was teaching Paddy O'Brien.

My Auntie Ellen was a very influential concertina player, but she was never recorded either. When I think about some of the stuff she used to play, she was incredibly fast, she had real Irish soul, when she played, she gave you the feeling that the whole of Ireland was dancing. When she tapped her foot it was as hard as a hammer, it was tighter than any drum machine, tighter than a nun's cunt. You had this old woman in a dress and a hairstyle she hadn't changed since the 1920s, because that was when she entered her middle ages, but you got her rocking on that concertina and every limb in her body would be shaking and the foot banging time would be like that classic rocker's Chelsea boot, hammering out the time, like Elvis, she used to rock like a fucking bitch. She knew a few slow tunes but she wasn't into playing that old crap, that old ethereal bollocks.

I'm going to go out one day and catch a banshee and cut her hair off and she'll bawl and wail her fucking head off and I'm going to record it and put it out as the original Enya . . .

Well, by the time they started recording, Topic, and Grapevine, and people like that, the ballad groups had brought back interest in traditional Irish music, and people were rushing around the countryside going, 'Everybody go to Clare! Everybody go to Clare!' . . . know what I mean? Nobody went to Tipperary. So, my Uncle Mikey never got to record, because Paddy O'Brien left Tipperary, and went to Clare. Everybody had to go to Clare to get picked up. They thought it only happened in the west. They thought Irish was only spoken in the west. Like, have you ever heard of a famous Waterford piper? Or Waterford accordion player? Or Waterford fiddle player? You know what I mean, they don't go to Waterford, they don't think Waterford is . . . In fact, Waterford is a very traditional Irish county. And has a border with Tipperary, and it goes on through to Tipperary, and gets wilder as you go west. Until you hit my bit. Which is as far as you can go.

I couldn't teach James any kind of Irish accordion style. The Tipperary one was the one I was trying to, cause that's the one I know. And it's very easy for a beginner, if you get him young enough. But it's very difficult for an adult, because it uses the black notes, black buttons, as percussion. And they'd use that with a bodhran, which had been banned by Ceoltas. All the real musicians, country musicians, used bodhrans, but you wouldn't see a bodhran in Clare. Until Sean O'Riada said, 'Fuck it . . . I'm gonna conduct this bunch of idiots, who wouldn't be able to play a note without my fucking genius.' You know what I mean? He was a modest man, Sean O'Riada. 'I'm gonna play the bodhran, and be a conductor', and that's what he did. That's what he did and he shocked Ceoltas, horrifically. Ceoltas are like the official organization for Irish music.

And he also used an orchestra who were drunk and out of tune. Ceoltas disapproved of him as a rebel and as far as they were concerned the bodhran is completely out. There is no percussion in Irish music. There's only the upright piano, the harp, the pipes, and the fiddle, and a tenor voice, if you were going to use your voice, like McCormack. So you can imagine the fucking wailing caterwauling fucking shite that was coming out on records, y'know, and on the radio, before O'Riada came along. And O'Riada played the music . . . arranged all the old tunes, and wrote several Masses in Irish, which Ceoltas also disapproved of. Cause like, who had the right to . . . you know he used the old hymns, but he wrote his own music. It was like, 'Who was he to come along and write a new Mass in Irish?!?!' And he used the bodhran to write his Mass in Irish! This was all rebellion, know what I mean. And Ceoltas would've done anything to destroy him, but he was instantly loved by everybody. He got on Radio Eireann. He bullied his way on to Radio Eireann. He was a driven man, like me, or Christy, or Michael Flatley, y'know, he was a driven man, he said fuck the rules! From the mid-1950s to the early 1960s, O'Riada was the sound of Ireland, to most Irish people, and certainly to most Irish Americans. Apart from the singers, who he had a lot to do with recording, like Maggie Barry. Maggie Barry, the 'Queen of the Gypsies'. She used to piss herself on stage, she was so drunk. She was an old fucking tinker woman. He fucking had her singing with him. And any fucking around from the traditional musicians, and they just got the boot. He said, 'I could go down to fucking Kerry tomorrow and get three hundred of you. But this orchestra is unique, and I'm unique, so you behave youself, and stop fucking showing off, and play what you're told to play!'

—**And is that the way you were?**

—I didn't have to be like that with the Pogues, you see. Everybody really liked each other. We were all mates, drinking pals for years. And they accepted that I knew more about the music than they did. I mean, Spider knew lots of the Irish songs, from jukeboxes in Irish pubs. Country Jem was in there to bring a country influence, with his bluegrass banjo. And that did power it along with a sort of different sound. Cause like, the old acoustic guitar just strumming away, unless it's played really well, is not the proper instrument for it. The upright piano is the ceilidh instrument. And what we were playing was ceilidh. The bass simply came in because we were playing in rock venues. It was to strengthen the beat. And to strengthen the chord pattern, it's just meant to go, 'Boom boom, boom boom'; cause James couldn't play the black notes on the accordion. Cait was playing what a good Irish accordion player would be playing on the accordion. She was putting in the black notes. And she also looked good, and all that was taken into account. It was a plan. It was a carefully planned operation. It was a crusade on my part. And like, supposedly on the rest of their part. I think, looking back, obviously, it was a crusade on the rest of their parts to get rich.

It was a crusade on my part to fuck over the sort of progressive Irish fusion shit that was going down. Like, I'd seen Moving Hearts with Christy Moore trying to be a rock singer. You know what I mean?!?! Saxophone! And they made a bloody God-awful noise on stage. They were really loud. Horribly loud! They just sounded like a pile of shit. In the session scene in London, it was all wimpy fucking eternal bodhran players. I mean you'd get the occasional inspired band like, a band that had planned it, and really had chemistry. Tom played in two: Dinglespike and Irish Mist. Who were both brilliant. And both got recorded, but on traditional labels.

Tom's parents' pub, The Favourite, was a mighty pub for Irish music, and the sessions there were recorded by Topic. They sold out three editions. Not just pressings. There's one out today, still selling. It's called *Paddy in the Smoke.* And you can hear a fifteen-year-old Tom on it, and other great Irish musicians of the day. And all people who Ceoltas wouldn't fucking give the time of the day to.

But the Pogues took the London-Irish scene over to Ireland, and gave the music a gigantic boot up the arse in its own country. Meanwhile, bringing out of the woodwork millions of Irish music fans. There are thousands . . . hundreds of thousands of Irish music fans in the British Isles generally, particularly in Scotland and the West Country, and Manchester, Birmingham, places like that which have huge Irish communities.

We were the hottest live act in . . . we were like the Pistols were at the end of '76, before they put out 'Anarchy'. Our first single was banned, because of our name. That made sure it sold out the first edition, and went into the second edition, and got picked up by Stiff Records. Who renamed us 'the Pogues'. Because the BBC wouldn't play us as 'Poguemahone' when they found out what it meant. This Irish lorry driver phoned in to the John Peel show when he was playing us one night. John Peel got really into us, and we did sessions with him, y'know. And he said, 'Do you know what the name means? Do you know what their name means? I think it's a mighty sound they're making. I think it's the best stuff you've had on for ages. Did you know what their name means in Irish?' And John Peel said, 'Oh, do enlighten us', and he says, 'It means kiss my arse!' And the bloke is hysterical laughing. And John Peel says, 'Well, I'm sure our listeners will be very interested to hear that, so here's the next number from "Kiss My Arse"!!!' And that got up to the ninety-year-old chairman of the BBC, right, that John Peel was playing a session by a band . . . an Irish band who had a name which in Irish means Kiss My Arse! Ban them! You know what I mean?! Don't play their records! Ban it!! No, don't ban it! Don't ban it, that'll make it sell more. Just don't play it. But it had already got into the press that it had been banned. You know, we made a huge thing of it in the press

P JUST LOOK
THEM
STRAIGHT
IN THE
EYE AND
SAY...........

POGUEMAHONE
AT THE
HOPE ⊕ ANCHOR
OCT 6TH.
-*- AND -*-
DULL ⊕ GATE
OCT 14TH + 27TH

COPYRIGHT © SIOBHAN MAC GOWAN 1998

that our name had to be changed; that the BBC wouldn't play the record.

That was Phil Hall, our publicist at Stiff, his first stroke of genius. I'd say Phil Hall had a hundred times more to do with us going from pub gigs to being a real contender than Frank had. And with us touring Europe and headlining and all that. That was Phil Hall's publicity. Phil Hall and Frank would argue continually about publicity. Frank wanted us all to look neat and tidy, and of course what people wanted was us in the suits, but after we'd been rolling around in a dustbin in them. Nah, they wanted us to look like people who'd gone out smartly dressed, but who'd been out all night drinking and dancing, and lost their ties, know what I mean. They wanted that Paddy chic. That is an Irish look. I mean, recently it's gone out of date . . . it's disappeared to a large extent. But then you could still spot an Irishman a hundred yards away. The haircut, quite apart from the racial features; the haircut, and the two-piece suit, and the high open-necked shirt. Not dirty or anything, but like, sort of casually worn. No t-shirts, no jeans, no fucking ties. That was our dress code, know what I mean. Time had frozen still since 1957. The year of my birth. Like the Beatles had never happened. Get what I mean? Rock and roll had happened, right. Country music was around, you know, fusion Irish, in the fifties and sixties. So we did country songs. But we never actually did a rock and roll song.

But that's what the press failed to see. The 'suss' press understood what was happening, that we were discarding rock music, after the death of Buddy Holly, and the death of Eddie Cochrane, and after Elvis went soft. And we were bringing Paddy-beat to take over the world. And Paddy-beat was being played by renegade show bandsmen, or Paddy-group men!

And we could do 'Connemara Let's Go' or 'Down in the Ground where the Dead Men Go', which it ended up being called. After 'Havana Let's Go', which was an annoying, ethnic, world music group at the time. They all wore Hawaiian shirts, and played steel-drum music, Kid Creole type shit. Like, we were reacting to all that shit, and to boring old pub rock, know what I mean. That was all you had, in the live circuit. So of course we tore it apart. 'Dark Streets of London' was a very catchy fucking song. I wanted to put out 'Streams of Whiskey' as the first single, but Stan pointed out that 'Streams of Whiskey' would probably automatically be not banned, but just quietly ignored by the BBC. Because of its blatant adulation of drunkenness. Its blatant adulation of an IRA man who became a writer, who made a lot of money, and who then drank himself to death. Oh yeah, and our suits and our shirts were exactly like Brendan Behan used to wear, cause that was what they all used to wear. That was what everybody used to wear in Ireland in those days. They still do, down in the country, you get over a certain age, and they still wear that. The majority of people above thirty just simply wear a sports coat and tie, and a neat haircut. Or the other thing is what I call the Paddy landed on a golf course look. Which is a green Fred Perry, and smart slacks.

My plan was to make the music hip everywhere, right. The real music. I wanted to destroy Ceoltas. And bring battering back, properly. And have the fleadh ceols happening again, like when I was a kid, in all the towns. Have young people knowing the songs. The only people that are playing it at the moment are me, Christy, and Ronnie Drew. And in America, me and Christy are the biggest things among the American-Irish. We're huge among the American-Irish. Like, they've got their own groups, like Black 47 and all that, but that's all fusion stuff.

I anticipated it being bigger on the east coast of America. Cause I knew all about the American-Irish, the New York Irish, and the New Jersey Irish . . . The east coast Irish. I have cousins over there. And lots of my aunties and uncles have gone to America, and died there. Lots of them have come back, too, so I learned all this as a kid.

I wanted to make it . . . I wanted to be paid a decent amount of money, for playing really good music, and get recorded. Not on folk labels. I wanted a decent crack at the charts, know what I mean. And that all worked out, but that wasn't because of Frank Murray. It wasn't because of Frank Murray that I wrote 'Fairytale of New York'. That's just one of those things. It was because of Frank Murray that we teamed up with the Dubliners, to make 'The Irish Rover'. That was an inspired piece of managing. I mean, I'm not saying he wasn't a creative manager, he was, yeah, but the point is, he should have worked with me as a creative manager, not against me. Instead, his idea of creative management is HE decides all the fucking moves.

We'd already done all our own graphics and stuff, and created our own image, without mentioning the IRA once. Like, we had Republican banners all over the fucking place at our gigs. All I said was that I was an Irish Republican and that was enough. And I said that one of my favourite writers was Brendan Behan. And that made them have an article about Brendan Behan in the *NME*. So we had already made it hip in England, and they were baying out for it in Ireland. Because it had gone over to Ireland. Everything that comes out in England comes out in Ireland. And everyone wanted to see the fucking band that had made 'The Dark Streets of London'. And then we followed it up with *Red Roses for Me*.

You know, Frank wasn't anything to do with us when we did 'Red Roses for Me'. Stan Brennan assumed he was managing us, but we never gave him that impression. We merely owed him a cut on the record, you know, cause he put foward the money towards recording it and pressing it. It was under our own Poguemahone label and was picked up by Stiff. But he insisted on producing the record . . . having something to do with the production of *Red Roses for Me*. That was my first frustration as a producer, right. I had so many arguments with Stan over the production. Because, as you know, having seen us, we had a thunderous sound, right? And my voice is very strong, and very raunchy, and loud. And you'd think from *Red Roses for Me* that I was Pinky and Perky, know what I mean. And you can't hear the bass at all, and the bass was really turned up quite loud. But despite all that, it's still a very exciting LP, you know.

Anyway, so after a really successful support tour, with Elvis Costello, we were ready to do our first tour of England . . . Britain. The headlining tour of Britain. And all that had been set up. So, shortly after that, we had done our first headlining tour of Britain, and it was a huge success. So, we had *Red Roses for Me*, and they picked up the option, and we were ready to make *Rum, Sodomy and the Lash*, when we finished our second tour of Britain. And it was at that point that Frank Murray started hanging around, drinking with us, and like being friendly, know what I mean.

I'd known Frank for ages, you know, but it seemed like he had never talked to me. You know what I mean, he was too important to talk to me. He was the Thin Lizzy road manager. Ha ha ha. But by then it was obvious to anyone but a chimpanzee, who had his ears cut off, that we were going to be huge. As long as we could keep it up on the second album. And as you know, the second album sold like, four times as many copies as the first album. And was our first platinum disc.

Me and Frank had a big row about the production. But by then I was busy worrying about him trying to stop me drinking so much. So I said, 'Fuck it! Let Costello produce it. I won't give him a minute's peace.' And Costello produced it. While he was fumbling with Cait on the set, me and the engineer fucking altered all the levels he'd set, and things like that. But we still couldn't get a good mix. We were doing it in Elephant Studios. Poxy little studio, know what I mean. But it came out pretty good.

And the idea for the title was Andrew's. That never got mentioned on the cover. It did get mentioned that the sleeve concept, the *Raft of the Medusa* spoof, was an original idea by Frank Murray. But we reckoned it was Marcia who had suggested it, yeah? And Jem who had proposed it. Whatever, from that moment, Jem hated his guts. And I never wanted him anyway.

His mother got run over by a bus, God rest her soul. He had a wonderful dad called Tommy, who's dead now, God rest his soul. And two wonderful brothers, and a wonderful sister. All really beautiful people. Really nice people. While Frank was charming everybody, backstage, in Dublin, I'd go over and talk to Pat, the brother. Pat was a trade union leader. So he was well off, y'know, working class turned middle class, by being a trade union leader. But he was a proper trade union leader, he wasn't a cheat, he wasn't a bent trade union leader. He wasn't always looking to put it in his pocket. And we were friendly, me and Pat. I was extremely friendly with Tommy, too, which I think really pissed Frank off. Tommy used to say, 'Get away, Frank, I want to talk to Shane.' And he used to make me take his arm, leading him across the road. He was a real gentleman. Both his brothers were real gentlemen, and his sister was a real lady. So where the fuck Frank came from, I'll never know.

I'm just saying that Frank was treating us like we were Thin Lizzy at the height of their sort of 'cock rock' period. He had me figured for a second Lynott. Maybe even bigger. But he wanted me on the road, where I couldn't mix with my friends in London, and drink a lot, and have a good time. Where I couldn't enjoy my money, know what I mean. I pleaded with him, I said, 'Right, I'm feeling really ill all the time, Frank. It's not good, playing night after night, with the amount of energy I put into each performance. And doing these gigantic tours of America ... I don't think we're going to crack it that way.' Because you don't crack America that way. You crack America with a hit single. Most bands go on for the rest of their lives touring America. The thing is, he was making twenty per cent of gross, on every gig we did. We'd cracked Germany, yeah. We made money in Germany, right, and then lost it all in America. Frank brought Terry Woods in, which was good, and he brought Philip Chevron in, which I think was bad.

—Why was that bad?

—Phil came in on banjo, originally, to help out because Jem was having a baby, and he was brilliant. He wasn't as good as Jem, obviously, but in a week he picked up the set and he stayed in time, didn't play a bum note, it was very impressive. And he put a lot of balls into it. He had the sort of balls that you'd expect from a guy who'd not only been one of the first punks in Dublin, but also openly admitted he was a faggot. And if he'd kept that attitude together, I wouldn't have minded, but once he joined the group, he took one of my jobs, which was rhythm guitar.

Now rhythm guitar, in Irish music, is not the sort of moron's job that it is in rock and roll. It's not a natural Irish instrument, of

course, which makes it harder, and not many people can play it well. I certainly didn't reckon he could play it better than me. If he had been improving what I had already written, then fine. For instance, on 'Lorelei', strangely enough, he kept it simple, like I would. It's like French cooking, playing rhythm guitar badly, there's loads of embellishment, but it's unnecessary and it doesn't taste good and it's not nourishing, it's got no guts. On his own stuff he does it exactly right, for his own stuff. For my stuff it's a different matter. But he's very good at what he does. Like 'Thousands Are Sailing', that's a great song, there's no way you can criticize that song, it's a brilliant song. Lyrically, I had to change a couple of lines, or else I would have refused to sing it altogether.
—Which ones?
—One line was 'Brendan Behan danced up and down the street'.
—Why?
—Because Brendan Behan wouldn't have danced. I did sing that on the record, but I sang it so viciously that it's obvious that he was kicking windows in at the same time. And on stage, I used to improvise and say pissed up and down the street, puked, crawled, shat, spewed, whatever came into my mind that night. But Phil never imposed any rubbish on the group while I was in it, apart from 'My Blue Heaven'. And I thought the stuff he did with the Radiators was really good.

As a person, Phil is a really nice guy, a really cool guy. A compassionate guy, as well. He has none of the bad qualities that some Dubliners sometimes exhibit.
—Like what?
—Bitchiness, sarcasm, chippiness.
—That's true.
—And 'Faithful Departed' is an Irish classic. And he's a good laugh to have a drink with. He can handle his drink, he's a proper Irish drinker. He can drink all day and all night and not repeat himself, not get violent, not get maudlin and he only tells funny jokes. He doesn't have the sort of toilet humour which is so prevalent on the road. People always regressed to school-outing kind of behaviour

and there's nothing as boring as endless gutter-level jokes. And Phil doesn't come out with any of that shit.

Now, Woods should have supported me in my crusade to keep the music hip, and keep the music happening. And I did keep it hip and happening, cause I knew it could be disastrous otherwise. But at least Woods' songs didn't sell out the fucking idea of the group. And, 'Fairytale of New York' didn't either. It was an Irish-based romantic ballad with an orchestra. That was the sort of Sean O'Riada thing again. Same with 'Broad Majestic Shannon'. It had the group's instruments imitating an orchestra. And using one phrase recurring. And the start-off phrase is a load of riffs. That was the obvious follow-up single to 'Fairytale of New York'. But Frank decided, No, it'll be 'If I Should Fall From Grace with God'. After 'Fairytale of New York', people would be expecting something slow or mid-tempo, sentimental, and very melodic. Instead they get a fucking psychotic hillbilly track. Very popular live. And as an album track. But a pretty senseless idea as a single, you know . . . throw it in the bin. But there was nothing I could do to stop him, because like, I couldn't get any of them to fucking vote against him. 'Yeah, let Frank take care of it. Frank's the manager. Fuck it.'

Spider voted for Frank as well. Cause Spider liked Frank, and was Frank's buddy, and all that. Mind you, I was meant to be Frank's buddy, as well.

Joey Cashman and him had been buddies too, right, but had a falling out. Joey could see that I was really ill, and could quite possibly die, know what I mean. And Joey was for taking at least six months off. And Joey was the guy who fucking rushed to fucking get a doctor when I puffed up in Italy, and it turned out to be hepatitis. But Joey was also the one who'd sneak me drinks when they'd put me on a drinks ban. I'd be told at the hotel bar that I wasn't allowed a drink, by orders of Mr Murray. And then Charlie MacLennan stepped in and was saying, 'You're fucking gonna get another Phil on your hands here. And I've had enough. I love Shane. And I don't want you to do the same thing to Shane.' You know, we saw him picking Frank up by the neck. Remember that? After he got me out of that Charter clinic or whatever it was. Charlie brought me round a couple of gin and tonics. And they were arguing in the van, all the way back home. Don't you remember, we were watching them arguing, by the van? Charlie went purple with rage, and picked Frank up by the throat, and lifted him up, really high up above the ground. And Frank was just going, 'Ach . . . ugh . . . Ach . . . Hey! Hey!!' And Charlie's self-preservation instinct locked in, just in time before he broke his windpipe. And he dropped him. Do you remember that?

—**Yeah. Charlie was good like that. Do you remember the time he kicked you in the ribs, for upsetting me?**

—Yeah. And then, when we moved in with Charlie, Charlie was supposed to be in charge of making sure I didn't take too many drugs!! So here we were in the flat, you, me, and Charlie . . . with bags of coke all over the place, and speed all over the fucking joint. The biggest television you've ever seen!!! A God of light, standing in the fucking sitting room! And baseball bats, that we got when we ran out to get a plunger to unblock the bog. And you notice Frank never dared visit that flat! Charlie had obviously told him, 'I'm looking after Shane now, Frank. And you're not coming round to see him. You're gonna leave him alone. And if he gets ill, I'll look after him. And you have nothing to do with this decision.' It's obviously what he did . . . stood up to him. I mean, at the end of the day, Charlie would always stand up to Frank. But the way Phil Lynott used to treat Frank was hysterical. He used to pour drinks over his head, and things like that, while he was just yabbering away. And he'd be like, 'Fuck off, Murray! The best part of you ran down your daddy's leg!'

—**So what did you want from Frank? What would have made you happy?**

—All I wanted off Frank was to be able to run the group the way I wanted it, musically . . . artistically. Which Jem had always left up to me, as well. He'd make suggestions, put in ideas, even write songs. Like, instrumentals, and things . . . good ones, but he left it up to me.

I objected to fucking being told by Frank, 'You're gonna sing "Johnny Come Lately".' When Spider wanted to sing it. 'No, Spider can't sing it. Spider won't be singing that. I decide who sings in this group, and who doesn't!' And then there were people saying that Spider couldn't play the whistle. And this was one of Frank's theories. He wanted me to just do what I was told. And of course, I never would. Because I still believed in the crusade.

The crusade was to make Irish music hip . . . for the Irish music to make the language hip again. And the literature hip. In other words, to build Irish self-esteem, right? And for the whole world to know what an incredible wealth of culture we've contributed to the world, for such a small nation. Also with 'Birmingham Six', I began singing songs about the atrocities by the British. I'd come to the stage where I could get away with that. You know, we were cut off on television during the beginning of a verse, cause they saw, suddenly, that it was about eight IRA who'd been shot by the SAS a few weeks before in Armagh. It wasn't about the Birmingham Six at all, the last verse, you know, 'While over in Ireland, eight more men lie dead. Kicked down and shot in the back of the head.' And like when they heard that, they freaked. And so they put the ads on. And everybody really noticed that. That was around the time we were doing Wembley for the first time. That was the time when I should have walked. But obviously it seemed stupid to me to walk while we were doing Wembley. I thought everything would be all right if we could get rid of Frank, and eventually we did part ways.

If you remember, I was feeling ill that day. Because I was always feeling ill in those days. The pressure of the whole fucking . . . it wasn't the pressure of writing, I could write songs till the cows come home, and play music till the cows come home. But I won't sit in a fucking bus for the whole of my life, going from one shitty gig to another, with no point to it. I'll do a tour of Ireland. I'll do a tour of Germany. I'll do a tour of places where they're really howling out for us, you know. And I'll do a tour of the east coast of America. That's where our following is, on the east coast of America. That's a big following.

I thought from the word go that he didn't really know that much about Irish music. He was a Dubliner. And he knew the Dubliners and stuff like that. And he knew what Phil had told him about it, you know, cause Phil knew a lot about Irish music. Being a black man, he was obsessed with the *The Book of Invasions* and all that. And, you know, the plight of the small farmers. He wrote songs all about things like that. But unfortunately he had an obsession with America. He'd made it! He'd made it . . . he was huge, right. He'd made it all over the world, except for America. He'd made it in England, Ireland, all over Europe. He'd made it twice, two huge hits, 'Whisky in the Jar', which he got publishing on, because he had arranged it. And 'The Boys Are Back in Town', which he got publishing on. And then the album that that came from sold masses. And the album after that.

—You're kind of going off on another tangent.

You know, I want to say now that all the crap about me being a self-destructive person is a load of rubbish. I was a person who had a vision, know what I mean. And a bunch of mates, who I thought all understood that vision. And Spider and Terry did understand it. Jem, I think, wanted to help. Well, he wanted to mix it with bluegrass, and I didn't have any objection, he wanted to see what Irish music would sound like on a bluegrass banjo, being a country music freak. And, you know, country music and Irish music are very similiar in a lot of ways. And the original line-up was a very good line-up of eccentric personalities. And we were pissed every night, out of our nuts when we were on stage. I said there was no way I was gonna go out stone-cold sober, in front of a crowd of drunks. And pretend to be drunk . . .

The thing that really started the legend of the Pogues being drunken, drug-taking scumbags was the Mat Snow piece, in the *NME*. He came along on our first American tour. He wrote about us taking drugs, and getting pissed, and Cait knocking Matt Dillon down a flight of stairs . . . six flights of stairs. And about how Spider could recite the whole of *Once Upon a Time in America*, from beginning to end, right. Four hours long.

—Wow!

—Five hours long, I mean.

—That's pretty impressive.

—Well, Spider had a photographic memory, you know. He only had to see a film a couple of times, and he could recite the whole thing, word perfect. But we were doing variations of it, in New York mafia accents. And we were talking about what we wanted to do to Elvis Costello. And I said we should send Cait his head, with his dick in his mouth. And he was furiously writing all this down. He must've been a really fast writer, y'know. And he must have thought he had a real scoop, know what I mean. And it was really going to upset Costello, and upset us, and all the rest of it. When in fact, it was a fucking brilliant article, you know what I mean, and it was meant to be a put down. But like, he'd done the same thing to Nick Cave, a bit earlier.

—What had he done?

—Well, he spent a lot of time going on about his drug addiction. Hardly mentioned his brilliance, and how he's committed to his poetry, and his music; his charisma, and all that. I think it made him out to be a fucking dirty fucking junkie. Typical fucking journalists! But the more some of them fucking slagged us, for being scumbags, the lowest kind of scum, the more the audience liked us.

The audience already loved us, because we used to fight on stage, and I used to insult them. Me and Spider used to insult them, and we were completely different from all the other bands at the time. And when articles like that came out, every article made the legend bigger. It backfired on us in the end. Because in the end, they never talked about anything except drink. But at the time it helped a lot. The more the press tried to fucking cut us down, the more it helped. And what's more, their racism helped a lot as well. The way they stereotyped us as drunken Paddys, you know what I mean. That really fucking annoyed loads of London-Irish kids, and they came out in force, out of the woodwork. With their Celtic banners, and tricolours, and all the rest of it. And it sort of united the London-Irish population on our side . . . because it was racist, y'know. Because we drank a lot, and were obviously out of it on stage . . . how many bands can you say that about now? Millions, you know.

At the time, you had the whole New Romantic thing, and the whole poofter and a guy with a synthesizer thing . . . you know who I mean, like Soft Cell, and Tears for Fears, and all the rest of it; and we were completely different. The Irish stuff wasn't new to the audience, the rock and roll wasn't new to the audience, but the mixture of the two was. The idea that you could headbang to your mum and dad's old records, to the Dubliners and stuff like that. And so we achieved what I set out to achieve, anyway. I achieved what I set out to, very quickly.

—**What was that?**

—Well, it was to bring Irish music out into the foreground . . . to make it part of popular music again. To make young people realize that in their own backyard there was really good music. And we were playing it. It had to be dragged into the twentieth century, you know what I mean. We just gave it a shot up the arse. We didn't take ourselves seriously at all, but we took the music seriously.

And because it's amazing dance music and we were an amazing dance band, we brought out the dance element in it very strongly. And the slower tunes were amazing emotional, and heart wrenching. And we had drunken yobs crying in the audience, swinging from side to side, and putting their hands up with peace signs and stuff. These were guys who normally beat each other shitless at gigs. Skinheads, psychobillys, punks . . . all getting their hair cut into Paddy quiffs, and getting old suits and white shirts, and turning up at the gigs looking like us. And so the more that the press said, 'They're a bunch of drunken louts who can't play', like the Sex Pistols thing, the more popular we became. The more people came to see us, to see this fucking freakshow. But instead of a freakshow, they came out loving the music, and howling for more. It brought out the animal in people, but it also brought out the soul and the heart in people, cause it hits you in the soul and the heart, in the beat, in the voice, in the intellect . . . all together. Whereas your faggot-with-synthesizer bands only hit the intellect.

Do you know what I mean, only hit the intellect? They were all about angst, and chic, and all of that. All those sort of posey things.

All the sort of things that are produced by the intellect, and the ego. Whereas we hit you in the gut, in the soul, in the heart, and in the beat, like Irish music does. It wasn't art. We weren't brilliant, we were just playing brilliant music. You know what I mean, we weren't that good at it, but we were playing it on rock and roll stages, at rock gigs, to young audiences. And we also appealed to older people, who loved the idea of their sons and daughters listening to the music that they loved. So the mums and dads loved us as well. And the grannies and grandads.

So, we'd not only get rock gigs, we played loads of Irish venues, and ballrooms and weddings, and things like that, where there would be three generations of people digging it. Like, at one gig, a priest introduced us. And we played with the Shillelagh Sisters, in the big hall in front, with the Kennedy picture, in the Camden Irish Centre. That's on the cover of our first album . . . us in front of the picture of Kennedy. And afterwards, the priest thanked us, because it was a charity gig. A priest thanked us and said what a brilliant band we were, and all the rest of it! It's surreal, you know! Spider had beat himself over the head, elbows, and knees with a beer tray, a total of about two hundred times during the gig.

—Why did he do that?

—Because it's a tradtional thing to do, play the beer tray, with your head, your elbows, and your knees. The trouble was, we never got a good beer tray. Cause, you're meant to get a beer tray which is really light, and makes a big crashing noise, that's how it's played. The beer tray is a traditional instrument, you know, like the bones, or the spoons, it's the same kind of concept. People pick up a beer tray and start joining in with the band. Spider also played the whistle, he was a natural on the whistle. But on numbers where we didn't use a whistle, he played the beer tray. But because we never turned up with our own beer tray, we'd just have to get the beer tray from behind the bar, so we always got heavy beer trays that made a dull noise. He'd have to hit himself really hard to get a good crash out of it. And he'd hit himself so hard that he ended up bruised and bloody at the end of the gig, you know. He was convinced that I was making him do it just to take the piss out of him.

—**And were you?**

—No, of course I wasn't. I thought it was a great noise, and I thought it looked great.

—**So it was your idea?**

—Yes it was my idea, yeah. I would've done it myself but I was playing guitar. I stopped playing guitar cause it was difficult to sing and keep time on the guitar – to sing such intense songs – with the sound we had in those days, which was very bad. I was putting off Andy Ranken on the drums a lot of the time, you know what I mean. I am a good rhythm guitarist, but I can't sing and play guitar at the same time. So they sacked me from playing the guitar and brought in Philip Chevron. But that's the problem with a democracy, know what I mean. And then he proceeded to write songs as well. But that's later. I offered to play the beer tray, cause I didn't want to stand and just sing, know what I mean. I'm a musician. So, I offered to play the beer tray, but the democracy decided that we had outgrown the beer tray.

—**Yeah?**

—That it wasn't a progressive move. That it was a reactionary move to bring back the beer tray. I might pick up the beer tray now that I'm a dictator. Now that I'm like, my own man, with a backing band, I can do what I want. I might go and get myself a really good beer tray, and you know, get into playing the beer tray.

—**Why not?**

—Yeah. I just keep forgetting to do it.

—**Tell about that time you took up the bodhran, that was funny.**

—I took up the bodhran, and I played it perfectly well. I mean, after being sacked on guitar, I wasn't into just standing there singing. I didn't want to do all rock and roll poses and jump around either. At the end of the set I did jump around and smash up the mic and all that, because I'd get really angry, cause all the songs at the end are sort of heavy. Very fast, but with heavy lyrics. But apart from that, I just got stuck standing there, know what I mean. So I started playing the bodhran. I played the bodhran for about a year.

—**And you used to break all the bodhrans.**

—I use to break one practically every night. Eventually . . .

—**I remember you playing it with your head.**

—I used to do all sorts of things with it. I didn't just stand there, in the end, I used to fucking change water into wine, or I used to pretend to crucify people, I used to bless the crowd, I used to do stupid dances . . .

—**Yeah, the stupid dances were good.**

—I used to do battering. A lot of battering, cause I was better at it than I am now. I'd like to get back into that, but I've got a dead leg now. For anybody who doesn't know, battering is improvised Irish dancing, like furious tap dancing, where you batter with your feet on the floor. It's done generally by men. And you put your hands against your sides, like in regular Irish dancing, but you don't follow any set steps. You turn around and jump up in the air and stuff like that. The main thing is that you batter in time, you have to batter your feet in time to the music. It's like, exhausting, but it's really fun. And if you get it right, it makes a really good form of percussion, you know, using your body as a percussion instrument. And there are masters of battering, in Ireland. Generally older men, cause it's starting to die out, unfortunately. And they have competitions for the best improviser, and the most exciting batterer. So I use to batter when I didn't have anything else to play.

The bodhran got phased out, because they had decided that I wasn't playing it well enough. I was playing it well enough, I played it very simply, and I wet it, because you're supposed to wet it before you play it. I was quite serious about it, you know. But the democracy, in the end, decided I wasn't allowed to play the bodhran any more.

Then I got really angry, and started playing the bazouka. Had another go at rhythm guitar, for a while. Then I started playing the banjo which really pissed off Jem, who was the banjo player. I started playing rhythm banjo, and I did that perfectly well. But they all . . . for some reason got phased out. In the end I played a Casio on stage, this was when I really didn't give a fuck any more, when the music had gotten so far away from what I wanted to do that all I was interested in was fucking them up.

So I used to play a Casio which made gun noises. And in the middle of solos by Terry Woods, or Jem, or whoever, I would start making gun noises, and fucking playing out of key and all the rest of it. Obviously the democracy didn't put up with that for very long. So I was always meaning to get a beer tray, but I never got around to it. I'm not very good at getting round to things like that, know what I mean, and like, nobody was gonna help me by going out and getting me a beer tray, cause the last thing they wanted was me playing the beer tray. But when Spider played the beer tray he was brilliant at it. And in the early days we were sensational on stage, what with the beer tray and fighting about what song to do next.

—**Didn't you find it odd that you all started off getting on so well and then ended up having such terrible relationships.**

—Of course I did. I mean, we were good friends. That just shows you – never work with friends. And like, we were all pretty grown up, or so I thought, so I didn't think that egomania would be a problem. But it became a problem. And the main trouble was that unlike the others, I wasn't interested in progression.

—**Progression?**

—Yeah.

—**How do you mean?**

—I wasn't interested in progression.

—**You mean, you weren't interested in changing.**

—That's right. I was interested in getting better at playing the music, and I was interested in being more adventurous in my songwriting, like using the influences of O'Carolan, and Sean O'Casey, which I did in 'Body of an American' and 'Broad Majestic Shannon'. A bit more intricate, a bit mellower . . . not mellower but a bit more – I don't know what the word is. They didn't progress from Irish music but they went from being straight headbangers and straight ballads to being like sort of . . . mini-Irish symphonies. You know what I mean? I know that sounds a bit pretentious, but things like 'Fairytale of New York' and 'Rainy Night in Soho'. I suppose the first one like that was 'Pair of Brown Eyes'. With lots of melodic and the weaving tunes . . .

> My name is O'Carolan
> Can you feel my proud heart?
> I'm known to the wise
> As the Irish Mozart.
> I played for the great lords
> I played what I chose.
> And I lived and I died
> By the side of the road.

But that's all a part of Irish music anyway. We started off playing the very basic stuff. That was enough progression for me. I didn't want to move away from Irish music, I didn't want to progress into some kind of mutation of Irish music. And they did. They all thought they were brilliant musicians now, and that they should be playing something more sophisticated than Irish music. Which was a terrific arrogance I thought, because you can't get any more sophisticated than Irish music. I mean it's been going for a few thousand years and it's as sophisticated as it needs to be. Considering that it's heart music, soul music . . . not classical music, or progressive rock.

They were trying to turn it into progressive rock. It was getting louder and louder, and more electric. More sort of rock solos in it. Songs the others were writing, we were doing more of them, and they didn't have anything to do with the basic Irish roots of it, know what I mean. I was becoming less professional, if that was possible, cause I was never professional in the first place. And they were trying to be professionals, I wasn't interested in being professional, I was interested in being real, you know what I mean. That's what got us where we got . . . by not being professional, but by being real. The same as the audience. Having one big party with the audience. To them it was a show.

—So you were never putting on a show, personally?

WHO DARES TO SPEAK OF
          DONEGAL
~~████~~ GET KICKS IN BARS
     AND IN THE BALLS
THE HARP THAT PLAYED
     IN TARA'S HALLS
IS BURNING ON THE DUMP
VIRGININIA IS A GIN TOWN
BELTURBOT IS A SIN TOWN
~~████~~ ALL THE BOYS
     FROM SKINTOWN
ARE IN ENGLAND ON THE
          LUMP
GOT PISSED IN LETTERKENNY
WITH DARLIN SPORTIN JENNY
SPENT ME VERY LAST PENNY

THE HURSBAND CAUGHT ME ②
IN THE BED
TRIED TO SHOOT ME IN THE
HEAD
I HAD TO SWIM THE STREAM
TO GET
THE DONEGAL EXPRESS

AS SURE AS I'M FR EMMETT
I'VE A KING DONG DOWN ME
                SEMMETT
AS ANY GIRL WILL TELL YOU
FROM CAVAN DOWN TO CLARE
BACK IN SWEET VIRGINIA
IN THE TOILET WITH LAVINIA
I NEARLY FUCKED HER BRAINS
                    OUT
AND TORE HER PARTY DRESS
A SHIT A SHAVE A SHOWER
A HALF # A PINT OF POWERS
THEN OFF AGAIN TO GET ON
        BOARD THE
            DONEGAL EXPRESS

—Nah, I've never put on a show! I just do what I do. I get up and sing songs. And to me, the audience . . . the buzz comes from the audience, and goes through me and goes back to the audience like a cycle, you know. Like without adrenaline from the audience, I don't have any adrenaline. And then my adrenaline picks up, and goes into the audience and gives them more adrenaline. Then it comes back into me, and gives me more adrenaline. So the adrenaline builds up and it gets more and more exciting and cathartic as the gig goes on.

—**And that's not a show?**

—No, it's a totally natural thing that happens.

—**Right.**

—It's not a show, no.

—**So, you're not a performer really.**

—I'm an entertainer, yeah. I mean it's a show in the sense that we're playing music. But I mean the audience are as interesting as us, know what I mean. I always thought that they had as much power as us to make a gig. It was a big party . . .

—**So it was more like a session?**

—Yeah, like a session, with loads . . . with hundreds of people. Thousands of people.

—**And what was the difference between that and what the Pogues wanted to do?**

—They wanted to put on a show, and be all professional, and make shapes and be big egomaniac rock stars, know what I mean? They had contempt for the audience, they were gonna play what they wanted to play, not what the audience wanted to hear. I used to get requests shouted by half the audience, and I'd have to shrug and go, 'We don't play it any more. We don't know it any more.' I was totally honest. I said it over the microphone, 'They can't play it any more.' Cause we hadn't played it for a while, and they couldn't remember things without rehearsing them. So like, sometimes I'd insist on doing an old number again, because there was so much shouting for it, know what I mean. And sometimes I'd get my way, but we'd have to rehearse it, y'know, we couldn't do it on the spot. I always wanted us to have a rehearsed repertoire, seeing as rehearsal was so important to them . . . And it was ridiculous, because if I forgot one word, the whole thing would grind to a halt.

—Why's that?

—Because they did everything by numbers, know what I mean! If I missed the fucking line, the whole thing would grind to a halt, instead of just playing on, round and round, you know, like natural musicians. They'd grind to a halt and I'd have fucked up the number by missing a line. I mean, the band I've got now, they play naturally, organically. So if I miss a line they just keep playing, then I come back in, y'know. I come in where I feel like it . . . when I get my balance back. And that is really professional, that is. Their idea of professional was being rehearsed like a machine. And doing everything by numbers, you know, counting everything. I'm not saying Terry Woods used to count everything, or even Andy. There were really good musicians in the band who didn't need to count everything. But there were lots of bad musicians in the band, even ones that appeared good, like James, was a good accordion player, but he wasn't a good . . . well, if you liked the sort of crap that he played . . . he didn't play Irish stuff, really. He used to annoy the shit out of me, the way he played, but like . . . he could play by numbers. He was a dots man, he could read music. He was a piano player, who played the accordion. So we ended up with mutual hatred, you know.

—Did it make you sad?

—It made me bewildered and sad, yeah. I didn't lose sleep over it, though, I was too busy being angry, and getting out of it, and fucking up the shows. I used to go into a rage some nights, I was so angry with everything. If I entered into this rage, everything was all right because it seemed like everything was going fine because I'd really put it across and it would be a dynamic gig, but if I was feeling self-pity and sadness, then I'd just drink myself stupid and all sorts of things could happen, like I could forget the words for the whole set, I could fall over on stage, I could suddenly find myself standing on the stage with my trousers around my ankles, that happened to me a few times. Quite a few times I was led off or carried off, not knowing where I was or what was happening.

—I remember. Charlie had to carry you off.

—Yeah, I felt very ashamed when that happened, I felt like I was ripping off the audience and I'm still very sorry that I did it but I think it should be taken into consideration, the incredible stress I was under and how it all seemed to be such a dead end.

I did my best to fucking deal with the situation, know what I mean. Even though every night I felt sick before I went on stage because I really didn't want to do it any more. There was no empathy between me and the band, it wasn't fun. We had a countdown before we went on stage and everyone did the same things every night, Spider doing his little routines, the same set every night, it was just like acting. We were totally against the flow.

And I think it's possible for a band to be successful without falling into that trap. Look at the Faces. The Faces were always untogether, drunk, playing the wrong chords, starting the wrong songs, even when they were playing in front of huge crowds in America. They never got too serious about themselves. And we were serious about ourselves. I wasn't into that. That was the last thing I was into. I could have kept it together though, if we hadn't fucking toured so much and it hadn't become no fun doing it. If something is no fun to do, but you're doing it all the time, what the hell are you doing it for? It was my livelihood, but I knew that I made more out of publishing than I did out of touring, so it wasn't the money, it was more out of a sense of responsibility that I kept on doing it, feeling that we'd all started out together, so we should stay together until we'd really cracked it. But I would never put myself in that situation again. I know the various mental stages I went through to get into that situation. The loneliness and paranoia. I experienced a lot of loneliness and paranoia, because everyone's in a bad mood all the time. Because everybody was fucked up and shagged out and overworked, but most people didn't even realize it. I was always saying it. It wears you down and takes away whatever inspiration you had from the music.

—**How long did that go on?**

—I suppose, the last three years, or something like that.

—**So when do you think was the turning point?**

—After 'If I Should Fall From Grace with God' really. After we had peaked with 'If I Should Fall From Grace with God' and 'Fairytale of New York'. That's when the big-headedness got worse. I guess they started thinking, 'He's making lots of money out of these songs', you know, 'We want to write songs'. Which is disastrous, you know. Because I write simple songs, know what I mean, with a melody and a beat, and lyrics. But if there was a hint of a reggae beat, they'd go over the top and play it reggae style, know what I mean. And that was their idea of progression. They were trying to divorce themselves from the Irish thing. They saw it as a limitation.

—**You vary it a bit, don't you, on your albums? Well, actually, you didn't vary too much on the last one.**

—No I didn't. And that's why it's one of the best ones I made, the last one. And I don't vary much on any of the good ones. When you vary it, it means you don't know what you're doing.

—**Yeah, but there was a period when you had like, a rockabilly track, a jazz track, an experimental track, and Irish traditional . . .**

—Yeah on *The Snake*, which is a crappy album in that respect.

—**But on a lot of the Pogues albums you varied . . .**

—That wasn't my fault, you know, that was the rest of them, putting their fucking oar in.

—**But even you used to write some stuff which . . . Like 'Fiesta'. I'm not saying there's anything wrong with 'Fiesta', but you know what I mean, you did have more varied musical styles all on one album.**

—I've always hated 'Fiesta', you know.

—**Have you?**

—Yeah. Your classic droning slow track, or your classic 'bippity, boppity, bippity, boppity, diddle-ee-didely-ee' stuff is what I do. That's what I do. That's all I do. I either do slow romantic ballads, or I do loud, fast, raucous, piss-artist songs, full of swear words and sexual innuendo, and . . . no, not even sexual innuendo, just fucking blatant fucking sexual obscenity. I go straight for the jugular, 'Come here, you fuck, come hell or high water. I might have fucked your missus, but I never fucked your daughter'. And like, 'A roving, a roving, a roving I'll go, for a pair of brown eyes', that's my slow-type song. Do you know what I mean? And that's what you get. That's what you get when you get a Shane MacGowan album. Like, some of the arty things I had to do when I was in the Pogues, I won't be held responsible for.

—Like what?

—Like 'Fiesta'.

—**But you did mess around with Spanishy stuff.**

—On *Hell's Ditch*, I couldn't write any Irish stuff.

—**No?**

—No.

—**Why not?**

—I just wasn't in the mood, and they wanted an album, you know. So I wrote some rock. And you know I don't like straight rock, so I put some Spanish influences in it. 'Summer in Siam', and stuff like that.

—**That's a good one, 'Summer in Siam'.**

—Yeah, it's a good one, yeah. But I wouldn't have put that out under the label of the Pogues, you know. I would have put that out as a solo single. It's a good track, I mean, it's a lot better than the stuff they wrote. It's a good track, but they fucked it up, you know. That was meant to be one verse, just one verse.

—**And that's it?**

—Yeah, and that's it, just the, 'When it's summer in Siam . . .' Just one verse, then . . .

—**Then that's the end?**

—Then that's the end. That's what it was meant to be.

—**It's like a musical haiku?**

—Yeah, a musical haiku, yeah. Well, not really a haiku, cause a haiku has only got three lines, but I know what you're getting at. Like 'Jonesburgh Illinois', by Tom Waits, just four lines, just four short lines. You only need to say it once. Everybody gets the message. You have the rippling piano at the beginning, and a rippling piano at the end. You set the mood, and then it's over. But they fucking insisted on stringing it out and putting a saxophone solo in it, and all the rest of it. It's like 'Five Green Queens and Jean' – it's the same. That was meant to be just like, four verses. Sung dead straight. With just an acoustic guitar. But they insisted on putting on a mambo beat to it, or some kind of bloody beat to it. Musos, you know.

—So there was a huge . . .

—Chasm between us.

—Yeah.

—Between what I was trying to do, and what they were trying to do.

—So why didn't you just get a different band?

—We'd been a long way together, we were supposed to be friends, you know.

—What's that got to do with it?

—Well, look . . . we were at the height of our success, it wouldn't have made sense to break up.

—Wouldn't it?

—Well, it didn't seem to make sense at the time.

—What kind of sense did it not make? Economically?

—Musically, we did achieve what we set out to achieve, but financially we didn't. We set out to popularize Irish music, make it into popular music. And financially we wanted to make it big, because we thought we deserved to. And we were on the way to making it after the third album and then we fucked up. Put out the wrong single after 'Fairytale of New York'. I wanted to put out 'Broad Majestic Shannon', but they wouldn't. That would have made me a pile and it would have made the group a pile. Of course there was always a lot of backbiting about that, too: they resented the fact that I was richer than they were. They used to say, 'It's all very well for you to not want to tour, you've got the publishing.' That was another excuse.

—When did you stop enjoying the whole process?

—I suppose . . . well, I was already pissed off to fuck with touring by the time we did 'Fairytale of New York'. I gradually started hating it. It didn't happen all at once, you know. It was a gradual thing, I didn't notice it was happening till it was too late.

—Why were you pissed off with touring?

—I didn't like touring.

—**You liked it in the beginning.**

—I liked it in the beginning, yeah, cause it was a novelty, you know.

—**So why did you stop liking it?**

—Because it's like, when you start eating chocolate, it's nice, but if you're force-fed it, it's sickening, you know what I mean?

—**So what was it about touring that you didn't like?**

—It was like being back at school, or in jail!

—**How?**

—I was bossed around! I was in a bus with loads of other blokes! I missed you! I missed fucking being at home with my mates. I missed fucking . . . the quality of life. There was no quality of life. I had this money, but all I could do was spend it on drink on the road. To blot out reality. It wasn't fun any more. I kept on asking for a year off or something. We could have afforded to take a year off. It wouldn't have killed us, you know. We had to tour after 'Fairytale of New York', yeah, but we didn't have to tour for fucking four years after it. We'd got there, we played Wembley Stadium. We hadn't broken America. That was the thing, y'know, we HAD to break America. So we endlessly toured in America. And I hated it. I hated America, you know.

—**Why did you hate America?**

—It's too big. It's full of idiots. It's like . . . it's soulless, y'know. I mean, I'm not saying the American people are . . . I'm talking about WASPs, you know. The Midwest, and the South, and all those horrible places that there are in America. If we had been playing to black audiences it might have been different, you know, but we weren't.

—**What about your Irish-American friends?**

—The Irish-American fans were great, you know. I always loved playing New York, Boston, even Chicago, know what I mean, yeah. But that was the Irish-American area. If we had concentrated on the Irish-American area, which would have made sense . . . we could've broken it, and they would've . . . well, at least we would have broken that part of America, you know what I mean. It was ridiculous to try and break the whole of America by touring. I knew it couldn't be done by touring. I had countless arguements with the band, and with Frank about it.

When we made one really dodgy album, *Peace and Love*, I started to really lose heart, I didn't think there was a way out. And that was confirmed by making a real dog of an album, *Hell's Ditch*, after that, compared to the first three alblums where I was in control. I had to really fight for control on the third album. It was already slipping, but I was fighting for control, I was still trying to keep control of the situation. Trying to salvage it, you know. But after *Peace and Love*, and all the squabbles about publishing money . . . they started hating me before I started hating them.

—**Why did they hate you?**

—Because I made more money than them, because I wrote the majority of the songs. And I was always out of it.

—**That must have been a big reason.**

—Yeah, it was a big reason. But I mean, in the early days we were all always out of it, you know?

—**Yeah.**

—We were all always out of it. Didn't do any harm. That was what people wanted. People didn't want another bunch of straights, playing 'world music'. People wanted the Pogues, which was a bunch of rowdy, out-of-it nutters playing headbanging Irish music. That was the stuff that got them going, you know. We could ponce around all we liked and get a mild reception for it, but it was only when we did the old favourites in the end – or when we did my new headbangers – that the crowd went nuts. We were meant to be a dance band, who also played emotional ballads. And they were trying to turn it into an intellectual thing.

But I still say half of *Peace and Love* is all right. The production is sort of . . . fenced in . . . but like half of it's all right. The half I wrote! I think we lost a lot of our original audience as we moved away from the original idea . . . I think they put up with the crap, so they could hear the good stuff, you know. And when a band has reached sort of legendary proportions, the audience will put up with just about anything. I mean, look at fucking Van Morrison. I mean honestly . . . look at Van Morrison, he could do anything . . . turns out really shitty gigs, you know what I mean. Boring, self-indulgent, too long . . . and people love it, because in their minds, he's playing 'Astral Weeks', or 'Moondance'.

And I still tried . . . I mean, I was still a crazy man on stage on a good night, you know what I mean.

—Yeah.

—I didn't do that many bum gigs. That was grossly overreported that, you know. But I did do a few. And like, the band expected perfection. The audience was far more forgiving.

—When did you start getting ill?

—It was the touring that made me ill. It was a bit after *Peace and Love*, I suppose. America was where I started getting ill. I always got ill in America. A fifty-two-date tour. Not eating properly. Psychosomatic I think it was, as well. I just wanted to be at home. Night after night after night, repeating the same routine. I felt like I was acting. I felt like I was faking, you know. I felt like the audience could see through it. So I got really paranoid. And I knew the band had nothing but contempt for me.

—For you?

—Yeah. So I didn't have any sort of backing from behind.

—Why did you not just quit?

—Because I'm an idiot. I'm a sucker for emotional blackmail, you know. Not any more I'm not, but then – I still thought of them as my friends, even though I knew they hated me. I tried to leave again and again and they just bawled and begged and said I couldn't leave them, you know, I'd brought them this far and it wasn't fair to just abandon them now. They really laid it on thick, as if I dragged them away from well-paid jobs, but I hadn't, some people were on the dole and some people had really lousy jobs, when we started. I had the best job, I was the one who sacrificed the best job, the best job I ever had, working in a collectors' record shop where I got paid just to play a collection of two thousand records and take my pick and sell them to people. That was the best job I ever had and I can never get it back and that sort of makes me feel sad.

I'm not going to say I'm self-sacrificing, or anything like that, though. I'd become institutionalized into touring with that group. I couldn't imagine a life where there would be no touring. I had sort of resigned myself to the fact that we would go on for ever. Like a prisoner, you know. It was all in my mind, obviously. I could have quit at any time. I didn't need to tour, I had plenty of money. And in the back of my mind, I'd always hoped there would be another hit, you know, another hit album. But I knew that would never happen after *Hell's Ditch*. Only God knows why I wasted all those years on the road. I'm frightened of change, and I knew it was going to be a big change, if I left. And it sort of frightened me in a way.

—**What did you think might happen?**

—I didn't know. And that's why I'm frightened of change.

—**Don't you have much faith?**

—In what?

—**Well, in things working out, generally?**

—I do now. I didn't then. I'm a lot stronger a person than I was. So many catastrophes that are made up in my head turn out to be nothing, you know what I mean.

—**Like what?**

—Well, I'm always thinking of . . . you know, every tiny problem turns into a massive catastrophe in my mind.

—**Why?**

—I don't know. I've got a terrible imagination, know what I mean, that blows things out of proportion.

—**Is that like, kind of a double-edged sword? Cause can't you use that to write songs too?**

—Yeah. I suppose that's the flip side of having an active imagination.

—**It's that you can imagine awful things too.**

—Yeah, I do imagine awful things, you know. Give me a simple problem, and I'll fucking turn it into a catastrophe in a matter of minutes.

—I've seen that. But then, if you're aware of that, surely you could, you know, modify it.

—I have modified it. But like, at the time I wasn't aware of it. My imagination was my reality. Remember, I was divorced from reality. Whenever you're on the road you lose touch with reality. The road, and the situation you're in, is the only reality there is. You're in a nightmare if you're not enjoying it. But you can't get out of it, any more than you can get out of a nightmare when you're asleep. All you've got to do is wake up! But you can't wake up in nightmares, you can't make yourself wake up. All I had to do was put myself outside the situation. Look at it and see that it was going nowhere, see that I was wasting my life, see that they were wrong, and I was right, see that they were fucking using me, taking the piss out of me. The friends I had in the end were the road crew. A lot of it was to do with the road crew. I got on with the road crew so well that I didn't want to leave them.

—But surely they could've left too.

—Well, I didn't know that our road crew was gonna leave and come with me, did I? Which is what happened in the end. It took a good while, though. I don't want to carry on talking about those things.

—No?

—So, nowadays I go out there drunk enough to have a good time, but not too drunk to fuck it up. But I only ever started fucking it up when I started hating what we were doing. It never broke me, though, because my vision had been achieved, I thought. I thought Irish music was safe, for at least another ten or twenty years, which was completely wrong.

When *The Snake* came out, I was ashamed of it. I'm not ashamed of it any more. There's some great songs on it. And some totally irreverent versions of old Irish songs which I personally find grating to the ear, but I knew would go down very well with headbangers. And that's great, you know what I mean, it's a party album. But there's more to it than that. Like one song has been covered by Christy Moore, 'Aisling', one of the serious love songs. And then there's my other song about you, 'Victoria', where we managed to recreate the Thin Lizzy dual guitar sound. I was pretty proud of doing that. I did that. I wrote the song. I conducted them while they played in the studio. And then ZTT totally lost interest and things just choked to a halt. And then we had a disastrous attempt to make *Crock of Gold*.

One more thing about Frank. Frank and Charlie worked in the same bands a lot. That's how they got to know each other. But Charlie always had rank over Frank. Frank was just a roadie, and Charlie was the tour manager. So it'd be, 'Oi, Frank, you get that guitar, you do this, you do that,' you know. 'Get me a cup of tea.' I suspect he desperately wanted to be a rock star, Frank. So I feel sorry for him, in a way.

Of course, six months later they sacked me. But I'd already had the first line-up of my new band together by the time they sacked me. We'd already been rehearsing, me, Mo and Bernie, and all of them.

Anyway, I had a nervous breakdown when *The Crock of Gold* went straight into the bin.

The *Twentieth Century Paddy* album is the most political one yet. It's the story of the twentieth century. It's not deep, high-brow political stuff, it's humorous or tragic, or whatever, it's . . . what I've always done. We're gonna be expanding the sound, and everything. And I'm gonna use the RTE Orchestra. We call it in Ireland the RTE 'Ork'. So I'm not gonna lose sleep.

Basically, I've been all the way up there. And it's fucking great up there, you know what I mean. And I've spent it, and I've spent it, and I've spent it and spent it, and there was always more. And I'm going to be back in the same position in about six months. But I see now that there's no point in Ireland getting the six counties back, if Irish culture has been totally forgotten and destroyed. That will have meant that they've won in the end. So I'm going to try and get involved as much as I can. I'm going to re-learn Irish, and spend as much time in Ireland as I can.

I met lots of Irish people in America, who think they can't go back to Ireland, because they're thinking of Ireland twenty years ago. They're thinking, 'The farm won't support me', know what I mean.

25 DECEMBER 1986
A HAPPY XMAS WITH A
            SPEEDBALL FIX
IN TIPPERARY AND WHEN
I GROW OLD
I THINK I'LL FIND IT
            THERE
THE CROCK OF GOLD

BUT I'LL KEEP SEARCHING
    FOR A CROCK OF GOLD
I'LL KEEP ON SEARCHING
FOR A CROCK OF GOLD
I WANT THE WOMAN
AND I WANT THE DOUGH →

DOWN THE DIRTY OLD STREET
THE ANGEL OF THE EAST IS
                    CALLING
AND WITH A TREMBLING HAND
I OPEN UP A CAN
I CAN HEAR A BABY BAWLING
BEFORE I OPEN UP MY EYES
~~────────────────────~~

I CAN FEEL HER THERE INSIDE
                         ME
BUT THEN I REALISE MY GIRL
        WITH GREEN EYES
IS NO LONGER ~~THERE~~
                    BESIDE ME
        _____
VICTORIA LEFT ME IN OPIUM
                 EUPHORIA
WITH A FAT MONK ~~────────~~
               SAYING A GLORIA
MY GIRL WITH GREEN EYES

ONLY YOU SEE THAT I AM LAZY
DON'T CARE ABOUT FAME
NOR MONEY LIKE A CHILD
AND I'M JUST LIKE A CHILD
THAT'S FORGOTTEN HOW TO SMILE
ALL THE PEOPLE ARE SO BUSY
I HAVE NOTHING TO BOTHER
                        ABOUT
IT SEEMS THAT I AM DIFFERENT
SEEMS THAT I AM STRANGE
I'M A BUMPKIN I'M A LOUT

SOMEDAY I KNOW
   I'LL PUT MY PIPE AWAY AND
                  HIT THE ROAD
HOWEVER FAR AWAY I HAVE TO
TO FIND MY GIRL WITH GREEN
                        EYES

They don't know that their fucking brothers are driving around in Maseratis now. But they have every right to fucking go back there, and live in their own fucking houses. And jobs are easy to get now. There's lots of money, jobs are easy to get, it's a rich country now, know what I mean. Even the small farmers, even if they don't do a stroke of work on their small farms they're being subsidized, and they're getting money from Europe. The Irish are getting paid to just sit in the pub and drink, you know, by Europeans. And the English are selling their gold, just to survive.

—**Don't you think you might be exaggerating slightly?**

—No.

—**Okay.**

The scorching sun sinks its weary way down behind a sumptuous and palatial motel, and a cool breeze, gently, displaces a somewhat isolated palm tree, as evening creeps up upon our hero and heroine. Clutching their travelling bags, they disembark, once again, and skip, eagerly, onwards, flushed with the efforts of their journey together and with anticipation of the motel's awaiting hospitality. We suggest, reader, that a cocktail might be appropriate at this point, for you, as our couple take a break and curl up in their luxurious penthouse, to watch television and similarly to ease away the worries of the day.

ACT SIX

First-class cabin, transatlantic aircraft, evening. A fierce and diminutive air-hostess approaches our couple, as they recline in their comfy armchairs, languidly. She eyes Shane's nose, suspiciously, as blood drips from it, copiously. Moments later, another stewardess approaches, determinedly, and requests that Shane and Victoria disembark the aircraft, immediately. The couple do so, indignantly, and find themselves back in the airport lounge, unexpectedly. Shane lights a cigarette, defiantly, and is asked to put it out, swiftly. Victoria sighs, resignedly.

—I think the stewardess thought your nose was bleeding because of coke.

—I don't give a fuck what she thought. I'm going to sue the bastards.

—Well, I'm sick of being thrown off airplanes.

—Are you taking their side?

—No, I'm just saying . . .

—Are you saying they're right?

—I just think that maybe if you looked more normal, we wouldn't get hassled so much, that's all.

—Look, I wasn't doing anything wrong, all right? THEY are the fascists.

Victoria frowns, irritably.

—All right. I know. Shall we change the subject? We haven't talked about writers yet, what do you think of Beckett?

Shane grins, suddenly.

—Yeah, I'll talk about Beckett. The reason why he's such a depressing, miserable bastard, so unlike any other Irish writer – cause any of the other Irish writers got some humour in them at least, y'know? I mean you could say Beckett had humour in him, but it's such black humour that it doesn't count as Irish humour, y'know?

—**Right.**

—So, the reason why he's such a miserable fat old bastard is because he wanted to play cricket for Ireland when he was a kid. And like, Ireland have got the worst cricket team in the world. Although they did beat the West Indies in 1954, y'know.

—**Which isn't bad going, is it?**

—Which wasn't bad going, no, but a real flash in the pan.

—**Yeah.**

—An exceptional year for Irish cricket. But they'd never beaten anybody else, y'know.

—**No.**

—And like, if I wanted to play cricket . . . if I had to shoulder the ambition of wanting to play cricket for Ireland, I'd be a miserable, fucked-up old cunt like Beckett as well.

—**Yeah.**

—Yeah.

—**Would you not just have gone ahead and done it?**

—What? Gone ahead and played cricket for Ireland?

—**Yeah.**

—Yeah, I would've gone ahead and done it, if I really wanted to.

—**So why didn't he?**

—Cause his family talked him out of it, know what I mean. He was a mollycoddled little git from Foxrock.

—**Was he?**

—Well, he wasn't mollycoddled, his family were all mad, y'know. His family were all mad, but he was very . . . he was a West Brit, y'know. Only West Brits play cricket for Ireland anyway. You don't get fucking Kerry men playing cricket for Ireland.

—**Maybe that's why they don't have a very good cricket team.**

—Of course it is, yes, but it's just not an Irish game. It's not the sort of game that Irish people are prepared to watch. When the Irish team are playing at home, there's nobody there, y'know. There's nobody fucking there cheering them on. Irish people aren't interested in cricket.

—No.

—But Samuel Beckettt was interested in cricket. So no wonder he ended up writing the most depressing plays ever written, and the most depressing books ever written, y'know.

—Do you like any of them?

—Yeah, I like *Malone Dies*.

—Why?

—Cause it's funny. Have you finished it yet?

—No. I couldn't get past the first couple of pages.

—You couldn't get past the first couple of pages?! Why, just cause it's stream of consciousness?

—No. I've read other stream of consciousness stuff that I like.

—It's very lightweight stream of consciousness.

—It just didn't grab me at all. Anyway . . .

—Did you get what was happening? There's an old man in a bed, with a piece of paper and a pencil, right, writing a story. And he knows he's dying, yeah. Which is a typical Beckett scenario, y'know, oh wow, great, yeah, lots of laughs in that! But he actually manages to squeeze out a few light laughs out of it, in *Malone Dies*, but that's the only book he manages . . . and there's a book called *More Pricks than Kicks*. Which is his first novel. Which was really funny. I mean, he's got a sense of humour, he just obviously hasn't got a sense of humour about cricket, y'know. And I don't blame him, cause if I was an Irish cricket supporter, I wouldn't have a sense of humour about cricket either. I mean it's all right to be an Irish rugby supporter, but like, that's not a totally West Brit game.

—Can we talk about Yeats?

—Well, Yeats was an old fairy, wasn't he?

—I thought he was in love with Maud Gonne McBride?

—Yeah! And have you seen the state of her face?! She's an ugly fucking cow! All the women he loved were fucking ugly bitches.

—Really?

—Yeah. And he wasn't into sexual love, he was into fucking kindred spirits, and like twinning of the intellects, you know what I mean, and all this shit.

—I've found a picture of her and she's not ugly. She's beautiful!

—Yeah, well, basically he fancied Hyde just as much as he fancied Maud Gonne, know what I mean. And it took him twenty-two years to write a poem about Roger Casement. Who was hanged, under the shadow of being a homosexual, by the Brits, to really fucking stick the nail in after the Sixteen Rising, know what I mean. Hung for being a traitor, because they regarded him as an Englishman for being a knight. And like, hung for being a homosexual, y'know like, not good enough to stand up and be shot like a man. Because they were trying to make out that he was a fairy, know what I mean. And it's all . . . people have researched it, and now people know that it wasn't true, that he wasn't a homosexual. Not that it matters. There's no law against homosexuals in the IRA, y'know.

—No.

—He was the man that got the guns over for the Sixteen Rising. And like, it took Yeats twenty-two years to write a pathetic poem about him. I mean, Yeats is like an Irish Wordsworth, y'know. There's sort of like, a few classics, right, but there's a mammoth amount of work. You know, there's like books and books and books of his stuff, and there's about three or four good poems.

—And what are they?

—What the good poems?

—Yeah.

—Uhmm . . . well not 'Roger Casement' for a start: 'Come speak your bit in public. Let some amends be made, to this most galant gentleman. Who is in quick lime, laid'. That's all he could come up with for Roger Casement!

—'Come all ye merry gentleman . . . let . . .' something. Is that the same?

—That's a Christmas carol.

—Yeah, that's it!

—[Sings] 'God rest ye merry gentlemen . . .'

—Yeah, that's it!! It's the same.

—Yeah, I guess, it is the same rhythm, yeah. So he used 'God rest ye merry gentlemen', y'know. Well, the good ones are, 'An Irish Airman Forsees his Death', and 'The Dancing Days are Gone', and 'I Am of Ireland', that's a good one.

—'I Am of Ireland'?

—Yeah.

—I think that's a really silly one, that.

—Nah, well, it's got a great lilt to it, y'know. [Recites] 'I am of Ireland. The holy land of Ireland. Time runs uncried she. Come out in charity. Come dance with me in Ireland.' It's only bits that are good. He goes on about his golden jug, and silver bag . . . y'know. There's bits where you can see the channelling coming through, y'know, the channelling comes through. When he channelled, he was good, but he didn't channel enough. He spent too much time thinking, to be a great poet. He didn't channel enough, he didn't just let his mind go blank, and let the thoughts come, you know. He was always thinking about Plato and crap like that. He talks about Plato, know what I mean?! Fuck me! Like we all didn't know Plato was basically just some Greek cunt. He had a bunch of tight-bunned little boys, and he philosophized about it.

—Why do you reckon that Yeats is so highly regarded? I mean he's supposed to be Ireland's most famous poet.

—He is Ireland's most famous poet, unfortunately.

—Why?

—Because he's Ireland's least Irish poet. He fooled a lot of the Irish people a lot of the time, but he fooled the rest of the people all of the time. The rest of the people all thought, 'Oh, this is Irish poetry. Oh, Yeats is Irish poetry.'

—So why isn't it Irish poetry?

—Because it's all about Plato, and the fucking swans in Coole Park, and stuff like that. It's like I said, him and Douglas Hyde.

—Tell us the story of Douglas Hyde. You'd better say who Douglas Hyde was, in case people don't know.

—Yeah. There was something called the Celtic Dawn, at the end of the nineteenth century, when all the Anglo-Irish got into preserving the Irish culture. Yeats was into it as well, before he got into all that other twisted new-age shit that he got into, and then into fascism, in the end. You know he ended up being a fascist in the end? So that's another thing I've got against the guy. He broadcasted for the Blueshirts.

ANYWAY, Douglas Hyde was a Roscommon vicar's son, right, a Protestant. And he knew Irish. He could speak Irish, properly, fluently – like a native, because of all the people who lived around him . . . he was in a deserted vicarage with his dad and his mum and a couple of sisters or brothers or something, and he used to go out and play with the locals. And they taught him Irish. Because in Roscommon, at the end of the nineteenth century, they didn't speak much English. So he had to learn Irish to fucking get on with it. Remember, this was at the time of the Celtic Dawn, when he grew up, with Yeats, and George Moore, and all that lot, and Lady Gregory. All fucking burrowing though the woods with Cathleen Ni Houlihan.

Burrowing through the wood, y'know, picking flowers as they walked through the woods, sort of going, 'This must be like how Cuchulainn felt, as he walked down to meet Ferdia at the bridge.' Know what I mean, stuff like that. And then Yeats would come out with a line like, 'And then Cuchulainn took his shining blade. And Ferdia's eyes were suddenly glazed and amazed.' And somebody would say, 'Oh no, that doesn't sound that good. Leave that one out, will ya. Keep Cuchulainn on ice for a while, yeah.' He did come out with Cuchulainn in the end, you know.

—**He did, yeah.**

—And it was almost as bad as that. But like, Douglas Hyde totally dedicated himself to preserving the Irish folk myths, which he learned in Irish from the Roscommon people. And they're not very nice stories. They're not nice stories like Cathleen Ni Houlihan. Like, not all Yeats's stories were nice, but they're all very romantic, y'know. Douglas Hyde's are real gritty, horrible Irish ghost stories. Irish nasty stories about people having to drag corpses on their backs for fucking twenty miles, and then, through the land of the half-living, and all the rest of it, know what I mean. Stuff like that. Stuff that sent you shrieking home to your bed, y'know. And he transcribed them all faithfully into English, to prove what a beautiful intelligent race the Irish were. Cause, y'know, he was an Irishman, but he wasn't a Paddy.

—**Right. He was a West Brit.**

—He was a West Brit, yeah, but he didn't have any of the airs and graces of the rest of them, know what I mean.

—**So some of them were all right.**

—He wasn't writing poetry. All he was doing was directly translating the stories he was told as a kid into English. From the Irish. Directly from the Irish. Using the vernacular of the Irish, like 'The Poor Mouth'.

—**Yeah.**

—Like, 'The Home', and 'The Crossing', and all that sort of stuff, y'know.

—**Yeah.**

—And like, he met Yeats. And he exchanged a couple of sentences with Yeats, who he didn't admire.

—**Didn't admire?**

—No. And Yeats really admired him. And Yeats came away saying what a wonderful bloke Hyde was, and Douglas Hyde came away saying, 'I don't ever want to talk to that bastard again'!

—**Is that true?**

—Yeah.

—**How do you know that?**

—Cause it's a well-known fact. It's a well-known fact. Douglas Hyde and Yeats like . . . Yeats licked his arse, y'know. Yeats would've done anything to be like Douglas Hyde.

—**Yeah?**

—To know Irish, for a start.

—**Why did he not learn Irish?**

—Cause he was too lazy, y'know, he was too fucking lazy. He just toyed around with English. So his whole 'Cathleen Ni Houlihan' is a bastardization of the Irish tongue anyway, the fucking name! The

WOMAN POWER IN THE WEST - I CAN FEEL IT COMING. SINCE PREHISTORIC TIMES, SINCE THE SHEILANAGLESHAIR, WOMEN HAVE BEEN WAITING TO PLAY THEIR PLACE IN SOCIETY. EXCEPT IN CHERISHED IRELAND, WHERE WOMEN HAVE WORN THEIR DRAWERS TOO LONG ANCESTRALLY. IT IS NOW TIME FOR THE MEN OF IRELAND TO GET A PAIR OF BALLS BETWEEN THEM AND HARANGUE THEIR MOTHERS FOR THEIR INDOCTRINATION, SELL THEIR WIVES TO VISITING ARABS IF THEY DO OFFEND MALE SUPREMACY, MARRY OFF THEIR DAUGHTERS TO RICH HOUSEHOLDS WHERE THEY WILL BE MADE TO WORK THEIR KEEP, HEAVING GREAT SACKS OF POTATOES ON THEIR BACKS AND SCRUBBING AND BOILING THEM IN STATEM PLACEDO IN PLACEBO), CURRA DISS, MOYLEM DO TRAILER RATION. . . . .

    YEATS' RAMBLINGS VOL 4, CHAPTER 6, STANZAS 18 TO
                                        17. -- - - - -

MOTHER MO CHROI, MOTHER MO CHROI, HOW OFTEN THE PEASANT BOYS TOLD ME OF THEE, AS I INTERRUPTED THEIR HOPSCOTCH GAME BY LANDING ON THE THREE, IT'S COMIN UP THREES ME BOYS, IT'S COMING UP THREES ME BOYS, MAY MADAME BLAVINSKY LOVE THEE, AS I DO, MY MOTHER MC CHROI' . . . . . .

    YEATS' POPULAR SONGS, VOL 6, CHAPTER 8, STANZAS 14 TO
                                  16. . . . .

NOW SEE O'DUFFY'S GALLANT VOLUNTEERS IN SHIRTS OF
                               BLUE
STEP NICELY TO A TUNE THEY SURELY KNEW
HAIL FRANCO AND THE REBELS OUT IN SPAIN
DEV'LL NEVER MAKE ME A BROADCASTER AGAIN
WHAT FOUL SMELLING HEINOUS BEAST
IS IT THE IRA? CHOOSE TO CREATE A WAFFRAY
WHAT ROUGH BEAST SLUMBERS TOWARDS BETHLEHEM TO
                               BE BORN

    YEATS - THE UNENDING IDIOCIES
           BROADCAST 1937

way he spells it. He would've done anything to be able to learn Irish, and to fucking be able to talk to Irish-speaking people, you know, like Douglas Hyde could. And drink with them. And have a laugh down in the pub with them, y'know. And get a story, and rush home and write it down in English. And then churn out book after book of fucking fantastic stories, know what I mean?

—Yeah.

—And that's what Douglas Hyde did. He was the blood and guts of the Celtic Dawn. He was the best of them all. And he couldn't stand Yeats, especially after he met him. Yeats was all done up in his foppish fucking outfit, with his Oscar Wilde jacket on, and his Oscar Wilde . . . he dressed just like Oscar Wilde at the time. And wore those fucking stupid glasses. He looked like a right idiot. Douglas Hyde would just dress in black. And he had a black moustache. He looked like a right Black-Irishman. And was a right Black-Irishman, despite being a Protestant, y'know.

—**So anyway, about Yeats. You said he wasn't really an Irish poet.**

—No, he was an Irish poet.

—**You said that was the reason . . .**

—Well . . . I mean, being Irish isn't everything, is it?

—**No, it isn't.**

—If you're full of shit, you're full of shit, you know.

—**Right.**

—I mean, O'Brien's full of shit, right, but O'Brien's about as Irish as they come, y'know. But everything he says is shit, know what I mean. And like, and what he says is generally anti-Irish, at heart. Because he's so full of shit, he's ashamed of being Irish. And Yeats is ashamed of being Irish, too, in a way.

—**You think so?**

—Yeah. Yeats had to relate the Irish myths to the Greek myths. He couldn't just stick to the basics, like Douglas Hyde. He couldn't just go out and learn the language, and talk to the people around him. He's from the west as well, y'know. They're both from the west. One of them, from the time he was a small child, went and played with the natives, y'know, played with the locals, although he was from a big house . Yeats is from a big house. But you know, his brother was the real talent.

—Yeah.

—Yeah, his brother, Jack B. Yeats. He was definitely a great Irish painter. I just think Yeats is terribly overrated, y'know. I think the good stuff is great, but like, most of it is shit. And if you want to get into all that sort of Celtic Dawn stuff, that was going on at the end of the nineteenth century, it's far better to get into Douglas Hyde. And you'll get far more of the spirit of Douglas Hyde from a painting by Jack B. Yeats then you do out of W.B. Yeats's poetry, know what I mean. He also painted, Yeats. W.B. Yeats.

—He painted?

—Yeah, but his paintings are terrible. His paintings are absolutely awful, y'know. It's all Coole Park. He was brought up on a nice groovy piece of land. A nice big piece of land, y'know.

—No, that was her house, Lady Gregory's.

—Oh yeah, Coole Park was Lady Gregory's. But his bit of land, that he was brought up on was all right as well.

—He was brought up in Dublin.

—He wasn't brought up in Dublin, he was brought up in the west.

—Hmmm.

—He wasn't brought up in Dublin!

—Yeah, he was.

—No, he wasn't.

—Well, they had a place in Dublin.

—And they had a place out in the west!

—Oh . . . He bought a place in the west himself?

—No, they had a place in the west!

—Did they?

—Yes.

—Oh.

—But the worst thing he did was go on the radio, right, in 1937. The beginning of the Spanish Civil War, and support the Blueshirts against the IRA. Support the fascists, against the socialists. Because he was into order, right, he couldn't handle fucking anarchy. He couldn't handle a bit of blood and guts, y'know. He didn't like getting his foppish clothes fucking messy. Douglas Hyde was well into blood and guts, y'know. There's blood and guts in every one of his stories. They're not his stories, they're old Irish stories, but they're stories that he preserved for us, y'know. They're probably not even told any more, in the Irish tongue.

—No.

—And like, when the Rising happened, Yeats was appalled. And when the war of independence happened Yeats was appalled. It took him ten years to make up his mind on what he thought about that.

—**Yeah?**

—Yeah, well before he wrote anything about it.

—**Yeah. He wrote a poem about that.**

—Yeah, he wrote a few poems about that, y'know. But it was mostly about how the swans weren't at Coole Park any more, know what I mean. Cause they got rid of her bloody swans during the war of independence.

—**Why?**

—Cause as far as they were concerned, Lady Gregory was a fucking West Brit fucking landlord, know what I mean. And that's what she was, for fuck's sake.

—**Of course. So getting rid of the swans . . . or rather, the poem about the swans being gone, is that a metaphor for the English being chucked out?**

—It was a metaphor for . . . I think it was a metaphor for the order that the English had maintained, y'know.

—**Yeah.**

—You know, like the way everything was in its place.

—**Civilized.**

—Yeah, you know, you had English people at the top of the heap . . .

—**In their big houses.**

—Yeah, the big houses. You had Anglo-Irish people a bit further down. You had sort of, civil servants, and the middle classes, y'know, and the big landlords. And then you had the peasantry.

—Yeah.

—And everybody knew where they stood. But like, after liberation, nobody knew where they stood any more. And he didn't like that, y'know. He couldn't handle it. It was too much for his brain. He couldn't go burrowing through the woods any more, spouting about Cuchulainn, you know. Cause in two savage years of like, bloody fucking conflict, the whole thing had been turned round on it's side. There was a civil war, and the Blueshirts were supposed to be restoring order, y'know, like all fascists, are supposed to. That's how fascism starts in any country, y'know, with a load of aggro that people can't handle. But fascism never really got a toehold in Ireland at all. You can't imagine Irish fascists, can you? I mean, there were Irish fascists, but I've never met one. I've never met an ex-Blueshirt, know what I mean. No no . . . I have met Irish fascists, yeah . . . I have met Irish fascists!

—**I'm an Irish fascist. Who are your favourite Irish writers?**

—Well, my favourites are O'Casey, and Behan, and Frank O'Connor and Edna O'Brien, and Martin McDonagh, and Pat McCabe, and Frank McCourt.

—**I knew that.**

—And Flann O'Brien.

—**Oh yeah, Flann O'Brien.**

—On the subject of Frank McCourt, I thought that we were going to be left with *Nothing To Say* by Mannix Flynn as the last great Irish book of the twentieth century, since *A Pagan Place* by Edna O'Brien and *Amongst Women* by John McGahern. The classic Irish novel seemed to have died out, in the second half of the twentieth century, but just in time *Angela's Ashes* came along and I personally think it's the greatest Irish novel of the twentieth century and therefore the greatest Irish novel ever.

—**Better than Joyce?**

—Yes. Joyce is difficult to read. And if you're not an Irish Catholic, large parts of it are absolutely meaningless. Not to say that they're not great books. But *Angela's Ashes* is absolutely truthful, totally lacking in sentimentality or O'Casey style romanticism. It's easily read by anybody and easily understood. It's hysterically funny all the way through.

—There's some sad bits.

—Even the sad bits are funny. And any human being who has been brutalized by fanatical religious sadism or fascistic, moronic teaching or bloody pure starvation can identify with all the characters in the book.

—What about Maeve Binchy?

—Well, I'm more of an Edna O'Brien freak, y'know.

—Yeah. What do you like about Edna O'Brien?

—Her total honesty. Like she's not the funniest Irish writer, you know, but like she's totally honest. It gets more and more honest as the books go on, y'know. It starts off fairly wet, and by the time you get the girls into *Married Bliss* it's gone savage. And by the time you get to *Pagan Place* it's blasphemy, you know what I mean. It got banned in Ireland. So I took great pleasure in smuggling a copy over there, and reading it over there.

—Your mum introduced you to that, didn't she?

—To Edna O'Brien? Yeah. It's about the only good writer my mum likes.

—That's not saying very nice things about your mum's taste in books.

—Well, my mum has got different taste in books than me, y'know. She's into Dickens . . . and she's into stuff like *Vanity Fair*.

—Well, we enjoy that, don't we?

—No. But we agree on Edna O'Brien, y'know. We agree on films, she likes thrillers and horror movies, and things like that.

—Yeah. Let's keep with the Irish literature for a minute. Do you think Joyce is overrated?

—No.

—What do you think about James Joyce?

—I think he's underrated.

—Do you?

—Yeah.

—Even though he's supposed to be the greatest . . .

263

—He's underrated, apart from by the Americans, you know. Like all the greatest commentators on Joyce are American. The world's greatest expert on Joyce is Richard Ellman, who's American, y'know. In fact the only book I've read about Joyce is Richard Ellman's book. And it's an amazing book. It really gives you some insights into the guy. The guy had a fantastic tenor voice, y'know. And he left Ireland in 1901, when he was twenty-three or something like that. Twenty-one. And he never went back. But he never wrote about anything else for the rest of his life.

—**Hmmm.**

—And he used to write home, to check out if he got the details right, when he was writing *Ulysses*. Like what kind of trees were there on Raglan Road, and things like that, y'know. Know what I mean? He used to write home about things like that, and ask his brother or his old man, while he was still alive.

—**They must have been driven demented. Were they?**

—Yeah. Like, they'd write back saying, 'Yes, there's such and such trees on Raglan Road, and such and such trees on . . . or, there aren't any trees at all on this road . . .', y'know.

—**So they must have been quite pissed off.**

—Well, they probably didn't realize they were contributing to a masterpiece.

—**Probably not. They probably thought he was just a pain in the ass.**

—Yes. They probably thought he was just being a pain in the arse. His kid brother always believed in him though.

—**Stanislas?**

—Yeah, Stanislas.

—**The one who gave him the money all the time.**

—Yeah, the one who gave him the money all the time, yeah, and became a doctor. The one who earned all the money for the family.

—**So why is James Joyce considered the greatest, and why do you like him so much? Why do you think he's so good?**

—Cause he really rearranged the English language, because he didn't like it the way it was, know what I mean? So he said, 'Fuck this. I'm getting rid of it the way it is. I'm gonna write the way I want.' And he wrote the way he wanted, not the way somebody told him to write, not the way he was taught to write. He totally turned it around. And he upset so many people. Virginia Woolf, and D.H. Lawrence, and all the great English writers of the period, all hated his guts. They all thought he was a fucking vulgar ignorant pig, know what I mean. They were all disgusted by the obscenities . . . the so-called obscenities in *Ulysses*, which is simply people doing what they normally do: having sex, and pissing against walls, y'know, getting pissed in pubs, having fights, wanking off over young women, y'know . . . whatever. Virginia Woolf and D.H. Lawrence, and all that lot, they all formed a movement against Joyce to stop it getting published, y'know.

—**They did?!**

—Yeah yeah yeah yeah.

—**No way!**

—It was largely down to them that *Ulysses* wasn't published in England until 1940 or something like that.

—**Wow!**

—It was originally published in Paris, y'know.

—**Yeah.**

—In English, y'know.

—**Right, but I didn't realize . . .**

—Or in Joycean.

—**I didn't realize that they had done . . .**

—Cause he made up his own language, that's what I like about him, y'know. Which is a mixture of Irish and English, and Latin and Greek, and just being pissed. Cause he's a total piss artist, you know.

—**Is that why you like him? Partly?**

—I admire all creative piss artists. I admire creative people, y'know. They don't have to be piss artists. I'm just saying that, like, a lot of his language development . . . like Richard Ellman would never have said that. Richard Ellman used to skirt over the fact that Joyce had a drink problem, y'know what I mean.

—**Did he?**

—Yeah yeah. And all the other American writers have written about it. You know, there have been hundreds and hundreds of books written by Americans – about Joyce, about *Ulysses*, about *Finnegans Wake*, about . . . I mean, there have been more books written about Joyce than about any other subject under the sun. By Americans, I mean. They're obsessed with him. But Richard Ellman is the most famous. And Richard Ellman, in his book, says James Joyce's drinking problem was still there but he carried on regardless. Know what I mean, just put that in every now and then, y'know. And like, he had countless affairs.

—**Who did?**

—Joyce.

—**Did he?**

—Yeah.

—**Wow. Did Nora not get pissed off at him?**

—Nora stuck by him through thick and thin, y'know. And not only did he used to chat them up, but he used to sing them up with his fabulous tenor voice. He used to get a few jobs, and then do a hymn, or a piece of opera, or an old Irish ballad, know what I mean . . . in this fabulous tenor voice, and the girls would melt, know what I mean, into his arms, and he'd have it away with them. He was an opportunist like that. And he had a long-suffering wife who put up with it all. And the ridiculous thing is, that when she died, which was a few years after him – he died tragically early – when she died a few years after him, she was laid in an unconsecrated grave, y'know . . .

—**Yeah?**

—. . . with a sign over her saying, 'God help this poor sinner'. Know what I mean!?

—**Ahhhhh . . .**

—And what a saintly woman, y'know. And she never fucking had support, y'know.

—**Oohhhh. Where is she buried.**

—She's buried in Trieste, or somewhere like that. They were both buried abroad. They never came back. She gave him a hand job on

Victoria and Shane on holiday
in Thailand in the 1980's.

Victoria and Shane
at home in 1991.

Top left: At the Lady Owen Arms in Islington.

Top right: Shane and Victoria in 1999.

Left: On stage at The Forum in Kentish Town.

Opposite page: Portraits by Victoria Clarke, taken in Kentish Town in the late 80s.

More holidays in Thailand.

Jock Scott at Shane's house.

Ronnie Wood with Shane in Dublin.

Victoria, Shane, Gerry Adams and Joey Cashman in West Belfast.

Andrew Catlin's portrait of Shane taken in Spain on the set of *Straight to Hell*.

Shane by Andrew Catlin.

Above: Andrew Catlin took this too.

Right: A Tim Wainwright
picture taken for the cover of
Rainy Night in Soho

the beach, the first day they went out for a date, so he fell in love with her. Two days later they were on a ship to Europe. Married.

—Did they get married?

—Yeah, they got married. Yeah.

—So why did the grave say that?

—Because of the man she was married to, y'know.

—But he didn't commit a mortal sin, did he?

—Well, in the eyes of the Catholic Church in Ireland he did, you know.

—Yeah?

—And in the eyes of the Catholic Church in general he did.

—What was the mortal sin?

—The mortal sin was to talk about sex openly, you know. You know what I mean . . . not like D.H. Lawrence did it, all climax climax climax, they climaxed together and all that shit, know what I mean. Not that stuff, 'He rubbed his manhood against her', and all that stuff, but like good, old-fashioned, plunging it in stuff. And what's more, Nora Barnacle was the woman he consulted when he was writing Molly Bloom's soliloquy. Which is the part of *Ulysses* that offends people the most. Which is a woman's fantasies, or rather, memories, of getting fucked by Blazes Boylan. And her life, you know, how she'd been fucked around. And he used her mercilessly, y'know, he said like, 'How did you feel when I fucked that woman?', know what I mean. 'Tell me exactly how you felt', and things like that. And he'd write that into the soliloquy, y'know, the way she said it.

So it's Nora Barnacle's voice talking to you at the end of *Ulysses*. It's his wife talking to you. It's all her fantasies, all her memories, all her . . . cause he didn't know anything about female sexuality . . . he was a man. And he didn't have the arrogance to try and do it on his own, y'know. So he plugged Nora for all the details. And he asked her sort of stuff like, 'When I got off with that little bird last week, how did you feel about that? Can you tell me exactly? And how do you feel about getting off with another man? How do you feel about this that and the other?'

I meant to mention Seamus Heaney.

—**Yes. Go on then.**

—Well, I've mentioned him now.

—**That's it? What have you got to say about him?**

—He's a really great Irish writer.

—**Why?**

—I don't know why.

—**I mean, what's great about him?**

—What?

—**What's great about him?**

—He is quintessentially Irish, but he doesn't go on about being beaten up by the Christian Brothers all the time.

—**What about Oscar Wilde? He's another Irish writer.**

—I don't think he's a very good Irish writer.

—**He's very popular.**

—Well, that about says it all, doesn't it?

—**Sometimes the popular ones are good. Why don't you like *The Importance of Being Earnest*?**

—I hate *The Importance of Being Earnest*. I hate it to death.

—**What about *Dorian Gray*?**

—Yeah, it's all right. It's cute, y'know.

—**It was a good movie.**

—It's a good film, yeah. It's a good story. He wrote one good story, all right, okay, good ol' Oscar. Yeah.

—**What about his witticisms?**

—His witticisms are great. But they're not as good as Dorothy Parker. And what's more, he never wrote anything as good as her *Big Blonde*.

—**What about George Bernard Shaw?**

—Pretty average. They're both essentially English writers. I'm not saying they weren't Irish, I was saying that what they wrote was essentially English, do you know what I mean?

—**Okay, so you don't like George Bernard Shaw much. What about J.M. Synge?**

—I liked *Playboy of the Western World*, then you can keep him. Do you like the rest of Synge's stuff?

—No, I hate it.

—Because the rest of Synge's stuff is worse . . . like *Riders to the Sea*. Yeah.

—**What about Paddy Kavanagh? Apart from the fact that he used to chase women . . .**

—He used to chase young girls. But his poetry, I find personally . . . Seamus Heaney does it better. 'Bogman Poetry'.

—**Ha. Bogman Poetry. Do you like Austin Clarke?**

—Not a lot.

—**Do you like any others?**

—There's millions of them.

—**Who?**

—I don't particularly like modern Irish poetry.

—**No.**

—Apart from Seamus Heaney, I like the old Irish poetry.

—**Like who?**

—Like O'Rahaille. That stuff, and earlier. 'The Midnight Court'. Brian Merryman and O'Rahaille, and people like that. In fact, I've been quite heavily influenced by them in the way I write my songs.

—**O'Rahaille?**

—Yeah. And 'The Midnight Court' and all that stuff. O'Rahaille was seventeenth century, but I like earlier than that as well. 'Saint Patrick's Breast Plate'.

—**Who wrote that?**

—It's anonymous . . . The anonymous stuff, from the really early times moves gradually on down through the centuries and into lyrics of Irish songs. The earliest songs are about seventeenth century. 'Peggy Gordon', stuff like that.

—**Seventeenth century?**

—Yeah.

—**That's funny . . . they don't date . . .**

—No, they don't. The poetry doesn't date, either. It's an oral tradition. It was an oral tradition, and started being written down in, I suppose, the sixteenth century. But they were still carried by the people. They are all songs, really, all those old Irish poems.

'The Midnight Court' would have had a tune. Or it would have been lilted. That's why Irish songs don't date, because they come from the same tradition. That's why I'd much rather be remembered as an Irish songwriter than a rock songwriter.

—**Why?**

—Because it's immortality. To have one of your songs accepted into the tradition is a real honour. I find it a real honour anyway. I think that's why people are always calling me a poet, you know.

—**Why?**

—Because I just write in the traditional style, and people aren't used to it. They're used to listening to pop lyrics. But it's very annoying to be called a poet when you're a musician.

—**Is it?**

—Yeah.

—**Why is that?**

—Because it means you've wasted your time writing the music, you know.

—**Does it?**

—Well, yeah. Poetry doesn't have music.

—**But doesn't that mean that you're a poet as well? Isn't it an added bonus, and not a . . .**

—I don't know what they mean, but being called a poet when you're a musician is a pain in the arse. Because writing poetry is a hell of a lot simpler than writing a song.

—**Is it?**

—Yeah.

—**I suppose it would be, wouldn't it, yeah, cause songs have verses and choruses and . . .**

—Well, they don't have to . . . but they have to have music as well as words. And music says so much more than words.

—**Why?**

—Well, if there's a tune you like, or a song you like, you might not know . . . think about it . . . you might not know half the words. You might not know any of the words. You can make up your own words. But if it's a strong enough tune, you can carry it around in your head. A great piece of poetry is as strong as a great piece of music.

—Tell me a great piece of poetry.

—'An Irish Airman Forsees his Death' by Yeats is a great piece of poetry.

—Why is it great?

—Because it's like a song.

—But . . . why is it like a song, what do you mean?

—Because the words go jingle jangle, you know . . . they lilt.

—Tell me, I've forgotten it.

—It's something like, 'The place I come from is Kiltartan Cross. My people are called Kiltartaners, poor. No light, the end, to bring them thus. And leave them happier than before . . .'

—It's the musical intonation, isn't it?

—Yeah. Do you want me to find it?

—I think I know what you mean. The sound makes a . . .

—The sound makes a tune in your head.

—An emotional impact.

—Yeah.

—Without you necessarily knowing what it means.

—No, but you do know what it means! If it's a great piece of poetry you do know what it means!

—Shane, your nose has snot hanging out of it now.

Shane wipes his nose on his sleeve, sulkily.

—I think you should use a handkerchief.

—Oh shut up.

—Fuck off.

—You fuck off.

Silence descends in the deserted airport lounge, as the couple wait, twitchily, to be allowed to board an aircraft home.

GHOST HORSE
ON THE
GALLÁGH

ACT SEVEN

Shannon Airport, Ireland, morning. An immense, immeasurable expanse of verdant land rises up to meet our couple, as their plane lands on friendly soil, finally. The broad, majestic Shannon sparkles and dazzles and vocalizes a greeting, mightly. A hundred thousand small birds take up the chorus, joyously. Shane and Victoria disembark, gratefully, and kiss the ground, reverently, before adjoining to the bar, fastidiously.

—**What does being Irish mean to you?**

—The Pogues would never have existed if I wasn't Irish. Ireland means everything to me. I always felt guilty because I didn't lay down my life for Ireland, I didn't join up. Not that I would have helped the situation, probably. But I felt ashamed that I didn't have the guts to join the IRA. And the Pogues was my way of overcoming that guilt. And looking back on it, I think maybe I made the right choice.

Ireland is the greatest nation in the world and the Irish are the most important race in the world. We're travelling people. That song, 'The Travelling People', which is about tinkers or itinerants or whatever you want to call them, could be about any Irish people. The Irish people are travelling people, we all travel, we've always travelled. We all leave home and go back and leave again and our influence has spread all over the world and this has been going on for thousands of years. In the early days of Christianity, the missionary monks were nearly all Irish. And it was said that if a man could speak Greek and Latin he was probably Irish. Behan said it. A proud and intelligent people. Wonderful sense of humour, brilliant imagination. I'm proud of everything the Irish do well. Even Che

273

Guevara's military hero was Michael Collins. But we can be treacherous people. As Collins discovered. Collins was an example of an honourable Irishman. Honourable and dead.

I wouldn't join the IRA now under any circumstances. I don't agree with killing civilians. I don't think I'd be any good in the IRA, is another reason. You find your task in life and you do that. I haven't got the qualifications to be an IRA man, I have the qualifications to be an Irish musician. And I've still got a few kicks in the arses ready for the boring old farts of Irish music. They're still there, the ones who couldn't handle the Pogues.

But what a talented race. I'm proud to be one of them. Great sportsmen, great soldiers, great musicians, great lovers, great artists. Nobody loves like an Irishman. And women always find Irishmen attractive. I think women are attracted by the fact that Irishmen are so much more intelligent than Englishmen. That's a bit of a generalization, of course. There are some glaring exceptions to that rule. There's no bigger bastard than an Irish bastard. And most Irish-Americans are great, but an Irish-American bastard is a real bastard.

The Irish are backstabbing, gossiping and begrudging, with a tendency to mindless violence. But they're faults that all people have. You can't say the Irish are any worse than anyone else. Their faults are very few. But the last thing the Irish are is perfectionists. And they're more interested in having a good time than in making millions. Lazy.

There is a section of the Irish people that is very obnoxious, also. The rich Irish are obnoxious. I don't mind stage Irishmen like Terry Wogan, though, and Val Doonican. Gay Byrne. They're funny because they don't realize they're so bad. The plain simple people of Ireland are the ones I really like. I'd rather be a plain simple person. I'm not a boring rich one. I'm not rich enough. An Irish person has to be very rich before they become boring.

I want to talk about Frank Ryan now.

—Okay. Who's Frank Ryan?

—Who was Frank Ryan? Frank was the laughing cavalier of the old

IRA. He was a womanizer, a drinker, a bold figure of a man. He was a Limerick boy.

—I thought you didn't like Limerick.

—No, that's not true.

—You said some derogatory things about Limerick people earlier on in your book.

—Well, I want to take them all out.

—Do you?

—Yeah. I've got nothing against Limerick people. Anyway, he's from Limerick County, not Limerick City. He's from Knocklong. And he went to school in Tipperary anyway.

—And what's so special about him?

—First, he fought in the Irish war of independence, then he fought in the Irish civil war, then he fought in the Spanish Civil War. And he was a passionate, Irish-speaking Republican socialist.

—Can you do him?

—Yeah, except I can't speak Irish. I wish I could, but I can't. Apart from the odd phrase, you know. He could speak it fluently, and write it fluently. And he was a great orator. And he could stir the hearts of man, you know, with his voice. With his oratory.

—You can do that.

—No I can't. I can only do it in song. Like, I don't know what kind of a singer he was.

—Maybe he wasn't as good a singer as you.

—Probably wasn't, you know, most people aren't. He could wow the ladies.

—Was he a good-looking bloke? He doesn't look very attractive in the pictures.

—Well, he had a cocky way of handling himself, y'know. And the gift of the gab. And like, he had no enemies.

—Why did he have no enemies if he was in wars?

—Well, apart from General O'Duffy.

—Who was General O'Duffy?

—The leader of the Blueshirts. Well, apart from the Blueshirts he had no enemies. He was universally liked. He fought in the Irish

MY NAME IS JOE BYRNE
I ~~AND~~ SPENT NGATAU D DAY
WITH A POLICING SQUAD
OF THE BOLD IRA
IF YOU'RE KIDS ON THE JUNK
THEY'RE ~~WE'RE ONLY TRY'S TO~~ STEP IN
A SLUG IN EACH KNEE
HE WON'T DO IT AGAIN
IT'S QUICK AND IT'S PAINFUL
WE'RE CRUEL TO BE KIND
WE ~~STROKE OF~~ PUNISH FOR HIS CRIMES
AND WE GIVE HIM A BEATING
~~HE COMES~~ TILL HE'S SURE THAT THE IS DYING
ONE NIGHT WE WENT A GUY WHO SOLD GRASS
TOOLED UP AND WEARING BLACK BALAKLAVA MASKS
WE GOT OUT OUR HURLEYS OUR BATS AND ~~THE~~ PIPES
WE BROKE EVERY BONE IN HIS BODY THAT NIGHT
THE CAPTAIN ~~SAID~~ ~~SEE~~ "DO YOU KNOW WHY WE'RE DOIN THIS TO YOU
A CONFESSION AND REPENTANCE WILL MAKE IT EASY ON YOU
YOU'VE POISONED YOUR OWN PEOPLE AND INJURED THE CAUSE
WE'RE HERE TO NOW TO TEACH YOU IRISH WAYS AND LAWS"
SEE THE BRITS BROUGHT US TORTURE AND THEY BROUGHT IN
                                        THE DRUGS
TO STEAL YOUNG FOLKS SOULS N MAKE EM MURDERERS N THUGS
TO CLEAN UP THE MESS THAT THE RUC LEFT
WE ~~YOU~~ HAVE TO BE BRAVE AND TAKE EXTREME STEPS
A PUNISHMENT BEATING LEAVES A MAN NEARLY DEAD
AND HE'LL GET A FEW VISITS IN HIS HOSPITAL BED
HE'LL PRAY FOR FORGIVENESS WHILE HE'S DOIN HIS TIME
AND WHEN HE GETS OUT GOD HELP HIM IF HE GOES BACK
                                        TO CRIME
A FEW HARDMEN WERE HAVING LATE DRINKS AT THE
                                        BAR
THOUGH THE LANDLORD WAS FREAKING HE WAS SERVING
ONE OF THEM SHOUTED OUT "IT'S A GREAT JOB THEM JARS
                                YOU'RE DOING
SAVING OLD IRELAND FROM THE BRITS AND FROM RUIN
BEATING ONE OF YOUR OWN AND YOU'RE NOT FINISHED YET
NOW THE LADS WITH THE BROWNINGS PLAY RUSSIAN ROULETTE
THE CAPTAIN GLARED AT HIM DIDN'T KNOW WHAT'S TO SAY
WE ALL GOT THE FEELING HE WAS IRA
THE CAPTAIN GROWLED "MIND YOUR OWN OR YOU'LL BE
THE MAN GRINNED SAID "I'M NOT REALLY BE NEXT"
YOU'D GET HURT MAY BE KILLED SO SAVE YOUR
                                        OLD THREATS

movement for independence, and he fought in the Irish civil war, on the Republican side. And he was one of the most important movers in the movement of the IRA to the left.

—**How did they become socialists? They didn't start out as socialists, did they?**

—They didn't start out as socialists, no. But in the thirties, they had to take sides.

—**De Valera wasn't a socialist, was he?**

—No, de Valera wasn't a socialist, no. De Valera was never a socialist. De Valera was a fucking right-wing bastard. De Valera was rich, yeah? But that isn't why he wasn't a socialist, know what I mean, lots of socialists have been rich. In fact more socialists than not, have been rich.

—**Champagne socialists?**

—I don't call people like Karl Marx and Lenin champagne socialists. There is, nowadays, a breed of people that you could call champagne socialists. I'm not a champagne socialist. I've always been a socialist.

—**So why did he become a socialist?**

—Because he had the brains to become a socialist. Like, the IRA split down the middle in the 1930s, between the socialist faction and the right-wing faction. The hardliners. And he went to Spain to fight in the Spanish Civil War. On the Republican side, obviously. Against Franco. Which is where most of the Irish people went to fight, against Franco, in the Spanish Civil War. Some Irish Blueshirts went to fight for Franco. They were sent home with a letter from Franco saying thank you to Ireland for its support, but that General O'Duffy was the worst alcoholic he'd ever come across and he was completely useless as a soldier.

—**What do we know about the Blueshirts? For the benefit of the readers who are ignorant.**

—The Blueshirts were the fascist party of Ireland. They were the strong-arm boys of Cumann Na Gael. Which turned into Finegael. That's why Finegael supporters are called Blueshirts.

—**And would they support Oswald Mosley, and people like that?**

—They were in with them, yeah. They were in with them, Franco,

Mussolini and Hitler. Finegael are a fascist party, you know. To this day they're a fascist party. The Blueshirts were their bully-boys. They used to parade and give the fascist salute, and wear blue shirts. Really ridiculous colour for Irish people to wear, know what I mean, who were meant to be nationalistic. Blue shirt. But they'd run out of colours. Couldn't wear green shirts, cause the Fianna wore green shirts. The IRA volunteers . . . the young IRA volunteers wore green shirts. So, they couldn't wear green shirts, they had to wear blue shirts. And they were led by General Owen O'Duffy. Who was a ridiculous character. And when de Valera got into power, he got the IRA into his office and he said, 'Listen, boys, do me a favour, get those bastards off my arse, will ya! Get the Blueshirts off my arse!' So, the Blueshirts had a march on a Saturday, and the IRA turned up and fired a few shots over their heads, and they all ran like fuck. And that was the end of the Blueshirts as a mass movement. If there ever was a mass movement. Irish fascism doesn't make sense, so it didn't have much of a popular draw to it. But even the loonies who were fucking involved with it shat themselves when the real boys turned up. The real bang-bang men. Know what I mean?

But they did go over and fight on the other side in the Spanish Civil War, but in very small numbers. Huge amounts of IRA men, and ordinary Irishmen went over to fight in the Spanish Civil War on the Republican side; along with Englishmen, Americans, French, and Spanish, obviously. No Germans, and no Italians. Quite a lot of Brits. The 1930s was a period when you had to declare your allegiance to fascism or socialism. And so the IRA had to declare its allegiance to fascism or socialism. And Frank Ryan was a socialist Republican. So, he went to fight in the Spanish Civil War, and he got captured, right, after a few spirited battles, he got captured, and sentenced to death.

So he wrote home a letter in code. You were only allowed to write in Spanish or French, so if you didn't know Spanish or French you were fucked. Luckily he knew French. But he also knew Irish, so he put words of Irish in, as code-words. Saying, 'I am under sentence of death.' In this perfectly innocent-looking letter to his sister, saying like, 'Things are wonderful over here. I've been eating figs from the tree, and the sun is baking down. It's hotter than Kerry in July . . .', and all the rest of it, he really said, 'I am under sentence of death.' In code. Using the Irish language. And to tell de Valera. And the word got to de Valera. And the whole nation looked to de Valera to get him out. So de Valera, being half-Spanish, pulled a couple of strings with Franco, and got him released from a sentence of death. So then he was gonna rot in a Spanish jail for the rest of his life. But the Germans wanted him. The war broke out, and the Germans wanted him.

—**What for?**

—To collaborate with them against the English. So the Germans did a kind of fake escape for him, from the Spanish jail, into Germany. And they kept him on hold there, like, 'Yes, Paddy. You just stay there, Paddy.' And they kept him in Germany.

—**So, did he collaborate with the Nazis?**

—Of course he collaborated. England's misfortune is Ireland's opportunity, you know.

—**But . . . does that mean he was on the side of the Nazis?**

—He was on the side of the Germans. The Nazis, yeah.

—**So that means he was killing Jews.**

—He didn't know anything about the Jews.

—**Did he not?**

—No.

—**How do you know?**

—The Germans that were in charge of collaboration with the Irish, didn't have anything to do with the SS, or any of those people. They were purely German soldiers. They weren't party members. They weren't Nazis. They were just Germans. And Sean Russell, the leader of the IRA, came over to Germany, and they teamed up. And they were going over to Ireland in a German submarine, to plot the downfall of England, through the back door, through Ireland. But Sean Russell got peritonitis and died, in the submarine. He had to be buried at sea. And, so the submarine turned back, and took Frank back to Germany. He was only fucking twenty-five miles away from

the coast of Galway, when Sean Russell died. And when they didn't
have the leader of the IRA any more, they just took him back to
Germany.

—**And then what happened?**

—Well, he spent the rest of the war in Germany. He died before the
end of the war. He died at the age of forty-two. It's a tragic ending to
a brilliant career. He had bad arthritis, and it developed into
pleurisy.

—**Arthritis turned into pleurisy???**

—Well . . . you've got to remember, this is the medicine of like fifty
years ago. He'd developed bad athritis in the jail in Spain, where the
conditions weren't very good.

—**You've got in one of your songs, 'Frank Ryan brought you
whiskey . . .'**

—'In a brothel in Madrid'.

—**'And you decked some fucking Blackshirt . . .**

—'Who was cursing all the Yids'.

—**So what was that all about then?**

—That's about a similar kind of character. Except he's an old dosser,
and he's dying. He lives longer than Frank Ryan. He lives to be an
old man. It's about how every old dosser you meet on the street has
got a history. He's got a history of probably fighting in a couple
world wars, maybe the Spanish Civil War. The character in that is an
Irish guy who's fought in all the wars that Frank Ryan fought in. And
that's why it mentions Frank Ryan.

—**And also Frank Ryan stayed at your house.**

—In the house my mum and dad have got at the moment, it used to
be a safehouse for Frank Ryan. It used to be one of the places he
stayed. But, I wrote 'Sick Bed' before they got that house.

—**So you were already a fan.**

—Yeah. Yeah. Is that what we were talking about?

—**Yeah.**

—Right.

—**What other heroes do you have?**

—Luke Kelly.

—And what do you know about him?

—Luke Kelly? Well, Luke Kelly was a great Irish singer, who hitched around the world, and like, picked up songs from all over the place. Played the banjo . . .

—Was he a tinker?

—He wasn't a tinker, no. He lived like a tinker. He wasn't a tinker. He acted like a tinker. No, I'm not saying he acted like a tinker.

—Why not?

—There's nothing wrong with being a tinker anyway.

—So, what else do you know about him?

—Well, he was a very strong influence on the way I sing, y'know. I've done it subconsciously. He's got a rasp in his throat. He's not a real tinker, like, Tom Waits isn't a real tinker, but Tom Waits goes on like a tinker.

—You couldn't have an American tinker.

—No, but if you could have an American tinker it would be Tom Waits, wouldn't it? Trailer trash.

—Who are your other heroes?

—John McCormack. Count John McCormack. He's a papal count. He was made a count by the Pope.

—Which Pope?

—Which Pope? Pope Pious. Twenty-third, was it? What, are you counting? You counting Piouses?!?

—I don't think there was a twenty-fourth Pious.

—Then it was Pope Pious the twenty-third. Are you sure there was a twenty-third though?

—Yeah, I know there was a twenty-third.

—Well then . . . that was him. Pope Pious lived a very long time. And he's the one that most people remember, that are alive today . . . apart from the ones that came after him. What I mean is, he's the oldest one that a living person would remember.

—Why was he made a papal count?

—It must've been something to do with his art. Cause he went and sang for the Pope. He went and sang for the Pope, and the Pope made him a papal count on the spot. It must've been a great day!

—Would you like that to happen to you some day?

—I'd love it to happen to me.

—Would you?

—Yeah.

—If they elect an Irish Pope, I'm sure it will happen to you.

—Yeah, if they ever elect an Irish pope I'm in with a chance.

—So, anyway, what do you like about John McCormack?

—Well, apart from the fact that he was a papal count?

—Yeah.

—The only Irish papal count. He's the closest Ireland's ever got to having a Pope. And what I like about him is, he's got the most beautiful Irish tenor voice I've ever heard. Take the piss if you want, but it brings tears to my eyes.

—What's your favourite?

—'The Days of the Kerry Dancing': [sings] 'Ah, the days of the Kerry Dancing . . .'

—Are you a tenor?

—I'm a tenor, yeah.

—So you could do an album of John McCormack. Couldn't you?

—I could, yeah. I've done 'Danny Boy'.

—Yes you have, beautifully.

—Done it properly. Stitched it up properly.

—I thought you did it very well.

—Well, there you go. I could do a whole album of that stuff.

—That would be great! That would sell too, wouldn't it?

—Yeah, I could knock Daniel O'Donnell off his throne with that.

—Yeah, you could be on the cover with an Aran sweater . . . and a pipe.

—Irish tenors don't wear Aran sweaters.

—What do they wear?

—They wear Armani suits, and good ties.

—You could do Vegas with a collection of songs like that. Would you like to sing in Vegas?

—I'd love to sing in Vegas. I'd love to be a crooner. Do 'Rainy Night in Soho', and all that, 'Pair of Brown Eyes'.

—When did you first sing in public?

—I did my first public performance at the age of three. Every weekend, I performed after that. I learned my crowd technique at a very early age so crowds have never worried me. On a Friday, Saturday and Sunday night, it was open house, for music, singing and dancing in our house. Anybody from anywhere could just walk in the door, it was open all night and there was a constant card game going on around the kitchen table. I would be put up in the middle of the table while the men carried on playing cards and I'd be made to sing 'Kevin Barry'.

—Weren't you nervous?

—As a kid I was nervous about singing, of course, and I'd say I was still nervous, but not really nervous. None of this getting sick before you go on rubbish. I just used to get put on the table and away I went. I used to think the sooner I get it started the sooner it's over. I started enjoying it after a couple of verses and by the time I'd finished I was really enjoying it.

—So you knew you'd be a musician when you grew up.

—So in the back of my head was always the thought that I was going to be a musician one day.

—Do you think you'd need to train your voice if you were going to sing like John McCormack?

—No.

—Don't they have to do a lot of exercises?

—I'd have to train my voice a little to be an Irish tenor. A proper Irish tenor. I mean, to be anything like in the same league as John McCormack. I could never be in the same league as John McCormack, he's like Caruso, or someone like that. But being Irish, he isn't as famous.

—He's very famous though.

—Yeah, but he's not as famous as Caruso, or Placido Domingo.

—The Italians are always the most popular, aren't they?

—Yeah. It's just bigotry really, you know. Bigotry. Caruso wasn't even a tenor actually, he was a baritone. McCormack could sing opera, he could sing hymns, he could sing Irish 'Come all ye's', y'know. I like him singing Irish 'Come all ye's'. Cause that's the kind of guy I am. [Sings again] 'Oh, the days of the Kerry Dancing . . .' I love clear, free, beautiful singing, without any pretension to it.

—He probably didn't smoke.

—If you're born with a beautiful voice, leave it alone, yeah. Don't smoke, don't drink. Well . . . drink. There's nothing wrong with drinking. But don't smoke, if you're born with a beautiful voice, cause it will only break it up. But if you're born with a voice just good enough to carry a tune, you know, a good voice, then smoking will give it depth, and a rasp, and give it a lived-in feel. I mean, you can tell that John McCormack didn't smoke.

—Yes, you can tell that. Cause he has a very clear, pure . . .

—Yeah, a very clear, pure, voice, totally like pure water. It's just like pure water. But if you're born with a voice that's like . . . muddy water, right, a bit muddy; then make it muddier. Accentuate the features of your voice that give it its character.

—Like John Lydon?

—Well, we're not talking about a voice there, we're talking about a delivery.

—He has got a very distinctive voice.

—Yeah, but it's not a singing voice. He's got his phrasing, and delivery, and character, and . . . he doesn't smoke either, actually.

—He doesn't smoke?

—No.

—Really?

—Nah. I think if he did it would sound a bit better, actually. He went to singing lessons, you know.

—Oh yeah, that's right. With . . . I can't remember her name. She's famous.

—But it didn't do him any good.

—Have you ever had singing lessons?

—No. Johnny can't sing. He hasn't got . . . he can't keep in tune, and he hasn't got much air, he can't hold his breath, you know what I mean, and stuff like that. But he can take a song, and he can rip it to shreds, he can really do his own job on it. So it will never be the same again. So you can never listen to anybody else sing it again, with a straight face. And he's got . . . in fact some of the high notes that he hits are quite awesome. Some of the 'AAAAAAAhhhhhhhhhh's' that he gets, know what I mean, are really sort of fucking . . . I don't know how that will come across in print. But stuff like 'Memories' and 'Death Disco', Public Image stuff; some of the stuff he does with his voice in that is really amazing. But he's using it as an instrument, it's not like he's using it as a human voice, know what I mean. It doesn't sound human, it sounds like a dalek.

—**And which do you think is the more important? Having the good voice, or what you do with it?**

—It all depends on the mood you're in. I'd rather listen to John McCormack than John Lydon. But lots of people . . . a hell of lot of people disagree with me. But like, I still love listening to John Lydon, because he's done a hell of a lot with it. He knows he can't sing, and he doesn't care. And like, he's put amazing amounts of energy into what he does with it. And imagination, and like, guts. Guts and balls! He's a really ballsy singer. He really penetrates, know what I mean?

—**What other rock singers do you like? Or hate?**

—Well, would you count Tom Waits as a rock singer?

—**Yes.**

—Well, Tom Waits is my favourite rock singer.

—**Is he? Your favourite . . . ever?**

—Nah, he's not my favourite rock singer ever. One of my favourite rock singers. And Steve Marriot. Stevie Winwood.

—**How about John Lennon?**

—John Lennon, yeah. Jagger's a load of rubbish. Completely dismissable. Dylan's a load of rubbish too.

—**Why don't you like Bob Dylan?**

—Well, I don't NOT like Bob Dylan, I'm just saying that as a singer he's a waste of time.

—**Why? A lot of people like him.**

—He hasn't got a voice, and he doesn't do anything with it. What he has got, he doesn't use. He just makes a nasal whine, y'know.

—Who else do you like? Who do like more, and why do you like them? Like, why do you like Tom Waits?

—Cause he's got an amazing voice.

—Yeah, but he's not really a singer.

—Oh, he is a singer. He's a singer, yeah. 'There's a place for us. Somewhere, a place for us . . .'

—He's a baritone, right?

—Yeah, he's a baritone, yeah. He's like Ronnie Drew. Ronnie Drew and Tom Waits are more or less the same kind of thing. He's just got the voice he's got, and like . . . he uses it. He gives it his everything. He gives it all in the delivery. And there's nothing wrong with the voice he's got. There's nothing wrong with the voice Ronnie Drew's got. But a lot of people would say that Ronnie Drew couldn't sing. A lot of people would say that Tom Waits couldn't sing. A lot of people like Rod Stewart would say that they couldn't sing.

—Do you like Rod Stewart?

—No!

—What? Not any of it? You must like 'Maggie May'.

—I like the early stuff, yeah. Yeah, he had a great voice. He had a great rasping tenor, he's like Luke Kelly.

—Do you like Bryan Ferry?

—Bryan Ferry? Yeah. Yeah. A lot of style. Yeah. A lot of style, but there's a voice there as well. It's not all style. There's heart in it.

—Yeah, there is. Especially in ones like 'Jealous Guy', stuff like that.

—Yeah, stuff like that, yeah, yeah.

—He was obviously very unhappy.

—Yeah.

—Do you think it's important for a singer to have experienced a really intense range of emotions in their own life?

—Yes.

—You do?

—Yeah.

—Is that why you think boy bands are crap?

—Yeah. They've never lived, y'know. But then you get people like Michael Jackson. Michael Jackson was an incredible singer when he was ten years old. Eleven years old. And he's had a tough life. Yeah, he was brought up in Gary, Indiana. Gary, Indiana, right! The youngest member of a fucking black family, know what I mean!

—**So, no wonder he screams.**

—So, he knew how to shriek soul.

—**That's all it takes, really, isn't it?**

—Yeah, yeah . . . you need to have lived, right.

—**Yeah, so he lived.**

—Yeah.

—**Can you think of a really good singer who hasn't?**

—Not really, no.

—**Little Stevie. Little Stevie Wonder.**

—But Little Stevie Wonder's the same thing. He's out of a black ghetto. I mean, black singers . . . they've all lived, you know what I mean. Black people . . . black Americans, especially, have usually lived most of the horrors that any fucking sort of normal average white kid would experience in a lifetime, by the time they're ten. They've been kicked around, fucked around, pissed around. And what's more, they've been infused with the glory of the holy ghost. In the gospel choir, you know. Black American singers anyway, and black Jamaican singers, they're all coming from that church thing. That's a mixture of the holy ghost and the devil. You know what I mean, meeting each other, in a furious outburst.

—**Who are your favourite black singers?**

—I love them all.

—**Not them all?**

—Well, I can't think of any I don't like.

—**Do you like Whitney Houston?**

—Yeah.

—**All right then, which is your favourite? You can only pick five all-time favourites.**

—I can't! I can't do that sort of shit! That's like the sort of thing newspapers do. I'm not gonna do that.

—**Do you like Al Green?**

—Of course I like Al Green.

—Have you ever tried to sing like that? Soul?

—Yeah, I've tried. I can't do it. I'm not black.

—No, but Van Morrison can do it.

—Van Morrison can't do it.

—Yeah he can.

—He can't! He might think he can, but he can't. But he can do Van Morrison . . . we've been through this one. He's a one-off, y'know, Van Morrison.

—Yeah, we agree on that. Is that why you can't do it? Sing soul? Cause you're not black.

—I think it's most of the reason, yeah.

—What about Mick Hucknall?

—He can't sing full stop!

—He was voted soul singer of the year, 1996.

—Who by?

—The Music of Black Origin Awards.

—Well, he's the wrong colour for a start.

—Yeah, I know that. But he's soul singer of the year.

—Well, I mean, that just shows what the music business has come to.

—Do you like Terence Trent D'Arby?

—Yes! He's brilliant! He's a black American.

—I thought he was English. He's English.

—Terence Trent D'Arby?

—He's English.

—He's not English. He's American. He won the fucking Golden Gloves in the American army. He's a boxer as well as a singer, yeah. He won the Golden Gloves. You have to be American to win the Golden Gloves.

—Okay then . . . Do you like Sade?

—That is, in fact, an example of a black singer that I don't like, and I was going to bring it up.

—Sade?

—Yeah. Well, she's an English black singer. And that's why I said black American or Jamaican.

—Why do you think a lot of the English ones are crap?

—Probably because they weren't fucking beaten up enough as kids. And they didn't fucking go to church enough as kids. Didn't sing in the choir. That's where they all learned to sing, Marvin Gaye, and everybody else . . . they all learned to sing in baptist choirs.

—So if you had kids, would you make them go to church and beat them up?

—Yeah. That's how John McCormack learned to sing, you know.

—How?

—By being beaten up, and fucking going to church.

—Is it?

—Yeah. Classic Irish upbringing. Classic Irish voice.

—But you weren't beaten up.

—I was beaten up, and made to go to church. I wasn't beaten up as much as I should've been. But I was beaten up a bit. And I was made to go to church a lot.

—Did you enjoy church?

—Yes, I loved it.

—Why?

—Cause it's a beautiful experience. The Roman Catholic Mass is one of the most beautiful experiences a human being can be subjected to. And I use the words 'be subjected to' advisedly. It's not something you want to do, it's something you're beaten into doing. But then once you're there, right, the whole thing takes you over, and like, you go . . . WOW! OH OH OH.

—So are you intimately aquainted with the holy spirit then?

—I like to think so, yeah.

—You look like you are. Were you an altar boy?

—I wasn't, no.

—You weren't an altar boy?

—No, I wasn't enough of a 'suit' to be an altar boy.

—Were you a choirboy?

—I wasn't a choirboy. I sang in the choir, but I wasn't a choirboy.

—What's the difference?

—I mean I sang in church, but I wasn't a choirboy. I sang hymns in church . . .

—Why do you think so many rock stars die when they're twenty-seven?

—Only about three of them died when they were twenty-seven.

—**Kurt Cobain, Gram Parsons . . .**

—Jimi Hendrix, Janis Joplin, Jim Morrison . . .

—**That's five.**

—That's it.

—**There's more.**

—Name them. It's also a really stupid question.

—**I just wondered.**

—A few people have died when they were twenty-seven, a few people have died when they were fucking . . . a lot more people died when they were forty or fifty, y'know. Musicians.

—**Which female singers do you like?**

—Aretha Franklin. Miriam Makeba.

—**Who's that?**

—She's a South African. She does clicking with her tongue. Minnie Ripperton, Maria Muldaur, [sings] 'Midnight at the Oasis. Put your camel to bed.' Maggie Barry. Maggie Barry, the Queen of the Gypsies. Yeah. Irish singer.

—**Who else?!?!**

—Delores Keane. Uhm . . . my mum!

—**Do you like Patti Smith?**

—She's not a singer.

—**Yeah she is. I've heard her sing.**

—She's a sort of singer.

—**Do you like Joan Jett?**

—She's definitely not a singer.

—**Joan Jett's definitely not a singer? Yes she is. I think she's great. Do you like . . . Laura Nyro?**

—Yeah, you know I like Laura Nyro. Cause she's a soulful, sweet little Jewish bitch from the fucking wrong side of New York.

—**She might not like to be described like that.**

—Well, that's what she is. She's a road apple.

—**What's a road apple?**

—It's an apple that falls in the road.

—Why? What does that mean?

—Bruised and beautiful.

—Yeah?

—Yeah.

—Do you like Janis Joplin?

—I particularly like *Gonna Take a Miracle* by Laura Nyro. That's my favourite album by her. Put Patti LaBelle and the Blue Belles behind her. And got her to do all the great girlie songs of the fucking twentieth century. But like, on the front cover of the album, you can see she doesn't look well . . . they put her in a pink dress, and she can't keep it on properly, know what I mean, cause she's so skinny. And like . . . her face is skeletal. And like, she's got big black rings under her eyes. And you compare it to the first album, which was only four years before; where she's like . . . this really wholesome-looking, young Jewish kid, from New York. Smiling serenely at you.

—So, why do you suppose that happened?

—The music biz.

—Ah, the music biz. The music biz does that to you? Okay. So why does the music business fuck you up?

—I was talking about Laura Nyro. I was talking about how this took a young girl, full of talent, probably not very sussed, you know, and it looks like it turned her into a fucking wreck, in a matter of four years. It's like it squeezed everything out of her, and spat out the fucking remainder. And she still came out with, *Gonna Take a Miracle*, you know, at the end of it. But then, she couldn't even get a fucking pink dress to stay on her fucking shoulders. That's what the business does to some people. That's what it did to Kurt Cobain. Hasn't done it to me.

—How come?

—Cause I'm tougher than them.

—But did it nearly do it to you?

—Nah. It didn't nearly do it to me.

—But you did have a hard time.

—I had a good time.

—And you had a few nervous breakdowns too.

—I didn't notice, I was too out of it. There were breakdowns coming and going, but I've always been too out of it to notice. I had my first nervous breakdown when I was six years old, you know.

—Six?

—Yeah.

—Your first nervous breakdown?

—Yeah, when they dragged me out of the bush and took me off to England.

—How did it manifest itself?

—What?

—The nervous breakdown, what were the symptoms?

—Anxiety, depression, and like, paranoia, you know. Didn't realize it was called a nervous breakdown at the time. Crying myself to sleep thinking about Ireland, y'know. So it'll take more than the fucking music business to fucking screw me up.

—Why does the music business do it to so many people? Cause it seems to do it to a lot of people, like, look at Elvis Presley, he started out fairly normal, didn't he?

—Well, what they did to Presley, Presley was ripe for . . . cause Presley was a mummy's boy. You know what I mean? Presley was a mummy's boy. He went in there that first day to make a record for his mother, you know. For her birthday. That's how he got discovered. Talk about . . . you know, he had about as much suss as a fucking hedgehog, know what I mean.

—So why does it do that? Why does the music business in particular fuck people up?

—Why does it eat them up and spew them out again?

—Yeah.

—Because it's just a conveyer belt, fucking canned meat fucking business . . . like any other business, know what I mean. Except you're dealing with people's lives . . . nah, you're dealing with people's lives in any fucking business. All businesses are like that, you know.

—Not in the tinned soup business.

—In the tinned soup business it's people putting soup into tins! That must drive fucking hundreds of people round the twist, you know.

—That's all done with machinery, isn't it? Putting the soup into tins?

—Somebody's got to put the labels on.

—Machines do that too. Anyway . . .

—Somebody's got to operate the machines, you know. Someone's got to push the button.

—Yeah. Okay, then, so why is it that the music business . . . is it just because there's more money in it that it turns out more spectacularly fucked-up cases?

—No, they're just more famous.

—Just more famous?

—Yeah.

—But they seem to do more drugs. Maybe that's because they've got more money.

—Yeah, they've got more money.

—Would you say that there would be roughly the same amount of people who get fucked up in the acting as in the music business?

—No, I wouldn't say that, cause actors are fucked up to start off with. Anybody who wants to be an actor is a fuck-up.

—And why is that?

—What?

—Why do you say that?

—Because they haven't got a personality of their own.

—Don't they?

—No. An actor has to be a blank piece of paper, you know. I mean, is there anything more boring than watching an actor being interviewed on television?!

—No. Not much. I've seen the odd one, but they're usually writers as well, or directors as well. They're really talented.

—No, directors are a different matter. Directors are the people with the fucking ideas. No . . . I'm not saying actors don't have ideas. Well, I am saying actors don't have ideas, they have to be blank pieces of paper for the director to fucking scrawl all over. But they have to be happy like that. And they are happy like that. I mean, I adore Robert de Niro, right. But I wouldn't really like to go out to dinner with him, you know what I mean? I don't think he'd be that much fun.

—I bet Dennis Hopper would be fun, and . . .

—Dennis Hopper's a director as well. And what's more, Dennis Hopper is a one-off, know what I mean? Some actors, right, are booked to be themselves. There's two types of actors, right, there's actors, like real actors, and there's character actors, yeah? Like real actors, right, that can play any role, you know what I mean, are generally, fairly dull people, as far as I can see. Or, need to be, you know, cause they need to be pliable. They need to be able to take on any personality. They need to be able to make something convincing without even knowing what they're saying.

Then you get intelligent actors, who don't really get very far. Except for people like Dennis Hopper, but Dennis Hopper is not exactly a blockbuster, teen matinée idol, is he? He's done all right, but it took him bloody years to get there. He directed a movie in 1969, which was a ground-breaking movie. Then there was basically nothing much heard of him again for ages, know what I mean, after *Easy Rider*. Then he walked straight back in and just got character parts all over the place. He's a pyschopath, you know what I mean, cause he is a psychopath. I mean Dennis Hopper is like Martin Scorsese being an actor. You know what I mean? He's an unusual actor, Dennis Hopper, he's not a typical actor. It's like letting Martin Scorsese be a movie star.

—So you said there are two kinds.

—Yeah, there's character actors like Dennis Hopper or Steve Buscemi, or Michael Madsen, who just walk on and you just have to look at them, and you go, 'Oh wow, yeah. Fucking great. Brilliant.' You know, they don't have to do anything. Like Nicholas Cage, yeah. They don't have to do anything. It doesn't matter what kind of poxy script they're handed, you'll watch them, know what I mean, from the beginning of the movie to the end. Because you can't take your eyes off them.

—Why can't you take your eyes off them? What is it about the person that makes you not able to take your eyes off them?

—Because they've got such massive personalities.

—Do rock stars have massive personalities?

—Good ones do, yeah, but there are very few good ones. I don't think Sting has a massive personality, or Elton John.

—Elton John seemed to be a nice bloke. We met him, remember . . .

—Yeah, but he hasn't got a massive personality. You wouldn't describe him as having a massive personality, you know.

—Jerry Lee Lewis?

—He's got a massive personality, yeah. All he's got to do is walk on stage, know what I mean. He could take a dump, and walk off again, and people would go mad.

—Yeah. But what is that then? What is it that makes them so charismatic? You're interested in personalities . . . to study them, aren't you? You've read *The Development of Personality* . . .

—That's by Jung, that's not about what we were talking about.

—It's not?

—No, that's about every normal Joe's personality. It's about normal people, it applies to everybody, that. The book, *The Development of Personality*, is about how you become who you are. And that applies to anyone, it's not about film stars, or rock stars, it's not about massive personalities, it's about normal personalities.

—So where do massive personalities come from do you think?

—I think they're made in heaven.

—Do you?

—Yeah . . . or hell. Probably hell. Charlie had a massive personality, you know.

—Yeah.

—You could have put Charlie in any film you can think of, right, and he would have been the star of the show. It wouldn't have mattered what he said or anything. You just couldn't take your eyes off him, and like, every time he opened his mouth, he goes, 'Grrrrrrrrrhhhhhhhh . . .' And that's all he'd have to say. He wouldn't have to use words even, Charlie. There is a fucking film star that got wasted, you know what I mean . . . in every sense of the word.

—**What about you? You have a massive personality, and you haven't decided to become a character actor.**

—It's very nice of you to say that I have a massive personality.

—**You know you have.**

—Well, I'm quite happy being a musician. That's what moves me, man.

—**Yeah. So . . . anyway we were talking about the music business and people getting fucked up. Do you think it's because of their egos?**

—No, it's not because of their egos. I told you why it was. It's because it's a fucking business. People go into it thinking it's something artistic, and it's not. It's a business. It's just a fucking business, you know, just like any other business. It's like throwing shit at a wall, and some of it sticks. Nobody in there knows what they're doing, you know. The music business has probably got every fucking horrific aspect of every other business in it. It's got all the advertising, all the fucking hype, all the fucking selling you shit and dressing it up as fucking roses – constantly going on all the time.

What it's doing is, it's treating music – which is fucking sublime and ethereal, and to do with your higher self – treating music, and people who make music, just like corned beef, know what I mean. So of course people who are very highly tuned will get fucked up. You know, like a harp is a very sensitive instrument. You don't get a harp and put it through a fucking Frey Bentos mixer, and expect it to sound all right when it comes out the other end. You don't get a highly tuned person, like Kurt Cobain or Laura Nyro, and just shove them through a fucking mincing machine. They certainly won't come out at the other end, like, finely tuned, without a blemish, no, they'll come out all fucking mangled up, and fucked up. It's like putting a harp in a blender . . . a massive blender.

—**Do you think those people would be less fucked up, and maybe wouldn't kill themselves or whatever, had they not chosen that** business, had they chosen to be painters or decorators, or shop assistants?

—Sure.

—**Really?**

—Yeah.

—**You don't think they were like, fucked up anyway? Like Kurt?**

—No.

—**He had already talked about killing himself before he ever got into the music business.**

—So did lots of people, you know. People who talk about wanting to kill themselves generally don't. Let's face it, people who want to kill themselves do it. And I don't believe for a minute that he killed himself.

—**Don't you?**

—No.

—**What do you think happened to him?**

—I think he was murdered.

—**Why would anyone want him murdered?**

—Seventy-seven million dollars, that's why! If you go around with a price tag like that around your neck and you haven't got fucking bodyguards, you're going to end up dead, you know.

—**Bono's not dead.**

—Bono has bodyguards.

—**He hasn't. Come on, we've met him loads of times without bodyguards.**

—All right . . . Bono hasn't got bodyguards. Bono's just a lucky guy, you know.

—**Well, a lot of people don't get killed who are worth millions, come on. None of the Stones have been murdered. Actually, a lot of really, really . . .**

—What are you talking about?! Brian Jones died in a fucking swimming pool when he was twenty-eight years old.

—**Twenty-seven, twenty-seven, twenty-seven!**

—Twenty-eight.

—**No, twenty-seven, all right. But an awful lot of very rich** musicians wander around. David Bowie's one of the richest musicians in the world.

—David Bowie exploits the business to its maximum potential, know what I mean. David Bowie knows how to play the game.

—**Do you think that that's an advantage in the music business? It must be.**

—Of course it's an advantage. It's the only thing that keeps you afloat, you know.

—**Cynicism?**

—No, not cynicism, just fucking suss. David Bowie has more suss than the fucking people that are trying to put him through the mincer. He always has, you know. And Bono's got a manager who is so sussed that like, it's a case of, 'Anybody touches my boy and you've got me to deal with!' It's a fascist's industry, and you have to be more of a fascist than the industry itself, to survive.

—**Do you think it takes a lot of strength to survive it without compromising what you do?**

—You can't survive it without compromising.

—**Can't you?**

—No. It's got an instant safety valve in it. Anybody who fucks around too much gets wasted, know what I mean.

—**Yeah?**

—Yeah. One way or another. There's a hundred fucking assholes you gotta lick, there's a hundred fucking well-oiled machines you've got to keep moving, you've gotta have eyes in the back of your head, you know. It's a jungle. It's like a jungle sometimes . . .

—**Nick Cave doesn't compromise, does he?**

—Nick Cave is still in the same financial position he was in like, ten years ago.

—**But maybe he doesn't necessarily want to make much more money. In fact, he doesn't seem to worry that much about money. Do you compromise?**

—What?

—**Do you compromise your art?**

—Yes, I've compromised, yeah.

—Do you regret compromising?

—Yeah.

—Which bits did you compromise on?

—I don't regret compromising – but it didn't make me feel very good at the time.

—No? What things did you do that you didn't want to do?

—Lots of things. I didn't want to do a version of 'My Way'.

—What else?

—I didn't want to do lots of things. I didn't want to get Frank in as the manager, you know.

—So you did them all for money, basically?

—All the compromises I made were for an easier life, not just money. I knew they weren't the right thing to do, but like, people hassled me so much that I did them. Or else people paid me enough that I did them. I have no regrets. [Sings] 'Je ne regrette rien . . .' If I could do it all over again, I'd do it all over you.

—Surely all those people that whinge about the music business being exploitative and stuff, they don't have to do it professionally, do they? I mean, they can just do it for the love of it. They want the money.

—You can only be exploited if you want money. Nobody can exploit you if you're gonna do something for nothing.

—No they can't, can they. So, in a way, Kurt Cobain and Laura Nyro were just as much involved in their own exploitation as whoever was paying them.

—Sure.

—So they could have just decided to say fuck the music business, and we're just gonna sing. And they could've just sang and people could've come to see them for free.

—Look . . . if someone waves a fat fucking cheque in front of you – in front of your face, it's amazing what you will do. And then you think about it afterwards. I mean, you can get someone rubbed out for a thousand pounds, you know. You don't hear contract killers whingeing about how they are being exploited.

—No you don't!

—But they are being exploited. A human life costs more than fucking a thousand pounds. Whatever kind of animal you are, you know. But people who think that art is going to be treated any differently to dogfood, right, are the people who get hurt. I never thought art was going to get treated any differently to dogfood. I knew I'd have to compromise. I knew that I was going to slave my guts out, it's lucky I'm not a perfectionist.

—**So, therefore you didn't mind . . .**

—Of course I minded. Everybody minds compromising, you know what I mean, when they've got a dream. You're dealing with people's dreams here, you know, not just your dreams . . . you're dealing with the people who are listening to the music's dreams, you're dealing with the people who are making the music's dreams. And in between, there are a bunch of bastards, right, who don't even dream. Who just think about it like dogfood. Who don't give a fuck. The lowest individuals in the world are in the music business. The biggest scumbags you are ever going to meet are in the music business, you know.

—**Why?**

—God knows why! Because it should be different, you know, it should be different. But people still go into it thinking it should be different, so it will be different. But it won't be different. Just because it should be different doesn't mean it will be different. Your dreams will still be treated like dogfood. And the dreams of your audience will still be treated like dogfood, by the dreamless bastards – who don't even dream.

—**That's a very strong opinion to hold. Don't you think it's possible that there are people with integrity in the music business, or that there could be?**

—What!? In the music BUSINESS?

—**Like in record companies? People selling the music?**

—No.

—**Why not?**

—I don't know why not. Like I said, it should be different.

—**So you don't think it's possible?**

—There's your David KatzNelsons about, but his hands are tied by a hundred morons, you know. People who are on a higher level than him, or like, the same level as him, who don't give a shit, who want to listen to Alanis Morrisette.

—**But obviously an awful lot of very good music has made it through the system, because we've got a record collection . . .**

—Less and less as the years go by.

—**Yes, that's true.**

—In the early days of record companies there were some good people. I'm talking about the forties, fifties, and sixties, yeah, there were some remarkable individuals around, like . . .

—**Like Berry Gordy.**

—Yeah, like Berry Gordy. But Berry Gordy was just a dirty old man you know, at the end of the day.

—**Who had great taste in music.**

—Yeah, he had great taste in music. But Berry got old and fat. And like now the Motown label . . . what comes out on it now? Fuck all. Fucking rubbish. You can get to a stage where, because of that, someone like Mick Hucknall can get voted . . . what was it?

—**Best male soul singer in Britain.**

—No, best male singer of music of black origin, wasn't it?

—**It was the Music of Black Origin Awards that awarded him.**

—Yeah. Best male soul singer, you know what I mean! Give me a break. So, I mean soul, which has probably been the purest form of pop music ever, goes through the mincing machine and comes out the other end too. But whatever you do to Smokey Robinson, you can't take the Smokey Robinson out of him. Musicians themselves are pure, innocent, little darlings.

—**All musicians?**

—All good musicians are pure innocent little darlings. They get battered into warped old men and women by the university of hard knocks, you know. By constantly having to compromise, constantly having to be treated like dogfood. That will do anybody down at the end of the day. Unless you just set your sights really low. Like Nick Cave, you know.

—Well, he's comfortable. He has a house to live in and he doesn't have to work at a job he doesn't like, to pay for it. Neither do you.

—No, you can't think about it in terms like that. To make great music, you gotta have no interest in houses of any description. You don't care if you sleep in the fucking street, as long as they're playing my music, you know what I mean, that's the attitude you have to have. Like, you can't even think about a house, or a car, or fucking anything . . . you've just got to be fucking overwhelmed by the idea of getting your music on to a piece of fucking vinyl, or whatever they make compact discs out of. Metal or whatever it is.

—Plastic?

—Is it plastic? All right, well, plastic then. And be prepared not to get paid.

—Right. You've to be prepared not to get paid?

—Yeah. Just as long as you can get it out. You've got to have a strong urge to be heard. You've gotta have this welling up inside you like, wanting to be sick, you know. Then you've got to scream it out, you've got to sing it out, you've got to play it out, you've got to make music, know what I mean. That's what a musician is – a good musician has to put music before everything. And that's what I have always done. When I've made good music.

—So these people, who approach this as a career, and think in terms of making a decent living and all that . . .

—Forget it! Nobody who thinks like that is gonna make good music.

—People make a lot of money though, don't they, by thinking like that? But that's not really the point.

—People do make a lot of money thinking like that, yeah, but they don't make good music. And so they've got that as their karma. They've polluted the atmosphere with their shit, you know what I mean, with their money-making shit. And they've shoved a load of real musicians out of the way to do it. Nick Cave's attitude is very pure, you know. He is a true musician. He doesn't give a shit what anybody wants to hear. He doesn't give a shit.

—You can tell that by listening to his records!

—I don't think he has ever made a bad record.

—**Come on!**

—I don't think he has ever made a bad record.

—**Some of the tracks on that last one.**

—What? *The Boatman's Call*? I think that's a brilliant album.

—**Yeah, so do I, but you don't think there are a few tracks on that which are a bit . . . turgid? Like the black hair one?**

—Nah. Not once you're in the mood, and the mood gets set straight off. Like thirty seconds into the album you know what you're gonna get. He doesn't fuck around. He doesn't make any attempts at compromise or anything like that, right. Thirty seconds into that album you know what it's going to be like for the rest of the album. It's not going to get any better than this. If that's the way you want to think about it. But personally, I think it's a fucking beautiful record. I think it's his masterpiece . . . so far. But he never ceases to astound me by what he is going to come up with next.

—**You like Nick, don't you?**

—Yeah. I first met Nick at what I call the *NME* Super Summit. There was me, Nick and Mark E. Smith being interviewed by Sean O'Hagan and James Brown. Mark E. Smith got really pissed and he was going on about how he hated Pakis. He said, 'If you were brought up on a council estate in Salford you'd hate Pakis too.' And he went on about how the English army had every right to be in Ireland and I got very angry about that. And Nick just sat there with a cup of tea, looking cool, being his usual self. Nick stole the interview by not saying anything. I thought he was great, I thought he was one of the coolest guys I'd ever met, he just was cool, some people are cool and some people aren't. I loved his music anyway and the fact that he lived up to his music by being really cool and I didn't like Mark E. Smith's music and he lived down to his music by being an arsehole.

—**I fancy Nick, do you?**

—Yeah, I know. I don't blame you. I'd shag him myself, if I could. And like, it's the same with Van Morrison. He doesn't fuck around. Thirty seconds into a Morrison album, you know the rest of the album. You know what it's going to be like, you know what you are getting, you know what mood he's in, you know what's coming out – and you just either take it off or you listen to it. That's what music should be like.

—Do you think he compromises?

—What, Van? No. Never.

—Well, he has managed to make a lot of money, without compromise. Even though he complains about the business, he's still managed to stay in it for a long time.

—It's taken him a lifetime, you know. He should have gone straight to Number One with the first fucking Them album, and stayed there for the rest of his life. He should've been monstrous from the word go. The first Them album is fucking brilliant, you know. Now he's got it too easy, that's the funny thing. He churns it out now, a bit. Well, he hasn't come out with anything for a while, you know, so I mean hopefully the next thing will be interesting.

—What's your favourite Van Morrison album?

—I haven't got one. It just depends on what you put on, you know. You just put one on and you just listen to it. But thirty seconds in, you know what I mean, you know what you're getting. There's no fucking around.

—When you say 'no fucking around', what do you mean?

—Well, there's no boring irrelevant crap going on. It just starts and you're in there. You're into the groove, and there's a melody, you know. He might not start singing for a while, but thirty seconds into it and you are into a groove. Everything he does has got a groove. Everything Nick Cave does has got a groove. Thirty seconds in, and you are into the groove, and you can either like that groove, or not like that groove. If you don't like that groove you can take the record off. But he's going to stay in that groove for the rest of the album, you know what I mean, you can tell that. You know that.

—Are we going to talk about Van?

—Well, Van depressed me, as well as being very funny he is also very depressing. At the end of the day he is funny though. I remember one time after we'd spent the day drinking together, I had to pick him up off the floor of the Clarence, which was not an easy job and

I'm sure that's not the only time that's happened. I stayed up drinking with him many nights and I always tried to convince Van what a wonderful life it was and what a wonderful life he was living or could live if he stopped being such a miserable fuck, but it didn't work.

There's a man who lived up to his public image, he was meant to be a miserable old git and he is a miserable git, but he is capable of having a really good laugh. There was a point when we were going to do an album together, with me singing his songs and him producing, but when he discovered it was going to come out on Warner Brothers he turned his back on the whole thing. But he was very impressed with what we did do and I was very flattered by that, obviously. The track we did was called 'Philosophy'. Most people don't know what 'Philosophy' is; 'Philosophy' is a track that only ever appeared on an EP, never on an album, never on the B-side of a single or anything like that. It is one of his greatest songs . . . 'you're gonna reap what you sow one of these days'.

I was a big fan of Van, for years, I thought he was Ireland's greatest living poet. 'My Lonely Sad Eyes', 'Hey Little Girl', 'Bad Or Good' and 'Don't Look Back' are my favourite songs, but I could go on forever, I like all his old stuff. He doesn't sing, he wails. I think that Them were definitely the best fucking band in the world, better than the Stones, better than the Beatles, better even than the Small Faces and a hundred times better than Oasis, better than the Spencer Davies Group. I think that's incredible, being an Irish group, and I regarded him as Ireland's greatest living poet and he was a great influence on my songwriting, but I did not expect much personality-wise.

—**What about the other famous people you know? You don't really like famous people, do you? Do you like Bono?**
—I just like people or don't like them, it doesn't make any difference to me if they're famous. Bono was kind enough to lend us his Martello Tower in Bray for a while and it turned out to be over-looking a house that was owned by Mary Coughlan. We went to the local pub a lot and we had quite a deep conversation with Bono in

there, once, about religion. He was confused about a lot of stuff and I wasn't . . . I don't regard myself as having the right to set people straight, but I think the knowledge I had was useful, I mean he told me it was to him . . . It was a good conversation, it went on for a long time, we had several pints of Guinness, there was no pretension on either side. I was glad to see that he wasn't as pretentious as I'd been told he was and he was very generous and he allowed us to stay in his place for a few months and he paid all our bills.

—**Which was nice of him.**

—Yeah. The tower was constructed in such a way as to have a glass roof built on the top, over the bedroom and it had a dangerous set of stairs leading up to it, so the ghosts couldn't get up the stairs to the bedroom, like a lighthouse stairs going around and around and around and you could easily slip and fall and of course, I did, and did myself some bad damage on the walls. I was trying to hit a guy and he ducked and I put the full weight of my body into this really thick wall which put my arm in plaster for at least three months.

So, anyway, when you get up to the top there's the master bedroom with a huge bed and there's just glass walls so all the neighbours can see you getting in and out of bed and see you dangling your wares. I would say good morning to Mary Coughlan by waving my donger at her. I was spotted by somebody passing by on the train, flashing at her and it was in the papers the next day, but the temptation to do it was unbearable.

We found one of the great man's condoms in the great man's bed, too. It was very comfortable sleeping in Bono's bed, it was a very comfortable bed.

—**It was a lovely bed.**

—Dublin was full of personalities at the time we were living in Bono's tower. My mate Rick came over to visit while we were there and he picked up an unnameable film star in Lillie's Bordello – which was a great club we used to go to, where they let you drink all night – and they went back to the film star's room at the Shelbourne and Rick says they went to bed together but I don't know whether that was Rick's imagination or not. I mean, I wasn't that interested,

I remember they were both very badly behaved and hammering the table and shouting and then he had a wrestling match with Rick and told Rick that he was like his little brother. It was around the same time that Lisa Stansfield broke my nose. I was having a conversation with somebody and there was lots of noise and there was you, me and Terry O'Neill, Robbie O'Neill and Barry Egan and I was having a chat with Barry Egan, I think, and Lisa Stansfield came and sat down beside me and started talking to me and I said, 'Give us a moment – I'm talking, having a conversation.' She got annoyed about that and punched me very hard in the face and my nose had already been broken three times at that time and she broke it for a fourth time and straightened it out again because it did have a bump on it at the time and there was blood everywhere and you were trying to mop up the blood and Lisa was trying to shove fucking ice cubes up my nostrils and trying to turn it into a Bloody Mary and you were saying, 'Can you fuck off – you've done enough', like you always do when somebody has a go at me, always supportive to me. Lisa Stansfield was saying, 'Oh, I just want to make it better' and there was blood gushing out of my nose and anyway after it all died down me and Lisa became friends and we saw her every night after that.

So we met a lot of different people. Dublin was full of personalities at the time, like I said. Jim Sheridan and Neil Jordan were always around. I'm sure Jim wouldn't mind me calling him a drunken old lecher, which makes him a great Paddy. Jim Sheridan is a great Paddy. *The Field* is a great film and *My Left Foot* is a great film. I don't like the one about Gerry Conlon, though. And Neil Jordan has done some good films, too. *We're No Angels* is a good film and *High Spirits* is a good film and *Mona Lisa*, that's a good film, and *Angel* his first film is brilliant, really good, with Stephen Rea.

He wanted to kill me one time. I think I went up and insulted him. It was the night he won his Oscar but I'd beaten him up before. The first time I ever met him was when he was doing a video for us and Kirsty MacColl. He had ordered these costumes and I didn't like them, I particularly didn't like my own one and somebody said to me, 'This is Neil Jordan and you must respect him' and I went up to him and said, 'Oh, Neil Jordan, so you're the wanker who fucking decided to dress me up in this costume' and he got taken aback by that and said yes he was and I said I thought it was full of shit and what's more I told him I'd stayed up all night especially to look like I was dead, because according to the storyline I'm dead and that there should have been a bullethole in the middle of my head and I wanted to put a bullethole in the middle of my head and he said that we couldn't afford to put a bullethole in the middle of my head, the BBC wouldn't like it and I said, 'Fuck the BBC, what kind of a director are you?' and I had especially stayed up all night, not that I wouldn't have anyway but I'd had a particularly hard night deliberately to look as much like a corpse as possible. I walked into make-up and said, 'Bullethole in the middle of the head please' and that's when Neil Jordan came in and vetoed it.

Then one time in Lillie's Bordello he called me a bastard and started fighting with me and I started beating the shit out of him and Terry O'Neill broke it up.

Mannix Flynn, now he should be given a film to write, produce and direct. I'd like him to do my film. Mannix Flynn is a great writer, playwright, actor and poet and criminal arsonist and he was put in a hall of correction as a kid then he came out and wrote a Behan-style, borstal-boy book called *Nothing to Say* and he's also written lots of plays and acted in lots of plays and you can always find him in some pub in Dublin, holding the floor, reciting in monologue and all the rest of it and demanding people buy him drinks. He is a good friend of mine and a great bloke.

—So what makes a great bloke?

—My criteria for somebody being a great bloke is pretty simple. A great bloke is entertaining, generous, can hold his drink, is unafraid to admit to being a homosexual or bisexual or a junkie or a criminal or a wanker. Somebody who doesn't just hang around great blokes sort of like hoping to get some of their glory, hoping that the power will rub off.

Terry O'Neill is a great bloke, Charlie MacLennan was a great bloke. I'd like to talk about Charlie. I'd known Charlie for years before he came to work for us but he didn't know me, really, because he was always drinking with Thin Lizzy and Robbo. I used to steal his food when he collapsed at the Speakeasy.

The Speakeasy was a late-night club in Margaret Street, really expensive cocktails. We'd get in with some record people that were hanging around with us because they wanted to know what was hip, they were desperate to be hip, they were desperately trying to find out what was going on on the street, so they would get us into clubs and in these clubs would be all the rock stars and roadies, Charlie and Phil Lynott and people like that would be down there, out of their brains. We'd be out of our brains too, but we'd be stealing, so we'd be more alert. We could drink their drinks and eat their food and take their drugs, when they passed out. I'd known Lemmy, as well, for years. I knew Lemmy since I was about fourteen, when I sort of muscled in on him and attached myself to him, like Danny Sugarman did to Jim Morrison and I used to be invited to his parties.

Charlie was one of Frank Murray's friends. Frank, I knew from Rock On, the record stall where I worked. All the work I got was from the Irish Murphia, running clubs, roadie-ing, working in the record shop, whatever. When the Nips first got signed, we signed up to an Irish Murphia label, Soho, run by Stan Brennan and Phil Gaston, who used to work for Ted Carroll and Frank was one of Ted Carroll's boys too, but Charlie was above all that because he was well in with Lizzy.

The first fairly long conversation I had with Charlie was at Self-Aid in Dublin and he was holding himself up by leaning against a trailer and he had a huge grin on his face. He managed to get off the trailer, I ended up with him in Geldof's caravan with Bill Brennan and Richie Morris. Someone was saying what a fat cunt Van Morrison was, how boring he was, he did a terrible set that night. Everyone was cracking jokes. Bob Geldof was being particularly funny, he's got a sardonic sense of humour, he's a really funny guy. Charlie was pissing himself. Then, about two weeks later, Charlie was working for us.

It was just after the launch for *Rum, Sodomy and the Lash* when we got dressed up in our eighteenth-century pirates' outfits and came across in a boat at Traitor's Gate and there was free booze and all the journalists got pissed and one of them fell out of the boat and had to be rescued by the police. Directly after that Charlie turned up. Basically, when people started working for us they just turned up, you might know them and you might not, I happened to know Charlie but it could be that a lot of people didn't know Charlie. Me and Charlie got on very well because we were the biggest space cadets around.

And then you get just plain nice blokes like Mark Hasler, you wouldn't say he was a great bloke but he is capable of being a great bloke, at the moment he is just a nice bloke. Spider is a nice bloke. Jock Scot is a really great bloke, Tom Waits is a great bloke, Joey Cashman is a great bloke, Jerry Lee Lewis is a *really* great bloke, he is a giant among great blokes. Jerry Lee was everything I had hoped for, when I first met him, every piece of the legend, he was a living legend. He had a gun in one hand and a bottle of rye in the other. The gist of what he said to me was drink with me or die by me. I drank with him. He was exactly what I expected, a shy and sensitive type of guy.

Quite a few people in my group are great blokes and they're all nice blokes and who knows what I am, that's for somebody else to judge. Matt Dillon is nearly a great bloke, Johnny Depp is a really great bloke, Nicholas Cage is a great bloke, Nick Nolte is a great bloke. Sean Penn very definitely a great bloke. Chris Penn is on the verge of being a great bloke but he's still just a nice bloke. No, actually I think I'd put him in the same category as Matt Dillon, not quite a great bloke yet. Pavarotti is a great bloke. I also admire in particular Gerry Adams, Michael Collins, Brendan Behan and Sean O'Casey as examples of great Irishmen. And an awful lot of musicians, too many to name. I do admire Gerry Adams, because he isn't a boring pretentious twat.

—**What about great women?**

—Dorothy Parker, Queen Maeve, Inion Dubh . . .

—What about me?!!!!!!
—Victoria Mary Clarke, Edna O'Brien, the list is endless.
—Okay then. Where were we? Varying the music . . . you don't believe in it.
—No. I don't believe in it, Van doesn't believe in it, Nick doesn't believe in it.
—Who else?
—Anybody good.
—Right.
—You do what you're best at, right.
—And stick to it.
—Yeah. I'm just gonna go on churning out the same stuff for the rest of my life, you know.
—Yeah?
—Yeah, I should never have wavered from the path, compromised. I compromised because of the rest of the group, and it took me a while to find my feet again.
—There was a time when you said that you really liked the idea of working in a democracy.
—I never liked the idea of working in a democracy.
—Oh yes you did. You always used to say that to me. You used to say that you believed in the idea of democracy, and you wanted the band you were in, the Pogues at the time, to be a democracy. And you didn't want to be a leader.
—Well, I was lying.
Shane chuckles, mischievously.
—You were lying? You said it a lot, that you had this sort of idealistic idea that you should be . . .
—I used to lie a lot!
—You would lie to me about something like that? Would you?
—I was lying to myself.
—Oh I see.
—No, I need to be in charge of it all, you know. I can't work otherwise . . . when I write stuff, I can't have any musical democracy involved in it. I can't have anybody telling me, 'It should go like this',

instead of the way I wrote it. When I write something, I make sure it's absolutely correct. That it's absolutely right. That it's a classic. Maybe you don't think it's a classic, but lots of other people do.

—No, I do . . .

—And like, then I used to have to teach them the bass part, and the fucking guitar part, and the fucking . . . The only person I didn't used to have to teach anything to was Terry Woods, in the Pogues. And the only person I don't have to teach anything to in the Popes is Tom. But the Popes are better, I mean, the Popes have got a better feel. They can pick up more on what I'm trying to do, without me telling them. That's cause they're not trying to put their own stuff in, you know what I mean. Maybe this is not the right direction to go in.

—**How do you go about writing songs?**

—I only write songs because I enjoy doing it, it's like painting or writing a story or doing a drawing or building a patio, building a wall. I don't know why, but human beings enjoy doing creative things. They enjoy doing things they're good at. They enjoy a challenge followed by some work. If you enjoy it, by definition it isn't really work but the creative process followed by a finished song, followed by the excitement of it all working is very satisfying. I also exorcized all my bitterness about Ireland, through songs.

In the case of a song, for me, it goes through different stages. I have the idea and then wrestle with the lyrics and the music. It can come very quickly or it can take ages and the lyrics and music can happen together or separately. It can be constructive or it can come out shit. And then the next thing is playing it as music with other musicians seeing if it works, if it sounds right. It never sounds exactly like you wanted it to sound, sometimes it sounds better, sometimes it sounds worse, in which case you have to work at it until it sounds good. It hardly ever sounds the same at the end as it did when you first imagined it. That's what's so good about singing other people's songs, they're already written and you just have the fun of interpreting them, which is different and doesn't involve as much work.

I get frustrated at not being able to play what's in my head, some of the time. That is frustrating. I can play my songs on the guitar, but not very well, although I did play guitar in the group in the early days. I had to stop because my co-ordination was suffering due to being drunk and I would have had to stay far more together to do it properly and I've got a lazy streak. Also I found I could sing much better without concentrating on the guitar as well. I did enjoy playing the guitar and singing, though, because it's a more satisfying feeling . . . it's more fun than just singing. It's the difference between having a wank and having a fuck.

But singing without an instrument is a different way of singing, you concentrate totally on your singing when you don't have an instrument, your voice is your instrument. Very few people play an instrument and sing seriously, people like Bob Dylan and Louis Armstrong, they're bad singers and they don't seriously play the guitar while they're singing, they're just strumming. Whereas Hendrix could do both, but Hendrix was a completely unique person. Hendrix could do things that nobody could do. Hendrix was in a completely different class. He is still the most influential musician for a long time.

I knew absolutely that I would never be able to play guitar like Hendrix. Because he was born with it as a gift and I haven't got that gift. No amount of practice could give me that gift. I think my gift is something like Tom Waits's gift, I communicate well and I'm very simple, the way I do things, and very unpretentious and I'm a good singer, I'm a singer you can get personally involved with. Like Jerry Lee Lewis, you sort of feel you know the guy when he's singing.

That isn't true of most singers, at all, it's not true of Tom Jones or Mick Jagger. I'm just a good singer and a good songwriter, that's my gift. I'm a visionary as well, I think.

I've taken singing for granted since I was three, in Ireland, and people got me to get up and sing at hooleys, 'Kevin Barry', 'The Foggy Dew', that sort of thing. I learned the songs from the old people. And everyone always told me I was good, so I never had occasion to doubt myself.

I had doubts on how good a pop singer I was, though, and I still do, but I think I'm a good Irish singer. I know I'm a good Irish singer but I think I'm a bit average as a pop singer. I've never worked at it, though, and I've had no formal music training either. Everything I've done I've done by ear. There's no need to read or write music because all really good musicians compose by ear and play by ear. Mozart could write music but he didn't need to, he carried the music around in his head. Without a piano or anything, without humming to himself or anything like that he could write out a whole symphony, a new one, make it up as he went along with no mistakes, no crossing out, none whatsoever, write it in music, in perfect notation, with no mistakes, from beginning to end, in one go. Because he played by ear and he had the music in his head. That's where it comes in. It comes into you through your ear, from where it's been floating around. Just floating around in the air, in the physical air, that's why you call a tune an air . . . it's in the air. You just need something like a voice to transmit the frequencies. We're receivers and we're transmitters.

—So you can hear music, in your head? I can't. And I think most people probably can't.

—I can hear the frequencies and I think everybody could, if they tried. If they wanted to. I do it because it's what I want to do. I'm normally humming all the time whether I make any noise or not. I have musical thoughts. I think about music more than anything else. It's kind of like leafing through a book of tunes in my head. There's tunes going through my head all the time. Right this minute, in my head is 'I'm Going to Leap Right Out of the Jukebox and Right into Your Heart'. And sometimes I hear tunes that I've never heard before. I choose the type that I want to write down, that's all. I hear beats a lot. You can do everything to a beat, your heart is beating all the time. Reggae is a little bit slower then your heartbeat, rock 'n' roll is faster than your heartbeat. No, rock 'n' roll is more or less the same beat as your heart.

I think an album is a beautiful thing, the whole thing is a beautiful thing. Every aspect, the music on it, the shape of it, the size of it, the cover, the quality of the vinyl are all things that add to the enjoyment of a record. I used to get very excited as a kid, if I bought a record, I'd look at it for hours. I look at a video for hours but they're nothing compared to records. A lot of videos are entertaining but they're not as important as records. Because music is the most important thing. I've got millions of tapes that I never listen to. They're all in bags. I never liked tapes, always thought they were unattractive. I prefer CDs, because they're more like records.

—**In your opinion, is it because what's in the record shops and what's played on the radio is generally so mundane and commerical, that that's what sells, or . . . ?**

—It's not commercial!!!

—**Well, what I mean is . . .**

—It's mundane, that's all it is. It's mundane and boring.

—**Right. Is that why that's what sells? Because that's what's being played on the radio and that's what's in the record shops?**

—Yeah!

—**It's not because that's what people want? Do you think people want boring stuff?**

—No, I don't think people want boring stuff.

—**So, do you think that if there was more interesting stuff actually played on the radio and in the shops, that people would buy more interesting stuff?**

—Of course they would, yeah.

—**So it's not down to the public having really crap taste.**

—No!

—**Really?**

—No. We've been here before, you know. Like, there was a time before the Sex Pistols, when everything was mundane and boring. And then the Sex Pistols came along, and nobody even knew that they wanted the Sex Pistols, until they heard the Sex Pistols, you know. They had to hear the Sex Pistols before they realized that that's what they wanted to really listen to, y'know. And everybody rushed out and bought the Sex Pistols.

—**Yeah. So, what about Oasis? When they came along they were something new, something a bit more lively.**

—Yeah, that's why they were successful, you know. I understand why they were successful.

—So, why do you suppose . . .

—But they weren't the Sex Pistols.

—No. But in that case, why do you suppose record companies put out boring stuff if it's not necessarily going to sell?

—Because people who work for record companies listen to Alanis Morrisette.

—So, it's because they are boring, or they like boring stuff.

—It's because what they like is boring, right, that they put out boring stuff, yeah.

—So why do you suppose they get into the record business at all? Is it because they think it's glamorous?

—Money, pussy, free drinks, drugs . . . They're just a fucking bunch of pen-pushers, who want a good salary. It's like saying, 'Why is murder so mundane and boring? Why don't people think of some more interesting ways of killing people?' Because lawyers and policemen haven't got the imagination to think of anything better.

—Lawyers and policemen?

—Yeah!

—But why lawyers and policemen? They don't . . .

—The murderers are the artists. Lawyers and policemen are the biz.

—That's not really . . .

—Like, if the policemen didn't spend their whole time arresting black people for nothing at all, they'd catch a lot more murderers, which would make a lot more interesting cases for lawyers to deal with. Which would mean that lawyers would be going around saying, 'You'll never guess what I fucking had today! This guy hashes up all these children, and he fucking strung their entrails all around the room, and there was brains all over the place!' And stuff like that, you know. That hardly ever happens. Consequently, because the police don't catch the interesting murderers, and the lawyers don't get the interesting murder cases . . . they're all bored! So, it's the same old murders, the same old crap. Lawyers are dealing with the same old crap, getting black youths off crack-dealing charges. That will go on for another century or so, you know. It's a sort of . . .

—Unusual analogy, my dear! So, do you think . . .

—If the policemen are too busy nicking black teenagers, right, to notice the guy who has just axed the whole family next door, then it never gets to the lawyers, and it never gets out in the press . . . It never gets out, and we never hear about it.

—Okay, I get your point. So, supposing you were in a position of power in the music business, what would you do differently?

—What would I do? I'd go around to grotty little clubs and pubs, and places like that, right, and I'd listen to bands.

—But don't they do that?

—No, they don't do that any more. Then I'd get them in the studio, and I'd do some serious production on them. Like a Phil Spector type production. A Tamla Motown type production. Production where I wouldn't let any bands in that didn't have a tune that you could fucking hum immediately after you heard it. I wouldn't let any bands in that couldn't sing. I wouldn't let any bands in that couldn't play.

—So you'd probably get rid of a lot of stuff . . .

—Yeah. They're just lazy bastards.

—Right.

BLACK MANDALA OF
NEW YORK
EVEN THE FLOWERS
GOT ██████
EYES

ACT EIGHT

A rugged Irish cottage, night. A fierce and loquacious wind still enjoys toying with the simple thatched roof and an equally enthusiastic fire still illuminates the kitchen, as once again we join Shane and Victoria for a chat. Shane, now attired in an Armani suit, handsomely, lights yet another cigarette and keeps an eye on Our Lady, devotedly, as conversation is resumed. Victoria brushes a crumb from her Gucci flares and crosses one Prada-shod foot over the other one, fashionably.

—We'd better talk about drink, seeing as people always ask me if I think you'll ever give it up. Do you think you will ever give it up? You have been in rehab a few times, now.

—Not by choice.

—So how did you end up in St John of God's? You've never explained that. I wasn't there at the time. I'd run away back to England and left you in Dublin, because I found you in bed with another woman in Bloom's hotel.

—St John of God's is a kind of loony bin for alcoholic nutters in Dublin. I was put in there in 1988 because I'd been drinking a lot of poteen and I collapsed. I woke up as they were putting me in an ambulance strapped to a stretcher thing and I said, What the hell's going on? Get this thing off me. They said, No, you're going into hospital. I said, No I'm not. I was perfectly all right. So they put me in, by force.

—How did you get out?

—At first I raged and screamed and yelled and banged my fists against the wall for a day or so and then I realized I'd have to do the usual play-acting crap so I became an incredibly co-operative patient and charmed everybody and said what an idiot I'd been and

319

I'd know in future and they let me out and I gave them chocolates and flowers.

At the airport on my way back to London, Carmel was travelling with me and the plane was delayed for six hours so I was drinking Long Island Iced Teas, Dublin airport style, and I had a blackout basically – I'd had a few and fallen asleep at the bar. When I woke up I just laid into this guy for no reason at all and he ran like fuck into the bog and went into one of the cubicles. So I crawled over the cubicle and started beating him over the cubicle. The police started watching me then, but they were saying, 'That's Shane MacGowan, you have to make allowances.' So this poor bastard didn't get any joy whatsoever out of them. He just thanked God when his plane was taking off and went running for the gate. But the incident that did it in the end was when I was walking across the floor and I slipped and went flying into this woman with a bag and sent her bag careering across the airport floor and she went screaming up to a copper and she was adamant she wanted me nicked. The copper said, 'Oh shit, I'm going to have to nick him now.' They didn't want to nick me, that was the last thing they wanted to do, with all the publicity and everything. So they offered me a choice between Mountjoy and St John of God's.

My cousin Carmel was with me at the time because she was supposed to be escorting me back to London. Charlie MacLennan – who was our road manager at the time – was waiting at the other end to pick me up. Carmel was just getting a free trip to London, once we were in London she could leave me with Charlie and fuck off and do what she wanted.

So, after I got nicked, Terry O'Neill – who was our publicist – was called in to reason with the police and he asked them if they wouldn't be prepared to overlook the incident. They said they would be willing to overlook the incident but the woman was pressing charges. It was the bloody woman pressing charges that was causing the problem and it had been a complete accident, I'd meant her no harm whatsoever. The other guy, I'd deliberately fucking attacked and he never pressed charges or anything. She just decided to take it personally.

So they tried to talk her into dropping the charges but they couldn't get it done overnight and they told me I had a choice of Mountjoy or St John of God's. And I suppose Carmel thought John of God's would be the safer option. I should have picked Mountjoy, of course, because the woman dropped the charges the next day, but instead of that I chose St John of God's because I'd been there before and I figured I could talk my way out of there again but this time they certified me insane and kept me in.

Can you imagine the rage I was in when I woke up the next morning in John of God's? I started screaming blue murder. I said, 'Give me my clothes, I want to go to the shop.' And they said, 'You can't have your clothes, you're certified, Mr MacGowan.' I was a certified raving lunatic. In Ireland they don't bother categorizing, they just call you a lunatic. I was a danger to myself and other people and a lunatic and as such they could keep me in there as long as they wanted. So I had to go to NA and group therapy.

—And it didn't work, obviously.

—I think it's a load of old crap, which is why it didn't work. Anything works, if you believe in it, but I don't personally believe God helps piss artists and junkies, I think he's too busy helping starving people. I think piss artists and junkies are whingeing toads who should help themselves. I've always helped myself.

—But surely God helps everybody?

—Yes, but I don't need to go to a meeting to ask God to help me, I can do that by myself.

—But he would help you, if you asked him to?

—Yes.

—So he's not too busy?

—No. He's not too busy. But they aren't trying to help themselves, they go there to whinge and they don't really believe in God, they go there to be reassured by all these other people that there is one. I don't need to be reassured by all these other people that there is one and I don't like whingeing, I think it's a disgusting habit.

—Why?

—Because it's self-pitying and I think self-pity is a disgusting habit.

It's useless. I'm not criticizing people who feel self-pity and I'm sure if you feel self-pity it's great to have an audience to whinge to, but don't you get bored listening to other people's self-pity? Which I have to do in pubs anyway and at least you get a drink in pubs and you can tell a guy to fuck off, which you can't do at a meeting. So actually they're great cos they keep people out of pubs. I'm one of those people that people tell their life stories to because they think I care, for some reason, and I don't care at all. Not at all. I've got no pity for wankers who whinge.

—I whinge!

—You're my girlfriend.

—**Am I a wanker?!!!!!**

—Yes!

—**No I'm not!!!**

—You have some of the make-up of a wanker, you're not all wanker. But then so do I. You're always telling me what a cunt I am to be with and how I can't get dressed and stay clean and how I'm lazy and untogether . . .

—**I'm sorry.**

—And I allow myself to get ripped off . . .

—**You do moan about that sometimes . . .**

—I moan to you and you moan to me. But moaning to anyone else is being a wanker.

—**Friends aren't for moaning to?**

—No. If a friend has serious problem, I like them to tell me about it and I try to help them, but that won't be by me whingeing at them, which is the solution they offer at meetings. 'So you think you've got problems? Listen to mine!!!!' Whingeing competitions, who's the biggest wanker competitions, that's all they are.

—**I see. Well, if you see it like that . . .**

—I've got a lot to be thankful to Dr Niall Joyce for, he's the one who put me in the straitjacket and put me in St John of God's. He once gave me two valium at *The Late Late Show* and Sinead O'Connor was there and she started shouting at him and saying he wasn't a real doctor if he gave me valium. He was going, 'I am a real doctor,

I'll go and get my case and show you.' And he showed her his case. He was furious and so was she and I was quite happy because I had my two valium. I had no idea Sinead was so anti-drugs and also that she was so protective towards me. I love her but I wouldn't stop her taking anything she wanted to take. I don't think there's any point. If you make people stop taking drugs in front of you they'll just go away and take them somewhere else. That's the pointlessness of stopping people taking drugs, they'll just go somewhere else and take more. Imagine getting Nick Cave to give you back two valium. It's the wrong way of going about things.

They were right, the old people who brought me up. They said let them have a drink, let them have a fag, let them have as much chocolate as they like, because then they won't go mad for it when they're older. I'd be much worse now, if I hadn't had the childhood I had.

The so-called Phantom of Death is meant to follow me, but I've always escaped perfectly unscathed.

—**Perfectly unscathed?**

—Yeah. Apart from close friends, y'know. The first fatality was Paul Verner, who was the nicest, kindest guy you could ever meet. He was also a two bottles of brandy a day alcoholic.

—**Brandy? That's bad that.**

—Well, I gotta make the point that you can forget about heroin, crack, and all the rest of it – brandy can kill you quicker than anything.

—**Why brandy in particular?**

—I don't know. It's very strong. It has a very high alcohol content, and it's very easy to drink. And people have died at a very young ages from brandy, you know.

—**So?**

—So, you can't say. Some people have got the constitution for it, and some people haven't. Paul was only thirty-nine when he died. On the other hand, my grandad – the one who died young – was only twenty-five. He died when my mother was three, and my uncle Sean was two. Which is why they were brought up on the farm, you know? I only grew up there till I was six. But I spent all my school holidays there. I still have dreams about that . . .

—**Okay, you've said all that before. What about going back to what we were talking about? Paul Verner and Dave Jordan.**

—When Paul Verner died, I was there . . .

—**Well, you better talk about who he was and stuff.**

—Paul Verner was our lighting engineer, and he had fantastic escapes from death. A ladder, right, a big ladder, a fucking huge thing fell on him and hit him on the head, y'know. And he survived it. So things like that, he survived. He wasn't into getting into fights, but if he was in a fight, he could kill you, y'know, he could crush you. He was a big man. And he was only thirty-nine years old when the brandy finished him off. And he'd been given a warning, a very heavy warning – stay off it or you die. And . . .

—**And it happened.**

—It happened. Dave Jordan died on the road, and that's all I've got to say about that. He was only thirty-eight or something like that. God bless him.

—**He was forty.**

—Was he forty, yeah? And that's what the road can do to people.

—**And what about you?**

—Like I said, I've always been able to cope with it. I've got the constitution, know what I mean, but you've gotta know that you've got the constitution for it. I've had hundreds of diseases, I've been knocked over, I've been in and out of hospitals, and I've had a hard time, but I've always recovered very quickly.

—**And why do you think that is?**

—Just, some people have got different constitutions than other people. I'm just saying that I've got a strong constitution, which runs in my family, on my mother's side.

—**But you told me already that your mother's father died when he was only twenty-five.**

—Yeah, I'm talking about . . . ahm . . . the maternal side. Not on my mother's father side, but on her mother's side.

—**Okay.**

—They all lived to very old ages, and they drank and smoked to their hearts' content.

—**So do you ever envisage a time when you'll give up drinking?**

—That's an impossible question to answer. I'm mortal – we're all mortal as far as I know – and drink is a wonderful thing when it makes people happy. I think it was put here by God for people to use for enjoyment and enlightenment. But it's addictive and it's a poison and, like all the best things in life, if you overdo it you stop enjoying it and in the end you'll probably die. But there's no shame in having a few drinks. If you feel guilty about it just don't do it: don't push it on other people.

—**So how do you feel about the idea of never drinking or taking any drugs at all? Just being a natural human being?**

—Uhm . . . I don't think it would suit me, y'know.

—**Why is that?**

—It's something I've been doing since I was fourteen, like, it's just a habit, you know, it's like smoking cigarettes. But I don't take tranquillizers heavily any more. And I am a very highly strung, nervous person, which comes out in my songs, I would have thought.

—**Yeah?**

—Yeah. And it's not fair to ask somebody who's going through that highly strung depression, and anxiety, to not take something . . . I think I should be allowed my tranquillizers, if I need to.

—**But what about conventional therapy?**

—And I think I should be allowed the odd drink.

—**Well, what some people would say is that if you're highly strung and depressed then you should see a therapist.**

—Well, I've seen therapists over the years, against my will.

—**You've seen psychiatrists. You haven't seen a therapist.**

—I've seen a hypnotherapist.

—**Yeah and he was good, wasn't he?**

—He was very good, yeah. I've forgotten his name, he really calmed me down.

—**How did he do that?**

—By hypnotizing me.

—**How did he hypnotize you? What did he do?**

—He just talked to me like one human being to another, you know. He didn't try to dominate me, or talk down to me. He just talked to me gently, know what I mean. And that was very good. And I must drop by and see him sometime.

—**Does it ever bother you that you can't feel good without all these drugs?**

—I can, now. But I would go to a Taoist or a Buddhist master, for therapy, if I was feeling really down. But just doing the *I Ching* or reading the *Tao Te Ching* or reading Alan Watts – who's the only Western writer on the subject who knows what he's talking about – helps. Western psychiatrists think of the mind as separate from everthing else, they don't belive in the soul, they don't believe in miracles, they're scientists. But I would go and see a Jungian psychotherapist. Only a Jungian one. Just reading Jung makes me feel better. And listening to Jim Morrison and Hendrix and Coltrane and Irish music. All good music, really, I find therapeutic. I think music is a spiritual, psychic thing and everybody is capable of making beautiful music but they have to unblock themselves, they have to break down the barriers, the mental prison that they've been put into by Western conditioning.

And that's a racial characteristic of the Irish, that they're aware of what you can't see and what you can't touch and they know there is more to life than there appears to be, with the five senses and that logic doesn't get you anywhere except the atom bomb.

It's a fact that all kinds of plants grow all over the world and from prehistoric times people have been using them to sort their heads out and your head is related to your body and your soul. It's a fact that all so-called primitive tribes have at least one potion made from plants. The ancient Egyptians used opium, the tribal Indians used to chew cocaine leaves, and take religious potions . . .

—**Yeah, but they only did that during ceremonial events. They didn't do that all day.**

—But they had those ceremonies all the time.

—Not every day, Shane. They didn't wake up in the morning and take drugs. This was like a ceremonial thing. They would do it for a purpose.

—Look, are we having an argument or are we writing a book?!?! Do you want to know what I think?

—**I want to know what you think.**

—If you're addicted to something, it's no use, it's a bind and that includes alcohol and cigarettes and chocolate and television and the internet and gambling . . .

—**What about sex?**

—Sex is perfectly natural and it's a perfectly natural thing, but if somebody doesn't think about anything but sex then that's an addiction. I know that promiscuity leaves you empty because I've done it. I've had a different woman every night for a while and now I'm completely monogamous. But that's just me. I think people should be allowed to do what they want with their own heads.

—**And bodies?**

—And bodies, yeah. All right. That's what I think, and nothing you say is gonna make me think differently, okay? In other words, I believe in freedom, I believe in democracy, I believe in personal human liberty, you know.

—**Yeah. I agree.**

—And I believe in people's right to choose their own individual way of living. And I don't think you have any right to yell at me over this, you can ask me my opinions, but if you continue to attack me about it, y'know, I won't talk to you any more about it.

—**I'm not attacking you about it. I'm just interested in how you see it. Because . . .**

—I just told you how I see it!!!

—**All right, I'm not talking about it from a legal point of view, but from a point of view of health. Don't you think it's better if people look after their health?**

—Yeah.

—**Yes, right . . . but does that include drinking and taking drugs?**

—Yeah. If you want to.

—You don't see that as a problem?

—I told you!!! I think brandy is a very dangerous drug.

—You think brandy is very dangerous. Do you think cocaine is?

—No.

—Why not?

—Well, I haven't seen any evidence of it. But . . . if you overdo it, it's dangerous. Crack is dangerous. Crack cocaine is dangerous. But coke's a different thing, y'know.

—Why is that? That coke isn't dangerous, but crack is?

—Because crack takes away your humanity.

—How?

—I don't know how it does it, it just does it.

—Well, in what way? I mean, describe it.

—Well, it can make you capable of killing your parents for the money to buy it.

—And heroin and coke don't do that?

—No.

—Why do you think that is?

—What?!?! What was that question!?!

—Why?

—I'm not a chemist!!! But I know from experience what crack does to you, and heroin and cocaine don't. I can't tell you why.

—Okay . . .

—I can't write you out a formula!

—All right. But most people don't know the difference between cocaine and crack.

—Because most people are stupid. What . . . do you want to know the difference? Is that it?

—Yeah.

—You take a rock of cocaine, and you take out all its impurities, and you smoke it as one rock, and in that case it's crack.

—But what's the difference in the sensation . . . ?

—They're completely different sensations.

—You can't tell.

—You can!

OH I'VE HAD FAME AND FORTUNE
I'VE DESTROYED RATIONAL THOUGHT
LIKE BILLY BURROUGHS SAID A PSYCHIC
                  COSMONAUT SHOULD DO
GOT STRUCK DOWN BY GREAT SICKNESS
COULDN'T EAT, COULDN'T THINK, SELF-HATRED
                  AND FEAR, THE BLACK
                  GRAVE OF THE BLUES

THE MONEY RUN OUT, ONCE MORE I WAS
                       BROKE

LIKE A CORN X PUNCH-LINE TO THIS LOUSY
                       SICK JOKE,

VICTORIA, MY PRECIOUS SAID SHE HAD ENOUGH
                  WATCH TRYING
SHE DIDN'T WANT ME DYING

—I didn't notice any difference. They had the same effect on me.

—The occasional use of crack has no more effect than the occasional use of cocaine. It's the continued use of crack that causes psychosis and paranoia, and turns you into a violent person.

—I think it's interesting that you don't realize that most people don't know anything about all this stuff.

—But don't ask me, I'm not a doctor.

—But you know a lot about it. You know more than most people.

—Well, I can tell you what happens, but I can't tell you why it happens. We both know people who got strung out on crack. They haven't killed their own parents. But they've gotten violent, and all the rest of it, more so than they would on . . .

—Yeah, we know lots of people, but I'm not talking about that. They all got over it, didn't they?

—I don't think it's as bad as brandy.

—Don't you?

—I think the worst drugs are brandy and nicotine.

—Yeah?

—Yeah.

—Well, the doctor at the clinic told me nicotine is the most addictive.

—But on a street level, crack can be lethal. Because it brings it into the black market circuit, y'know, so gangs get involved, and things like that.

—See, this brings us to . . .

—The illegality of crack is its problem. If crack was legal, it wouldn't be a problem. They should legalize all drugs.

—Do you think that people would take more drugs if they were legal?

—No.

—But people smoke a lot of cigarettes.

—Yeah. Nicotine is a very addictive drug. I think it's more addictive than crack.

—Do you think less people would smoke if it was less accessible?

—No. I think that if you illegalize smoking, you'd immediately start up a black market. I'm saying, legalize all drugs. It's the only answer.
—**Some people would say that if you did that, you'd get all the housewives rushing out to buy bottles of valium.**
—They can get bottles of valium anyway, legally, on prescription.
—**Not any more they can't.**
—They can.
—**They can't. They can only get prozac now. Doctors are only giving people prozac now.**
—That's not true.
—**I know loads of people who have been to the doctor, saying that they were depressed or something, and they got given prozac.**
—You should be going back and saying you're still depressed, and you'll get valium. I get tranquillizers easily, and I don't even ask for them. And I don't think tranquillizers are completely dangerous drugs. I said, if you don't want to know my view, then switch the tape off because there's no point.
—**I don't want to argue.**
—Well then, if you want my opinion, just let me give it.
—**Go ahead. Give your opinion.**
—Like I said before, I think the most dangerous drugs are brandy and crack.
—**And nicotine . . . you said before.**
—And nicotine.
—**So tell me, why is it that you don't like crack yourself?**
—It brings violence into the equation. A junkie dying for a hit will not go out and kill someone for it. He'll go out and steal something, y'know.
—**Supposing he has to kill somebody in order to . . .**
—He won't do it!
—**He won't do it?**
—No.
—**So he'll suffer the cold turkey.**
—Yes. He'd be too weak to kill anybody by the time cold turkey sets in. But a crack addict . . . crack makes you, it gives you a giant boost,

y'know. And if you can get a gun, you'll go and you'll kill somebody to get more crack. That's the thing about crack.

—**What do you think about heroin?**

—Uhmm . . . it destroys too many precious things in your life.

—**Like what?**

—Love.

—**How does it destroy love?**

—Not necessarily destroy it, but, attempts to destroy it.

—**How?**

—Because you're lying to the person you love all the time. And you're ignoring the person you love all the time. People are worth more than drugs. Seeing as you've brought it up, obviously heroin is just as dangerous as nicotine and brandy – particularly if you fix up. And if you have something you can't handle about yourself – if you're in mental pain – it's not going to cure that mental pain. Heroin, you have to realize, is incredibly addictive. If you are at all greedy or irresponsible and if you don't know who you're getting it off, there's a possibility, a strong possibility that you'll die on the spot. That's why drugs should be legal and you shouldn't be allowed to do them till you're sixteen. They should be controlled because pubs can't get away with putting poison in brandy bottles. Actually, if anyone offers you smack don't even think about buying it or taking it. But I know what the temptation's like to do anything illegal. So if you are going to do it, find someone who knows what they're doing and let them sort it out for you. Because nobody will tell you the truth about it, they don't educate people properly about it: it's not the same as hash or grass, but they tell kids it's the same thing. It's not. Like I said, if you're that unhappy, you should examine yourself and wonder why you want to take it and remember that you're gambling with your life.

If you are prepared to gamble with your life, at least consult an experienced gambler. That doesn't mean a hopeless junkie, that means someone who's done it and knows what they're doing.

—**Do you believe when somebody dies that it can be an accident or do you think God decides or fate?**

—I have no idea. I'm a human being, so I don't think I'm supposed to know that.

Just to make this absolutely clear: the reality of the situation is that alcohol and fags are legal and it's better to be safe than sorry, so stick to the legal stuff and remember that's going to kill you as well. It's incredibly stupid to smoke, for instance, but one cigarette won't kill you and it's a gradual, slow, horrific death. It's not 'bang' like smack. Usually alcohol is slow and horrific as well.

—**Okay then, do you believe in God?**

—I believe in a universal force of which we are all a part of, and which is in ourselves, which the Chinese and the Japanese call the Tao. And which is unnameable.

—**If it's unnameable, how is it called the Tao?**

—The minute you call it the Tao, it ceases to become the real Tao. And of course some people call it the Dao, because of the pronunciation.

—**That's right.**

—But in the Western world we call it the Tao, and Zen. And the Tao and Zen are the worship of . . . there's Tao magic, there's Tao philosophy, and there's Tao religion, but they're all different facets of the same thing. Which is what other religions call God, Allah . . . uh . . . I forgotten what the Jews call it . . . and I don't know what the Hindus call it either, except that Hinduism and Buddhism are both developments of Taoism . . . the same way that Christianity is a development of Judaism. The Tao can be understood in different ways. Like say, religious Taoism is the *I Ching*, and philosophical Taoism is Zen. It's things like Zen, or like the drunken way of Zen. There's like three hundred schools of Zen. Zen is . . .

—**What is Zen? What does it mean?**

—Zen is . . . when you've partly absorbed the Tao, and you're going with the flow, then you become incredibly bored, cause there's nothing else to do, yeah, and Zen is a set of games to play with your mind to reinforce your Taoism. It's a bit like the Jesuits in the Catholic Church, know what I mean. It's a bit like theology. Zen is like . . . it's a set of jokes and riddles, and it's also – depending on the school – it can be a set of jokes and riddles, it can be meditation and silence; meditation meaning sitting quietly, doing nothing. Taoist meditation means that. Taoist religion and Taoist magic are the steadfast belief in the unnameable, which is the proper word for the Tao, yeah, the unnameable.

—Isn't this . . . well, okay, yeah . . .

—What? Have you got a problem here?

—I don't really understand.

—Well, because the Tao that can be named is not the Tao.

—So how can you have a belief in something that can't be named?

—Because words are useless.

—So what is the Tao?

—The unnameable.

—What is *not* the Tao?

—The nameable.

—So I'm not the Tao, and the television is not the Tao, the table's not the Tao . . .

—They're all the Tao.

—But how are they? I thought you said they weren't?

—This is the riddle that Zen is about. This is the riddle, yeah. And there are a hundred thousand ways of approaching that riddle. Because if you name the Tao, you're naming it as something outside yourself, whereas you, yourself, are the Tao, know what I mean.

—So everything is the Tao.

—Everything is the Tao.

—Everything that is.

—Everything that is, is the Tao.

—Everything that was.

—Everything that was, everything that is, everything that will be, is the Tao. Everybody is the Tao, the Tao is in everybody. And therefore the most similar thing to it in Christianity is the Holy Ghost. The Holy Ghost is basically the Tao. The Holy Trinity was only made up by the Council of Nicaea, in the Middle Ages.

—And what did they have before that?

—They just had God the Father, and God the Son. And at the

Council of Nicaea, the Holy Ghost was revealed. And as a Taoist, I can only believe in the Holy Ghost.

—Why?

—Because the Holy Ghost is the Tao. The Holy Ghost is in everything, and it is everything.

—**What about Jesus?**

—Jesus was an enlightened human being.

—**So he was the Tao.**

—Being a human being obviously is the Tao. We're all the Tao.

—**So Jesus wasn't the son of God.**

—No.

—**No. So, do you pray to Jesus?**

—Yes.

—**Why do you pray to Jesus if he's not . . . ?**

—Because he was . . . for the same reason I pray to Buddha.

—**Right. And why is that?**

—He was a totally enlightened, holy human being.

—**Where is he now?**

—He's around.

—**What happened to him? Did he get resurrected or what?**

—Yeah.

—**So you believe that Jesus died . . .**

—And then he shot off into space.

—**So you believe that Jesus died on the cross?**

—Yeah.

—**And you believe he was resurrected?**

—Yeah.

—**Who resurrected him?**

—He resurrected himself.

—**He resurrected himself, so he'd obviously developed special powers.**

—Yeah. I think he went to the East, and developed Taoist powers. Tao magic. With Tao magic, a ninety-year-old man, who is enlightened, can move a boulder with his little finger. Whereas like, forty young, strong men, martial artists, couldn't move that boulder. In Taoism, the lack of force is stronger than the use of force. So, to use a really old example – a really old and boring example, which you've heard before – if I loosen my little finger, you won't be able to break it, but if I hold it out straight . . . like, if I try to keep it from being broken, you'll break it, y'know, but if it's loose you won't be able to break it. Same way as if you fall down a load of stairs and you're drunk, and you're loose, you don't generally get injured.

—**Right. So who else do you pray to?**

—I pray to the wind and the rain, because I was brought up a Roman Catholic. It's not fair to say I was a devout Roman Catholic, cause I was a religious maniac. And . . .

—**Tell me about that. When did you start being a religious maniac?**

—When I was very young.

—**How young?**

—I can't really remember.

—**What, four, five?**

—Four or five, yeah.

—**And who taught you that?**

—My Auntie Nora.

—**Right.**

—Younger than that. Two or three, something.

—**Right.**

—I talked at two. I walked at one, I talked at two.

—**And you read *My Fight for Irish Freedom* at . . . ?**

—Four.

—**So did you read the scriptures?**

—I read the New Testament, obviously not the Old Testament.

—**Why is that?**

—Because that's not part of Catholicism. And I was taught to believe the catechism, you know. The catechism is a bastardized version . . . a twisted version . . . taking all the bits out that they don't want you to read . . . of the New Testament. Like, the catechism is the bits they want Jesus to say, and they don't leave in the bits that they don't want him to say. Yeah, the catechism is the way the Catholic Church perverted the word of Jesus.

—Why did you believe in the Catholic Church?

—Because I was indoctrinated.

—**Right.**

—Because I believed the people who were telling me it. And the person in particular who was telling me it used to buy me cigarettes, back horses with me, do the Irish sweepstakes with me, and like . . . they were all devout Catholics in that household. They gave me booze, they gave me cigarettes, they gave me chocolates . . . they were kind, loving people, right, and I trusted them completely. So anything they told me, I believed. So, *My Fight for Irish Freedom*, and the catechism, were the two most important books that I ever read.

—**Right.**

—And the catechism had lurid, colour pictures of hell. You know, with the demons poking forks into you, and the fires burning you, and all the rest of it. And Christ on the cross . . . it was beautifully done. I'm a person who appreciates great art, and the catechism book was beautifully painted and drawn. Christ on the cross is a brilliant drawing. Shocking and horrifying, know what I mean. The dead rising from their graves, and all the rest of it . . . any child would go for that!

—**Wasn't it scary?**

—Hell scared the shit out of me, yeah.

—**Did it?**

—Yeah.

—**Did you think you were going to hell?**

—No.

—**Why not?**

—Because I was told I wasn't going to hell.

—**Who told you that?**

—They told me I wouldn't.

—**Your family told you?**

—Yeah.

—**Well, why not?**

—Because I wasn't doing anything wrong.

—**But supposing you did do something wrong?**

—If I did do something wrong, I might go to purgatory, if it was a venial sin.

—Tell me the difference between a venial sin, and a . . .

—A mortal sin.

—. . . cause I don't know the difference.

—A mortal sin is marrying a Protestant, uh . . . murder . . .

—In which order?

—There all on the same level. Murder. But I mean if you marry a Protestant, you know immediately that you're going to hell. So, you'll have to live with that for the rest of your life. Because you're excommunicated.

—What about murder?

—Murder . . .

—You can be forgiven for murder, can't you?

—You can be forgiven for murder, yeah.

—You can be absolved.

—You can be absolved for murder.

—But not for marrying a Protestant?

—But not for marrying a Protestant, no. A mortal sin is sex before marriage, a mortal sin is suicide . . . there aren't that many of them.

—So what's the other one?

—A venial sin is stealing, lying, roving.

—Were there any sins that you committed as a child, that were . . .

—That were what?

—That were any kind of . . . that you might have worried about?

—I commited venial sins. I lied, I stole, I bullied people, y'know . . .

—Did you take the name of God in vain?

—I took the name of God in vain a lot. That was a regular thing, y'know, every week I had to bring that one up. Every time I said, 'Jesus fucking Christ!' That's a venial sin. If you're not absolved of your venial sins, you end up in purgatory.

—Right, and what's that? What happens there?

—In purgatory, the only punishment really is that you're not in the light of God, you're not in heaven, yeah. And then there's limbo.

—I think that's been abolished.

—Which is where . . .

—**There's just purgatory.**

—Well, at the time I was learning about it, limbo still existed. Which is where the babies go that haven't been baptized.

—**Right.**

—And also people that didn't know . . . or weren't given the word of Christ. Like Julius Caesar and people like that. Gengis Khan. So they weren't given the chance to become Christians. They go to purgatory.

—**And what's it like, purgatory?**

—It's not like hell or anything. It's not uncomfortable or anything like that, it's . . . but you're constantly depressed, and crying your eyes out, and yearning to see God . . . you know, to meet God. And you never will.

—**And what's heaven like? What did you imagine heaven to be like?**

—But you could get out of purgatory.

—**Right.**

—Like if you spend a certain amount of time there. That's where it's a bit unclear, right, whether people like Gengis Khan ever have a chance to be baptized and all the rest of it . . . and go to confession and communion, do they stay in purgatory for ever or . . . ? I'm a bit unclear about that.

—**Right.**

—But's that the catechism anyway.

—**Anyway, about heaven? What was heaven like? What did you think heaven was like?**

—Heaven, you met all the people who had died that you knew were good, y'know. And like, everybody becomes angels.

—**Everybody?**

—Yeah, everyone. We all become angels.

—**What do we look like?**

—Well, we have wings, y'know.

—**So we look normal except we have wings?**

—Yeah.

—And are we wearing white dresses?

—Yeah.

—**Yeah?**

—And we just bask in the light of God for eternity.

—**Well, that sounds good.**

—Well, it sounded very boring to me, actually.[Laughs!] But I mean you could have anything you want.

—**Anything you want?!**

—Well, you couldn't have something that was a mortal sin!

—**Do they have mortal sin in heaven?**

—You can't sin in heaven.

—**You can't?**

—Well, that would be impossible, y'know.

—**So you can have whatever you want and it wouldn't be a sin?**

—No, you wouldn't be able to sin. Or if you did sin in heaven you'd be cast down into hell.

—**Right.**

—Yeah. Yeah.

—**So did that prospect appeal to you? Heaven?**

—Uhhm . . . it appealed to me more than hell or purgatory! [Laughs!] And I wanted to meet the people who had died, and I wanted to meet the people who were going to die. I wanted to meet all my friends and relatives again, you know what I mean, in the afterlife. And there was booze and cigarettes in heaven.

—**Was there?!**

—Yeah.

—**How do you know?**

—And there was horse racing!

—**How do you know there was booze and cigarettes, and horse-racing?**

—Because that's what I was told.

—**Who told you that?**

—THEY told me that.

—**Who's 'they'? Your parents? Your family?**

—My family. Not my parents.

—They told you there was booze and cigarettes in heaven?!

—Yeah.

—And did you believe them?!

—And you can sing Irish songs.

—Is drinking a sin?

—Drinking isn't a sin, no. So, I'm all right. Betting isn't a sin.

—Isn't it?

—No.

—What about food?

—Food, I never . . .

—You weren't interested?

—. . . I wasn't particularly interested in, y'know. Besides, I wasn't hungry.

—What about girls?

—No, I loved food as a kid, but I just assumed I would never be hungry, that it would be provided for me. It seemed like a place where everything was provided for you. As long as it wasn't a sin.

—Right.

—But if you wished for something that was a sin . . .

—Then you'd be chucked out.

—Then down you went, yeah.

—So, if you decided you wanted a shag?

—And you weren't married?

—You weren't married . . .

—To the person that you wanted to shag?

—Yeah.

—Down you went. I lapsed very early, though . . .

—How early did you lapse?

—Eleven.

—Eleven?

—Yeah.

—And why did you lapse?

—I was walking down a ravine one day, and it just suddenly happened in a flash. I just thought, 'Supposing it's all a load of crap!?' I'd been reading Marx and Trotsky and . . .

—You'd been reading Marx and Trotsky?

—Yeah.

—When you were eleven?

—Yeah.

—Wow, that's sophisticated.

—Well, no, I mean like, communism was always an obsession with me, and socialism, and why it was so bad, y'know? Why it was supposed to be so bad, know what I mean?

—Yeah.

—When it had always seemed fair to me. That's what led the way really. And I think that's the moment I grew up, sort of thing, and went to the next stage in my thinking. And I lapsed.

—So you thought at once it was all a load of crap. Then what happened?

—Then, the minute I thought that . . . the minute I lost my faith, I couldn't get it back. Well, I have my faith again now.

—But it's different.

—It's in a different form.

—Right. So what happened after that, after you lost your faith? Did you lose . . . did you not believe in God, or not believe in . . .

—Yeah, I became an atheist immediately.

—So what did you believe in as an atheist?

—Nothing. Oblivion. The lights went out and that was the end of that.

—Did that bother you?

—Of course it did, it frightened the shit out of me.

—Really?

—Yeah.

—Why?

—Because oblivion doesn't appeal to me, y'know.

—Why not?

—Why not?! Because I like myself too much. I like other people too much. I like . . . it meant, no trees, no plants, no rivers, no wind, no cigarettes, no booze, no girls, no boys, no wonderful old people who taught me the catechism, y'know. It meant that I'd never meet them again after they died. And some of them had already died.

—Did you really believe that?

—Yeah.

—Totally?

—I just got a sudden fucking . . . jolt. I had just completely lost faith.

—There was nothing? You didn't even have a hope that there was anything?

—I tried to fucking . . . I tried and tried to fucking regain my faith, but you can't.

—Why not?

—You can't make yourself have faith.

—Why not?

—Faith is something you either have or you don't. I have faith again now, though.

—How did you get it back?

—Through living, through experience, through thinking about it very carefully.

—And when . . .

—Through thinking about the fact that science held no real answers . . . I had to give up communism, y'know.

—Why?

—Because communism is atheistic. And like, I had to give up any kind of belief in logic, or science.

—So when did you stop being an atheist? What age?

—When I started taking drugs.

—When was that?

—When I was fourteen.

—So you were only an atheist for three years?

—Yeah.

—From eleven to fourteen.

—Yeah.

—Well, that's not so bad. So, you started taking drugs, and then what happened?

—Drugs helped my mind open. My subconscious, and my universal mind and all that.

—You better explain, what was that?

—Drugs opened up . . . can you get me a fucking Caffreys?! I'm dying of thirst. In a pint glass . . . also I started to mature. You know, at eleven it's like all black and white, it's either true or it's not, y'know. And then my Auntie Nora died. You know, the one who'd been the most instrumental in indoctrinating me. The one who bought me all the fags, and who I'd done all the betting with. They all used to bet, but I used to bet with my Auntie Nora because we were lucky, the both of us. And we used to do the Irish sweepstakes together. And like, y'know, I don't know how much she was manipulating me, or whether . . . I think she was just being herself. She was not what you would regard as a very holy woman. But she was a religious maniac. And like, she did the rosary every night. Anyway, as I matured . . . drugs brought back the beauty, to me, of the stained glass, and the beauty of the Mass.

—What kind of drugs?

—Acid, and downers, and speed, and drink.

—They brought out the beauty of the Mass, and of the stained glass?

—And of the whole religion, y'know. And when my Auntie Nora died, I just could not believe that I would never see her again. So I started to go back the other way again, know what I mean. And by the time I was sixteen or seventeen I was a practising Catholic again.

—Were you?

—Yeah.

—Wow. So how did that happen? You just suddenly . . .

—No, nothing happens suddenly. These things don't happen suddenly, not for me anyway. And I turned from being a stroppy little bastard who like . . . upset my relatives by asking them to prove to me the existence of God and all the rest of it, to being a traditional Irish devout Catholic again. I went from being a lapsed Catholic, to a bad Catholic.

—Right.

—I couldn't say I was a good Catholic again.

—What do you mean by a bad Catholic?

—Well, I didn't say the rosary every night. Well, that wasn't said in our house, you know, my mum and dad's house. It was only said in the house in Ireland. So I never got back into regularly going to Mass. But they were intending to make me be a priest!

—Who was?

—Well, because I was a very intelligent kid, most of them had me lined up for the priesthood. You know, there was a lot of pressure on my parents to fucking send me to a seminary. It was the last thing my parents wanted, but the rest of the family were heavily into it. Their wish was to have a priest in the family, instead of a drunk in the family . . . It was one step up for everybody if I became a priest. Up until the time I was eleven I was seriously considering it.

—What appealed to you about it?

—Well, I was told I should be a priest.

—No, but what appealed to YOU about it?

—What appealed to me about it? Free house, right? Like, every house I went to visit they'd give me loads of booze, know what I mean? I saw how priests lived. And I knew it was an easy number. Of course that appealed to me, y'know. And I was religious, so I mean, I wouldn't have to fake it. So what better thing to be? And like, the music, and the beauty of the Mass, and the stained glass, know what I mean. Even when I was really young I didn't believe that priests didn't really do it.

—Didn't really do what?

—'IT', you know.

—You mean sex?

—Yeah.

—You never believed that the priests didn't have sex?

—No.

—Why not?

—Because I didn't believe that anybody didn't have sex.

—Didn't you?

—No.

—Why?

—Because I knew that people had sex. It's a natural, human thing to do.

—Hmmm. Anyway, so when you got your faith back what things didn't you do? You didn't say the rosary . . .

—My faith came back with a raging support of the IRA.

—How can you reconcile the two?

—Easily.

—What? Thou shalt not kill?

—Priests absolve IRA men all the time, y'know.

—Do they?

—Yeah. Republican priests do, yeah.

—How can they do that?

—How can they do it? They do it.

—But, if the man who confesses . . .

—Who did he kill?! A British soldier. Well, then you're absolved.

—But supposing he says, 'But do you regret it?' Because you're supposed to regret your sins, aren't you? That's part of the confession thing . . . remorse.

—No, you don't have to regret it.

—You do. You have to have remorse otherwise it's not absolved. You can't be absolved without remorse.

—It wasn't regarded as a sin by these priests. To kill a British soldier.

—So did you regard it as a sin?

—No.

—No. Okay, so your new faith. You didn't say the rosary, did you go to Mass?

—Occasionally.

—Occasionally. So you didn't go to Mass every Sunday?

—No.

—Did you go to confession?

—No.

—Did you have sex?

—Yes.

—So you were committing loads of sins.

—Yeah.

—And you didn't go to confession?

—No I didn't. It was my own Catholic faith.

—**What was in your new faith? Was there God?**

—There was the Holy Ghost.

—**Just the Holy Ghost, not God?**

—And Jesus.

—**And Jesus.**

—And God the Father . . .

—**What about him?**

—I couldn't work that one out, until I discovered the Tao.

—**What about Mary?**

—Mary?

—**The Virgin Mary.**

—She's a saint.

—**She's a saint. Was she the mother of Jesus?**

—Yes.

—**Was she a virgin?**

—Yes.

—**She was?**

—Yes.

—**Did she have powers?**

—Yes.

—**So, do you pray to her?**

—Yes.

—**What other saints do you pray to?**

—St Martin de Porres, St Francis.

—**Why?**

—There's very few saints that I pray to, although I do pray to all the saints on occasion. St Martin de Porres was a black lay brother in the Dominican order, right, in Lima, in the seventeenth or sixteenth century, I can't remember. I had a subscription to the magazine when I was a kid. From the time I could read. That's what my Auntie Nora got me. And he wasn't allowed to do anything, like say Mass . . . he was a lay brother, y'know, but he was allowed to wear the outfit. He was black. There was racism, you know. Especially in Lima and Peru.

And he used to clean out the shitholes, you know, the bogs, clean them out every day, and do all the washing up, y'know. And then he'd go out at night, into Lima, and go among the poor and work miracles. And he woke someone from the dead. So that was cool, you know what I mean, that was a saint worth praying to. And St Francis was a Taoist, no doubt about it. He believed in . . . he believed that God was in everything, y'know, God was in the trees, and the wind, little insects, and cows, and the humans, and the little children, and the old people . . . and in the brooks, and the rain . . . y'know, all that. And he said, 'Brother Sun, Sister Moon'. He thought of the sun as his brother and the moon as his sister. Religious history. And he started the sacraments of the Franciscan order, who are the most problematic order in the Catholic Church, because they don't believe the Catholic Church should have all that wealth. They believe they should give all that wealth to the poor. And like, they used to collect, y'know, he started his order, and they collected. And they wore hemp.

—They collected what?

—They wore cloth sheets, like, really uncomfortable cassocks – not flash ones like most of them wore. And all the money they had collected never went to the Church, it went straight back to the poor. They collected from the rich and gave to the poor, y'know. So those are my two favourite saints.

—And what happens when you pray to them? Do they . . . what kinds of things do you pray for? And what happens?

—I pray for . . . like when I'm in a fix I pray like fuck, y'know. I pray for guidance, but not that much . . . not as much as I should. But I know that they're beautiful spirits, that are of course still living.

—Where are they living?

—Well, in another dimension, you know. I pray to them. But in this dimension they're dead, but their spirits aren't dead, their spirits are around, everywhere. These are very holy to me, you know. As holy as Jesus. And I pray to them whenever I'm in trouble, or depressed, or afraid, or . . . you know.

—What about if you just like need something? Like if you need money?

—I prayed for years for money, y'know, and eventually I got it. I prayed to Jesus, I prayed to Mary, I prayed to St Francis, I prayed to St Martin de Porres, I prayed to my dead relatives, who I regard as saints, you know.

—Have they answered your prayers?

—Generally, yeah.

—What kinds of things have they done for you?

—They've done this.

—I mean generally, what kind of things do they do?

—They give me inspiration, y'know, when I need inspiration. They give me strength when I need strength. When I'm really low, and like, feel really ill, and I'm really fucked up, they provide, y'know. When I lose things, they help me find them.

—So now that you're a Taoist, can you still be a Catholic?

—Can you be a Taoist, and a free-thinking Catholic as well? Yeah?

—Yeah.

—Because Taoism is a philosophy.

—Right.

—Although it can be practised as a religion.

—What's the difference?

—What?

—Between philosophy and religion? What's the difference?

—A religion has rituals and priests and rules and appeals to sheep mentality. Philosophy is . . . and I'm not talking about Western philosophy when I say philosophy, I'm talking about Eastern philosophy, y'know. Christ was a philosopher. St Francis was a philosopher. St Martin de Porres was not a philosopher.

—He wasn't?

—No, he simply did it. He just did it.

—He didn't talk about it.

—He didn't think about, or talk about it, or preach about it, y'know. But a philosopher is someone who tries to explain how things are, the way things are.

—Are you a philosopher?

—No. Philosopher is really the wrong word for me, so I'll try to remember another word that suits me. It's a way of thinking, that's what philosophy is. A philosophy is a way of thinking.
—**Right.**
—Know what I mean? A philosopher is an entirely different thing than philosophy. A philosopher is some boring old fart in fucking like, y'know, a cave . . . and all that crap.
—**So, for you now, you don't . . .**
—I go with the flow as a principle. That's the basic principle of Taoism, cause we are all part of each other.
—**How do you know that we are all part of each other?**
—I don't know.
—**You don't know?**
—No.
—**So why did you say it?**
—It's what I believe.
—**So there's a difference between knowing things, and believing them?**
—Yeah.
—**So what's the difference?**
—I couldn't tell you, because I've never known it.
—**Well, you know what you believe.**
—I thought I knew the difference in the past, but all I was doing was 'believing' there was a difference.
—**But you know what you believe.**
—I believe what I believe.
—**Okay then, why do you believe that we're all a part of everything?**
—Why not?
—**But what made you think that?**
—At first I started reading Taoist poetry, yeah?
—**Yeah.**
—And I got heavily into 'The Way of the Samurai', which is all Taoism, and Zen as well. And then I got into Zen, which is a development of Taoism. But I'm a basic Taoist.
—**But what I'm asking you is how come? How come you bel . . .**

—Zen is an intellectual version of Taoism.

—**Right, we've had that. But why? How come you believe in the Tao? How come?**

—I started reading . . .

—**The poetry, yes . . .**

—. . . yeah, the poetry. And got into 'The Way of the Samurai', and Eastern philosophy in general.

—**Right.**

—Then I discovered the Indian part of Eastern philosophy. Then I concentrated on the Chinese and Japanese part of Eastern philosophy. And the whole separate section on Buddhism, y'know, which is another development from Taoism. Then I read *Tao: The Watercourse Way*. It's a very short book, a very simple book, by Alan Watts. He's written loads of books, and I've read all his books. But with the first book I read on the Tao, it just clicked, y'know. I realized that that was what I believed.

—**So, if I was to ask you what you've learned about the meaning of life, for the benefit of the readers, what would you say, to sum it up?**

—Follow the rules of the Tao. Don't talk too much, don't argue, don't fight people. And try and go with the flow. Which I forget to do, a lot of the time. But when you go with the flow, you get your karma, so you don't argue or fight. When I was about fourteen, I did start enjoying living in England, but I was full of fury and anger and rage until then. And there was a part of me that said, 'If you're so full of fury and anger and rage, join the IRA.' And that part of me said if I didn't join I was a coward. Afraid to die, y'know what I mean. But I exorcized that by writing songs. I didn't want to write songs, to start with, because we were meant to be playing traditional stuff, but once I started writing the songs, they made me feel good. And I eventually came to a state of inner peace. At that time I was drawing mandalas all the time, which was a tip I picked up off Jung.

—**You mean Carl Jung?**

—Yeah. Jung, when he was in his late forties, after curing two thousand people of neuroses and psychoses and all the rest of it, by using basically Eastern medicine, suddenly felt completely empty, as if there was nothing to live for. And he went through a massive mental breakdown. But being a psychiatrist, he knew he was having a mental breakdown, so he treated himself as his own patient. He used all the knowledge he got from the two thousand cases. He'd recognized a shape that they described in all their dreams and when he went to the East he saw it. It was a mandala. Then he realized that all he had to do was draw mandalas and then he got heavily into it and read the *I Ching* and wrote the introduction to the original *I Ching* translation and became a happy man again. He'd rejected being a psychiatrist and he knew the mandala worked.

—What's a mandala?

—A mandala is a representation of your soul. If every day you draw a mandala, the nature of the mandala will show you the nature of your soul, that day. It just has to be a circle with four points on it, any kind of circle-based shape with four points on it. The swastika is a mandala, the cross is a mandala, that is, the Celtic cross.

When I drew mandalas every day, I stopped dreaming. When I slept, it was a pure black sleep, no nightmares and no dreams. Because I'd drawn my mandala. There were hundreds of cases of people with absolutely glorious mandalas in their dreams, but because they couldn't work out what they meant it made them neurotic. Don't try and think about what it means because you don't know. Just get into it. So Jung destroyed all Freud's theories completely and made shrinks a laughing stock all over the world, except for in America, I mean who takes a shrink seriously except Yanks? Jung, the greatest shrink of all, turned round and said it was all a load of bollocks. All you've got to do is draw mandalas, study the *I Ching* and follow the Tao. Go with the flow. He ended up saying exactly what all the Eastern yogis say. What Buddha had said. And Chuang Tzu and all the Tao masters. He ended up at the end of the twentieth century taking the whole thing back eight thousand years and showing that humanity had developed backwards, which it definitely has because we're blind now to things we used to be able to see. We don't see dragons any more. There are still enlightened people who see dragons and Tao masters who see dragons. Tao masters can push a boulder over with their little fingers. Or jump off a mountain and fly on a cloud. But we all used to be able to do that. The more man had tried to explain things, the more fucked up everything had got and that's what Jung was basically saying, in the end. Destroy all rational thought. Definitely. That was his conclusion.

For ages I drew mandalas, then at some point my heart broke. Towards the end of the Pogues. And I didn't want to do anything any more, except take drugs. But I tried to hold on to the basic principle of going with the flow. There are more things in Heaven and Earth than we can ever understand or accommodate in our tiny little minds. We're blind and the only way to cut through some of that blindness is to admit that you're blind. You're in the dark and you don't know where you're going or why you're going there. You're just going. That's the way of the Tao. But if you can get glimmers of light and you can shoot someone like Hitler, then it's your duty to do it. Because you can push the river, if it's stuck and it needs a push. One direct action, without thought, without hate, just 'This man has to die'. Why do you think all those Zen masters are able to kill you with one blow? Kill you without even touching you? Because they had to deal with bandits and robbers, unenlightened people. And why should they die, when they had the beauty of direct action with the minimum of force to overcome weaker people? Not physically weaker people, but people who were weaker because they were blinder.

The Taoist priests realized that incredible things could be done with the body and mind with this tremendous energy which makes up the universe, and which they were part of, that there were no barriers to what they should be able to do. That's how the martial arts were developed and through meditation they went further and further out. People were meditating for weeks on end. And some people are intrinsically evil, they just won't get the message even when it's as simple as the Tao, even when it's shown to them, so they become bandits, who don't give a shit. And continue to be violent and attack other people. The priests developed the martial arts so that they could defend themselves, because they didn't see any reason that their lives should be shortened by bandits. So they weren't soft. A lot of the stuff the Shaolin monks did was really heavy, like walking on nails. Overcoming pain was a challenge which they took on and got together.

Then Buddhism developed from Taoism. And the *I Ching*, which was written so that people could see inside themselves at any given time and know what was actually happening, what the Tao was doing, where they were in relation to everything else and what they should do, and it's written so that you can understand it. Although it isn't written literally, it's written in images, it's like interpreting dreams, but not as difficult. There's always a thing called the Superior Man, which usually means you, unless you're reading it for someone else. It tells you what the Superior Man has done and what he's doing and what he should be doing. But having been written thousands of years ago, the images are all of castles and fire and mountains and wind and rain and courage and swords and things like that, so it's a bit like the tarot. But you can never get a bad reading in the *I Ching*. You can get a duff one, you can get one that tells you not to do anything but you can't get one that says you're fucked. I believe you can't be fucked. But I believe you can believe you're fucked, and that can be bad because if you think you're fucked then you are fucked. But you're not really fucked. People escaped from Alcatraz and Devil's Island, people have done unbelievably dangerous things. Houdini got out of a chest with chains around it that had been thrown to the bottom of a river. Anybody else would have been fucked, but Houdini didn't believe he was fucked, so he wasn't. So lots of people use their minds to overcome situations, but people do have a tendency to think they're fucked. And they just go deeper into depression. I never let myself think I'm fucked. I'd kill someone before I'd let myself think I was fucked. I try and think like a Samurai. Samurais think in a very Zen way. Zen is a set of games that you can play with your mind and with nature, with the world. Some of the schools of Zen are very strict, but there's the Drunken School of Zen, where they get really drunk and then paint with their hair. Everybody who looks at the paintings knows what they're supposed to be, they're paintings of drunkenness. And they had a drunken martial art. I subscribe to the drunken school of Zen.

But I never get as drunk as these guys, these guys get ludicrously drunk, they believe being drunk unlocks their subconscious. And it does, it reveals the truth, all your emotions come out, all your anger. Everything becomes totally uninhibited. No hang-ups at all. They thought that was the best way to follow the flow because they thought the logical mind was a complete waste of time and had to be jettisoned. So to a large extent a lot of those monks are playing around because they become so enlightened they get bored with being enlightened and they play games, which is why they have all those koans in Zen, where the master asks the student a question and the student gives an obvious answer and the master knocks the student into the river with a stick. Then the master gives a much more Zen answer.

—What's a koan? Tell me one.

—I can't think of one at the moment, but the student gets knocked in the river every time, every fucking time. And they have to put up with that for years.

—Why?

—That's to teach them to jettison their logical minds and their preconceptions and their conditioning, which are traps. You're meant to be one with nature. And it does work, because in the end they become masters. And they get to do it to other people. They write poetry as well and the poetry is just very simple stuff about a crane crashing into the water while Lao Tzu drinks tea. But I've been blind most of my life, I've been one of the blindest bastards that ever lived. Which is why I'm not surprised that I couldn't hold on to inner peace for very long. As soon as I opened my eyes I started to shut them again. But I can remember it, so I know it's there. And I know how I got there. I think I can get back. Start drawing mandalas. I'm suspicious of this instant enlightenment crap that you're into, though, because it's not meant to be instant. You're not meant to put on a tape and become enlightened. If you played one of those instant enlightenment tapes to a Shaolin monk, he'd just piss himself laughing. He'd say, 'What the fuck is this rubbish? It doesn't rhyme, it isn't funny, you can't eat it.'

—I like my tapes.

—If it makes you happy, great. There must be hundreds of ways to the same place. I just think I might as well do it the way I know.

—How are you going to do it?

—There's two ways that I've got out there and one is meditation and the other is tripping. Tripping, I spent a lot of time in my subconscious, but I got higher than that sometimes and I saw a big huge light and I knew I was touching something really amazing, I was touching the Tao, or whatever, really touching it. When you're tripping, all your senses get mixed up, so I was smelling it and hearing it and feeling it as well as seeing it and I was laughing, and feeling very happy. And I was miles above myself. But it didn't last very long. I also saw my aura, while I was tripping. That was like a rainbow of colours, all around my body, in the shape of my body. At the time I didn't know what it was. You see, what you see when you're tripping is actually there. The tripping just unlocks your real sight, and gets you in touch with your higher self. And gives you total access to your subconscious. So everything you see when you're tripping is real. You see the movement in everything, you see that nothing is solid, everything is moving all the time and the air looks like strips of Playdo. Different colours. And you can fly.

One night, when I was living in Kathy Macmillan's house in the West End, I'd been out all night and I went home to play *Madam Butterfly*. So I decided to drop a tab of acid. Well, a blotter, or a section of blotters. I don't know how many, but it was very strong, the section that I got because I imagined the third world war starting and I was involved in a plane crash. And it came out with Ireland being the ruler of the world and I was Ireland's diplomatic attaché to the superpowers, like some kind of ambassador. I'd been a soldier in the war and the US were a write-off as a political power. And I was negotiating with the Soviet Union and China. So I started dishing out all the caviar I had around there. Not real caviar. Lumpfish roe.

I got out the vodka and caviar for the Russians. I was doing the diplomatic negotiations. I imagined that I was at a summit meeting in my flat. The kitchen was a disaster area. And the third world war had been started by our roadie, Charlie Malcolm, being shot in the band bus by Tone Loc, you know, who was in a bunker under the motorway singing 'Wild Thing'. So I started playing 'Wild Thing' over and over again and we decided to divide world power up between the blacks and the Irish. And in order to demonstrate the USA's cultural redundancy I ate my Beach Boys' *Greatest Hits* album.

Kathy knocked on the door and my mouth was covered in blood and she said that Frank Murray was on the phone and I had to be somewhere and I said, Go away, can't you see I'm involved in the future of the world here? She knew I'd flipped my lid when I threw my green guitar, my favourite guitar down the stairs after her.

I woke up and I thought the third world war had happened and I was in Vienna. I went out walking in the streets and I couldn't understand why everything looked so normal, with everyone just wandering around as usual. And it gradually dawned on me that I was in London and the third world war hadn't happened. Then I realized I'd eaten my Beach Boys record.

I was bored at the time and there was a lot of acid around, because acid house was happening. When you start taking it, it's startling and you feel like you've discovered something that you never knew before. Or you realize that you're seeing reality for the first time as it really is. But very soon you get to the stage where you can do a whole page of blotters and it just keeps you vaguely stoned, because after all it is only showing you reality the way it really is.

—What was the best trip you ever had?

—The best trip I ever had was the one where I flew around on a magic carpet in the air and there was lots of squiggly bits. Squiggly bits of, like, matter itself, colour and all the rest of it, that you could just use like Playdo. And a feeling of tremendous love and tranquillity. And everything is funny and there's no sadness and you can see that we're all one. And you can do things like wandering around inside people's wombs.

There was this little coloured ball with a doorflap on it with a little bunnyrabbit going 'Teeheehee'. Because thought and emotion and sight and hearing and the senses are all one. Because they are all one. It's just seeing it, having it revealed to you. Which is why we call it enlightenment. Acid is a short cut. Then you could call the other ways of doing it a long way around.

—**But can you sustain it, with acid?**

—You can sustain it if you keep taking the acid. I stopped because I didn't need it any more. And it wasn't working as a short cut any more. My senses were returning to their normal blocked-off state. However, having had the revelation, you always have the memory of it. For some reason it's not destined for us to have the intensity of the experience all the time. Well, I'm only guessing.

—**Why?**

—Why does it stop? Why do all the senses return to their normal blocked-off condition?

—**Yeah.**

—I think the intensity of the revelation is too much for the human mind to bear all of the time. In the same way as you have to meditate over and over again, you don't just meditate once and achieve Satori. And when you achieve Satori, then there's no reason to carry on living, really. Because there's no point to life apart from the achievement of continuous enlightenment. We're probably meant to teach other people how to achieve enlightenment, once we've achieved it. I think I already have been enlightened, but it didn't last, so it was Satori, not Nirvana.

—**Do you mean that you achieved enlightenment through drugs?**

—I used drugs because drugs are used in spiritual practices. Like Shamanism uses psychedelic drugs to achieve enlightenment. That's just one example. There are numerous spiritual practices that use psychadelic drugs. But it's incredibly dangerous if you're looking for a cure for depression, or you're anxious or afraid or miserable, you need to be at peace with yourself and you should never be alone, you should be with people you trust and I've always got fairly drunk before I've done it and the only time I didn't I had a massive bummer which was hell. Also, I'm a product of my generation, so luckily I was told to eat something, don't do it alone and get a bit pissed first. Having a bummer was hell and I thought about suicide for hours – that's the most frightened I've ever been in my life.

—**Same as me.**

—Yeah, but that's for a different reason.

—**Yeah, because I was fucked up anyway.**

—Exactly. So was I.

—**Yeah, but as we know the drugs wear off, so what's the point of getting enlightened by using drugs?**

—I think the point behind it is to show people what things are really like, so that when they return to a state of naturally blocked senses, they won't forget what things are really like.

—**So have you got to a state of enlightenment by meditating?**

—Yeah, but with meditation I've only got to a stage of total peace, in darkness. Some colours, but no blinding lights. But I wasn't expecting anything else, I was expecting a deep, dark sense of peace, so that's what I got. Like a dark room in my mind, where I could really find peace, that's how it felt. Like when you were a kid, just before you started to dream, and you made pictures in your mind, because that was a place where you could play. I was aware of my body, and my body was completely still, I was aware of the stillness. I did that for a long time, alone in my room. And I followed the rules of the Tao, like I said. Which I'll repeat. Don't talk too much, don't argue, don't start fights for no reason. And try and go with the flow.

—**Right.**

A satisfied grin illuminates the fine, angelic countenance of Shane MacGowan as he leans back in his chair, stretches his legs and sighs, contentedly. Victoria switches off her tape-recorder and winks, amicably. Outside, in the misty, mystical landscape, a chorus of banshees howl, approvingly.

TO BE CONTINUED

UNCODITIONAL APOLOGY

I WAS SPEAKING FROM THE HEART
WHEN I SPEWED THIS STUFF

I WAS A STRANGER IN MY OWN SOUL
TO THOSE WHO CAN ACCEPT IT
PARTICURLARLY THE POGUES
FAMILY
INCLUDING FRANK

I OFFER UNCODITIONAL LOVE — L-♡-V!
TO THOSE WHO CAN'T

I'LL SEE YOU AT THE GATES OF

HELL

Shane MacGowan